BRIGHTLY FADES THE DON

BRIGHTLY FADES
THE DON

By

J. H. FINGLETON

With a Foreword by

SIR NORMAN BIRKETT

COLLINS

ST JAMES'S PLACE LONDON

FIRST IMPRESSION,   JUNE, 1949
SECOND IMPRESSION,   JUNE, 1949

TO YOU, PIP!

CONTENTS

ILLUSTRATIONS

9

ACKNOWLEDGMENTS

The author and the publishers would like to express their thanks for permission to use in this book material the copyright of which is held by:—

The Times.
Mr. Lester B. Wilson and the *Sunday Despatch.*
The *Yorkshire Post.*
Mr. Arthur Mailey and the *Sydney Sunday Telegraph.*

For permission to reproduce the photographs in the text we are most grateful to:—

The Sport & General Press Agency, Ltd.
The *Manchester Evening News.*
The *Yorkshire Post* and *Yorkshire Evening Post.*
The *Truth* and *Daily Mirror* Feature Service, Sydney.
The *Daily Graphic.*
Press Association and Reuters.

FOREWORD

By SIR NORMAN BIRKETT

IT is a great personal pleasure to write a Foreword to this most excellent book, though I must disclaim any special qualification for the task. I am glad to call Mr. Fingleton my friend, but that cannot, in itself, atone for manifest shortcomings. Indeed, my limitations are such, that when Mr. John Arlott, for example, is broadcasting from Lord's or wherenot, and with breathless and unpunctuated fervour informs me of the disposition of Lindwall's field, the only general impression I retain is one of much congestion near the wicket. Happily for me, a love of cricket is not dependent upon technical excellence, and a life-long love of cricket with all its lovely associations must be my plea in mitigation, as I serve the office of a friend. For there is a quality of hero worship that resides in us all whatever our years may be. When the Rev. John Mitford made his famous visit to Beldham's cottage, he records that his hand trembled as he touched the sacred bat, and that he was moved to press it to his lips and return it to its sanctuary. To some that may seem to be the language of exaggeration, but I find it to be altogether fit and proper. I have always had much respect for that great English judge going the Northern Circuit who did very much the same thing at Manchester. The High Sheriff of the County and the civic dignitaries were there to meet him at the station, but there was also on the platform a truck piled high with the cricketing bags of the Lancashire team, who were starting out to play a match in a less-favoured county. Leaving the group of officials, the judge walked to the truck, and laying his hand on one of the bags came and said: "Now I can always say that this hand has touched the bag of Johnny Tyldesley." I confess to being made in the same mould. I can remember still the quickened beating of the heart when I first saw the majestic Maclaren take guard at Old Trafford; and even to this day I cannot watch a match, wherever it may be, but the opening overs are a time of the utmost tension, and I feel the glow and the excitement inseparable from a great encounter.

Despite all this, when Mr. Fingleton did me the honour of asking me to write this Foreword, I was a trifle hesitant. After all, he had once occupied the august position of opening batsman for Australia in Test Matches, and had participated in that tremendous moment, surely one of the greatest moments in any match, when the first pair come down the pavilion steps, and, to all outward seeming, walk serenely to the wicket. I recalled, too, not only his many centuries, one of them at least with the marks of Voce all over his body, but the memory of his quite wonderful fielding, and how that repository of all cricketing knowledge and wisdom—Sir Pelham Warner—had wished to award him first-class honours in that regard. But I reflected that a Foreword might give me the opportunity of saying something on behalf of that great company that can never hope to open an innings or field a ball, who yet love cricket with a great intensity, delight in its literature, and take infinite pleasure in watching it being played. For cricket has a strange power of uniting men of all degrees, skilled and unskilled, and binding them together in a common devotion to the game; and I write, therefore, as one of those who only stand and wait.

Mr. Fingleton is now an established author. His *Cricket Crisis*, published in 1946, received the highest praise from a great master in the art of writing on cricket. Mr. Neville Cardus has enriched the literature of cricket and given the deepest pleasure to cricketers everywhere, and he it was who praised the book, both for the manner of the writing and for the contribution to the cricketer's library. The present book may be commended on the same grounds and without change of language. As the title indicates, the book is a record of the Australian tour of this country last summer, with particular reference to Mr. Bradman (as he then was). It is written with the knowledge of one who has himself been "in the middle" on great occasions with all that phrase implies. It is full of insight and great understanding, replete with technical knowledge—the nature of the wicket, the disposition of the field, the resources of the bowling, the quality of the batsmanship, the elements of Captaincy, the weaknesses and the strengths, and all that makes up the fascinating story of a memorable tour. It is a record of the matches played, the great figures who took part in them, and a critical appraisement of the performances; but throughout the book the great figure of Bradman dominates the scene as he dominated the field on his last tour of this country. There is always a certain solemnity about doing something for the last time, when done consciously, and Mr. Fingleton has never lost sight of this. It was entirely fitting that throughout these pages there should be in the mind and the imagination the picture of the great man saying his last farewell to the places where his fame had been won, as he went to join Grace and Trumper, Hobbs and Macartney, and the great company of the Immortals.

Now I am one of those who believe that the love of cricket is one of the enduring ties binding Australia and Britain together in the Commonwealth of Nations. There is sometimes a tendency when writing of cricket to use the language of unreality, and to ascribe to cricket moral qualities and perfections that are not its sole prerogative; but the value of cricket to the Commonwealth is not to be denied. That great Australian, Mr. R. G. Menzies, a former Prime Minister of Australia and a passionate lover of cricket, would, I am sure, bear me out in this. But I also like to think that the tour of 1948, because of certain exceptional circumstances, has brought us nearer to each other than ever before. If I am right in this, as I think I am, Mr. Fingleton's book will be doubly valuable both here and in Australia. The nature of the welcome given to the Australian team in all parts of the country was quite remarkable. Conventional language scarcely does justice to it. It was, I believe, much more than the traditional welcome to our brethren from overseas; it was in some measure a thanksgiving that one of the great institutions of our common life had been restored. The great crowds that gathered wherever the Australians appeared did more than testify to their love of cricket; they did more than pay their affectionate tribute to a consummate captain of a great team; they did more than give expression to their joy in seeing that team once more in their midst; they gave utterance to their deep-seated satisfaction, after years of darkness and danger, that cricket had once more come into its kingdom in these great and historic encounters. For not the least of the deprivations of war is that the glory and the grace of cricket depart for a season, and the minds of men are turned from the days in the sun and the green earth and the blue sky, and all those gracious and lovely things associated with English cricket fields, whether they be at Lord's or the Oval, or where the "butcher bowls out the laundryman." To see the Australian team emerging once more from the pavilion after the years of war was to be filled with thankfulness and pride and happiness, and not a little emotion. The memories and associations of the past were combined with the pleasure of the present, and the long interval had added a quality to the pleasure of the rarest kind. Bradman was there before the eye but the heroes of bygone days were in the heart. It was natural, of course, that a very special welcome should be given to Mr. Bradman. He is already in the company of the very greatest cricketers of any age or clime. That he was appearing for the last time on English fields invested the occasion, as I say, with an undeniable tinge of sadness. The great warrior was putting off his harness, and the crowds were anxious to show him their abiding gratitude for the pleasure he had given to countless thousands, to render homage to his greatness, and to express their admiration and affection for the way he had borne himself amidst the world's acclamation. It was once said that "nothing in this world is precious until we know that it will soon be gone," but that was never true of the batting and the fielding of Mr. Bradman; nevertheless, the fact that he was being seen for the last time imparted an intensity to the feelings, which resulted in him being cheered all the way to the wicket. Thousands who did so had never seen him before, and thousands had seen him in his youthful strength and glory; but all alike were anxious to do him honour, and to make memorable the occasion of the task accomplished and the long day done. In this book, however, Mr. Fingleton is far from spending his time in indiscriminate praise. He has the courage in his writing that was found in his batting. He finds human weaknesses in the great men; he is outspoken about body-line bowling and bouncers; he turns a critical eye on the weakness of English cricket and prescribes the strengthening tonic; he brings the rich stores of his knowledge, gained in Australia and England, to the discussion of all matters connected with the game; and he writes both fearlessly and convincingly. But nowhere is the purely technical side allowed to take charge. Mr. Fingleton plainly knows that the charm of cricket is a very composite thing. He sees beyond the immediate task of making runs for the side, the setting of the game with its indefinable attraction. He believes in the fine saying of Mr. Cardus that "Cricket is sensitive to its habitation." He follows the precedent set by Nyren, and blends the practical and the technical with touches of brightness and colour that lend animation to the whole. His analysis of the merits of the Australian team is of the highest interest and value, and invites those with lengthening memories to compare the merits of Joe Darling's team which contained, in Mr. H. S. Altham's words, "that new star of unsurpassed brilliance and charm," Victor Trumper, perhaps the noblest Roman of them all. But when all is said and done, this book is really a farewell to Mr. Bradman. Mr. Fingleton collects some of the many tributes paid to him by admirers all over the world. Mr. Robert Lynd once said: "When Bradman came out of the pavilion with his bat, you could have guessed he was a man of genius even if you had never heard of him." It is in substance what Johnson said of Burke in the famous passage where he declared that if you had met Burke for the first time in the street, and had spoken to him for five minutes, you would have known him for an extraordinary man. And Mr. Fingleton brings another memorable saying about Burke to the mind when he speaks of Bradman, the veteran, saying farewell, and Neil Harvey, the lad of nineteen, opening his Test career, both in the same match, the one with dazzling triumphs behind him, the other with all his triumphs yet to come. Macaulay wrote of a similar situation when he said: "The House of Commons heard Pitt for the last time and Burke for the first time . . . it was indeed a splendid sunset and a splendid dawn." Here, then, for all lovers of cricket everywhere, for all hero worshippers, for all who play and for all who watch, is a book of absorbing interest and fascination. It will recall happy days in the sun and the memorable departure of one of the greatest figures in cricket history. I cannot quite go the length of the Rev. Mr. Mitford, who bewailed the fall of Troy and the ruin of Thebes whilst rejoicing in the permanence of cricket; but I can at least commend this book without reserve to all who love to read the brave and bright chronicle of enduring things.

NORMAN BIRKETT.

CHAPTER ONE

THE DON COMES ON

"H E'S ON!"
The call echoed along the passage-way of R.M.S. *Strathaird* on the afternoon of March 18, 1948, as the ship lay at the Fremantle wharf. It was one steward calling to another, and in his voice was unmistakable excitement. It reminded me of that call, "It's on!" that used to sweep through the far northern towns of Queensland in the war years when thirsty troops were tramping the streets in search of beer. When they found it (which wasn't often) there used to be the delirious and re-echoing shout of "It's on," and that could mean only one thing. So, too, could the call on the *Strathaird* mean only one thing. It meant that Don Bradman had come aboard, en route to England.

This was to be Bradman's fourth and final tour of England as a cricketer. He made that plain in Melbourne during the then current Australian season when he stated that the fifth Test against India would mark his final first-class appearance in Australian cricket.[1]

There was tragedy in that. When he made 57, Bradman suffered torn rib muscles and retired injured—a sad manner in which to retire from an Australian stage which he had graced and dominated since his second entry in 1928. I write second entry because it is interesting to know that the Australian selectors of that time dropped Bradman after his first Test against England, a game in which he made 18 and one. It was a poor start to the most meteoric career ever known in cricket, but in his failure in that game Bradman kept step with Woodfull, Ponsford, Kippax, Hendry, Kelleway and Ryder. In two innings Australia made 122 and 66, and Bradman's 18 was third top score in one innings. But in every age selectors have been unable to rise above a rout and so Bradman was dropped.

Bradman was never again dropped from an Australian team. He was reinstated for the third Test against Chapman's team and made 79 and 112 in Melbourne. That century will never be for-

---

[1] This did not quite prove the case. He played in three benefit games on his return from England—his own, the Kippax-Oldfield and the Arthur Richardson ones.

gotten in Melbourne or by those who saw it. Years afterwards, in 1948, I sat in his Blackpool home with Harold Larwood. George Duckworth was also there, and we looked through Larwood's photographic albums. This was Larwood's first tour of Australia and he kept a splendid photographic record of it (as he did, indeed, of his second and very unhappy visit in 1932). He turned the pages and came to a photograph, which occupied the whole page, of a grinning Bradman waving to the crowd.

"This was the greatest reception I have heard on any cricket field," said Larwood. "The crowd cheered for five minutes. We couldn't go on with the game."

The second figure in the photograph is Duckworth. He sits sprawled on the grass, waiting for the applause to subside. His gloved hands support him, his head is crowned with a huge white sun-hat and there is a wry smile on his face. "Aye, Lol," said Duckworth (all his friends call Larwood "Lol"), "I remember now what I thought of yon so-and-so. I remember saying to the crowd, ' Go on, cheer yourselves hoarse. We'll have to put up with lot o' this, laads, before we see back of yon so-and-so.'"

"Oah, aye," said Larwood, in that lovely expression of the North of England, "he was a great batsman."

Bradman, as I write, was never afterwards dropped from an Australian Eleven. He went to Adelaide and made 40 and 58 (being run out in the latter innings by a bad call from Oldfield when Australia, beaten by 12 runs in a thrilling finish, looked as if it would win through the Bradman blade); he came to Melbourne for 123 and 37 not out, and he went to England in 1930 for a season unparalleled in the whole history of the game. There he made 1,000 runs in May—the only Australian ever to achieve the feat—scored a century on his first Test appearance in England; completed three double centuries in the Test series, including the record 334 at Leeds; and reached the highest aggregate for one series of Tests (974).

It is not my intention to recapitulate the records Bradman has garnered in his two decades of first-class cricket. His career occupies a book in figures alone, but on only two other occasions since his initial omission has he been missing from the Australian side. One was in Sydney in 1932, when he withdrew, because of illness, from the first bodyline Test against Jardine's team; the other was when he declined, because of health and business reasons, the tour to South Africa in 1935-36.

Since 1928, Bradman had played Test cricket against the West Indies and the South Africans in Australia. He went to England again in 1934 and 1938, but the prickling decision he had to make after the Second Great War was whether he would play big cricket again.

He was invalided out of the Australian Army in 1942. He had doubts, expressed in a letter, whether he would be of any physical value other than as an "A.R.P. warden." From Adelaide, through 1943 and 1944, came stories that he had broken down very seriously in health, and there must have been many times when Bradman doubted whether he would ever play cricket again. His health caused him to withdraw from the first Test in 1932; there were fears for his well-being in 1934 when he was operated upon in London for appendicitis, and, in 1935 he refused the South African trip and captaincy because of his health.

Bradman's cricket, over the years, had taken toll of him. Nor is this to be wondered in one who has always exacted the maximum from his mind and body in consistently big scores. There was not, either, much peace and rest for him off the field. Where the average Test cricketer could slip into civilian clothes and be unrecognised off the field, Bradman was known, sought after, fêted, pestered for autographs or plied with invitations wherever he went. In moderation, this could be flattering and pleasant to the ordinary individual; in excess, as Bradman knew it all his cricketing life from 1928 onwards, it was overpowering, demanded too much of him and, in short, was embarrassing.

In the early 1946s, when his health was low and he was dispirited, Bradman must often have asked himself whether it had been worth it, and so, as he gradually improved in health, he must have pondered long on the importunate requests made to him to take up first-class cricket again where he had left off in the first year of the war. He began sport again quietly. He played a few rounds of golf and a game or two of tennis. He played for South Australia against Lindsay Hassett's returning team of Service cricketers. He made 112, an innings of quiet and comparative sobriety. As Hammond's M.C.C. team was en route to Australia the main topic of sporting conversation in Australia was whether Bradman would play against them. Bradman would not commit himself, but portents were to be seen in the frequent games of squash rackets he played.

Over the air and at their public functions in Perth, both

Hammond and Howard, the manager, expressed the wish that Bradman would play against them. All Australia hoped that too! Because of this, it was interesting to reflect upon the position which Bradman still held in the cricketing world. Though he had flayed them over the years with his bat, England's cricketing representatives still wanted more of Bradman. Like London during the blitz, they could take it! But what a stir, to be sure, there would have been in 1934 had Woodfull, landing at Tilbury with his team, expressed the hope that Larwood would play against his side!

It is a matter of history now how Bradman did play again against England and dominated the field as in days of old, but I often wonder what his future would have been had he been out at Brisbane in the first Test for 28 and not 187. In the calmness of afterwards, when the flurry and skirl of controversy die down, no harm is done in admitting to posterity that Bradman *was* out at 28, caught by Ikin in the slips, and given not out. This was a mistake which the best of umpires have made from time immemorial, but it probably had a profound influence upon Bradman's career after the war.

He did not return convincingly to cricket against England. He looked far from well. He made 76 against Hammond's men at Adelaide but it was a somewhat diffident innings which revealed that his footwork had lost much of its sparkle. He looked pasty and round-shouldered. Two weeks later, in Melbourne, he would not confirm or deny that he would play Test cricket again, and the decision—though anticipated in all quarters—was only official when Bradman's name appeared at the head of the Australian Test team a week or so before the game began.

It could be assumed, therefore, that Bradman was by no means confirmed in his decision to play the highest class of cricket again. It was thought that he would be influenced by what happened in Brisbane and whether he was still good enough to do his great reputation justice. In making 20 at Brisbane, Bradman played his most unconvincing Test innings. He appeared to be in great mental distress. Bedser worried him continuously and nearly all of the first twenty runs came from unintentional strokes through the slips.

In 1948, as we were travelling to England, I talked one evening with Bradman, and I asked him whether he was fully convinced that Bedser was as great a bowler as Bradman claimed him to

be.[1] Bradman gave me his Brisbane experiences as an example
and pointed out how Bedser had worried him. I agreed with that
but pointed out that Bradman was far from his real self—with
which he agreed.

In view of all this, therefore, it is interesting to reflect what
Bradman's future might have been had he been given out to the
disputed decision at 28. Taking the rest of his 187 innings away,
this would have meant that Bradman, of a certainty, would have
had to bat some time on that terrible Brisbane sticky pitch that
came for England. The huge score Australia amassed in the first
innings ensured England's follow-on; the time it took to make
placed England twice in line for the results of that awesome
storm of hail and lightning.

Assuming that Bradman had to bat on this sticky pitch and
that his lot (as his previous showings on such pitches would lead
one to expect) had been failure, would he have continued in Test
cricket? It is a point to be considered because it was obvious in
his first Test innings for ten years that Bradman, in Brisbane,
was suffering intense mental stress.

But the "might have's" count little in cricket. Bradman
went on to another tall-scoring season. He made 1,032 runs at
the average of 79·38 and his experiences of that season led him
to announce at the end of it that he had no intention of retiring
from the first-class sphere although he would not commit
himself on another English tour.

When the Indians came for the first time in cricketing history
to Australia in the following season, they began at Perth as the
English before them. In October of 1947, Amarnath, the captain,
and Gupta, the manager, expressed the pious hope that Bradman
would play against them. They wanted to learn from him. He
played all right and they learnt plenty! He made 156 at the rate
of a run a minute the first time he met them in Adelaide;
he made 172 (his hundredth first-class hundred) in Sydney
for an Australian Eleven; 185 in the first Test; 132 and 127
in the third; 201 in the fourth, and 57, retired hurt, in the
fifth.

In this usual welter of runs by Bradman it was interesting to
note that his only failures against India were on a sticky pitch.
He was not out 179 over-night in the first Test at Brisbane. Next
time he batted the pitch was sticky. He had added six runs when
he was out to the most remarkable stroke I have seen him play.

---

[1] At the end of the series, Bradman said Bedser was a better bowler than Tate.

He drew back behind his stumps to force Amarnath to the off. The ball did not rise high, as Bradman evidently expected, but it came through at normal height and in trying to get down to it, Bradman hit his off stump over from behind. A photograph was taken with the stump leaning up the pitch towards the bowler.

In Sydney, Hazare clean-bowled him on a jumpy pitch for 13, so that while Bradman averaged 168 against India in Tests on a good pitch, he averaged only 9·5 when the pitch assisted the bowlers. This revealed two things. Bradman was still human and he had not over the years rectified his weakness on a sticky pitch. In the preceding season against England there had been no sticky pitches for the Australians. This is written in no carping spirit but only to show that the bowlers *did* have hope against Bradman when the elements came to their aid. In that series against India, although most of his batsmen were hopelessly inefficient on a bad pitch, Bradman, as captain, twice avoided batting on a damaged pitch though the result of the game was assured in Australia's favour. This was all the more noticeable because players were on trial for England.

We saw two different Bradmans in Australia in the two big post-war seasons. He gave nothing away in his captaincy against England in the Tests. He retained control of the pitch in Sydney one day so that he could use the heavy roller and assist the pitch to crack if it was tending that way (Yardley twice returned that compliment to him—in Sydney, in the fifth Test, and again in 1948 at Leeds), and he satisfied himself undoubtedly with a draw in Adelaide when that gave his side the rubber. In view of Australia's overwhelming strength in what was known as a goodwill series, many thought that Bradman would have accepted the challenge which Hammond made in Adelaide, but Bradman brought with him through the war years the general conception of Test cricket between England and Australia.

Bradman showed a change against India. This side, without Merchant, Modi and Mushtaq Ali, was not a powerful team and the supremacy of the Australians was never seriously challenged. But in his general outlook on life and other things Bradman had undoubtedly mellowed. He seemed to get more fun out of life; he sought the company of his fellows more than in his earlier days, when it was said of him that he was not a team man and that he was satisfied with his own company. He disproved that in Australia in 1947-48. He mixed more with the players than he did pre-war and he was certainly a more popular leader and man with his players and the opposition.

But a post-war tour to England, his fourth to that country, made Bradman think hard. Unlike pre-war days, he had his own business in Adelaide and he was also a very happy family man with a charming wife and two small children. Another tour of England would be all the more exacting in that he would be ten years older. He would be captain. He would be expected to make innumerable speeches and there would be the usual lack of privacy in his life off the field. All the counties would want him to play, and six days' cricket a week to an Australian who, apart from a few first-class games, plays only on Saturday afternoons at home, was a tall order.

Bradman must have thought extremely hard in the Australian summer in 1947-48. He could have come to England in many capacities. One day in Fleet Street I was talking to an editor and he told me of his newspaper's attempts to attract Bradman to London to write on this 1948 tour of England (a newspaper which was very patriotic to the cause of English cricket, when one comes to think of it!). The editor told me an offer well above the normal "special" offers had been made Bradman. I asked him what it was. Looking furtively up and down Fleet Street, he drew me up a lane and whispered the sum. It staggered me.

Bradman is Bradman and no name before has ever had such appeal. The editor told me Bradman wrote back and explained his difficulties. Away went another offer—*doubling the first*—but it was as a cricketer that Bradman came to England in 1948.

He was in his fortieth year. That is old for an Australian cricketer, who departs the game much earlier in life than his English contemporary. In all history, only three Australians had led a side in England when older than Bradman. Blackham was forty in 1893; Gregory (Syd) was forty-two in 1912, and Armstrong was forty-two in 1921.

Bradman's acceptance of the post again meant that in his fortieth year he was attempting the deeds of his miraculous youth. Bradman, himself, would not have wanted it that way, but by virtue of his name and his records it would be construed as such because a champion must always be a champion. He is never allowed any latitude. Bradman's deeds of youth were such that he could not hope to surpass them. He could gain no more but, indeed, stood to lose much.

Hammond, in his last days in Australia, was a sad, a tragically sad, instance of a once-famous player fallen on evil days. The game gives and the game takes away, and in coming to England again in 1948 Bradman knew what he was risking in reputation and what was expected of him. The game of cricket had nothing more to give Bradman. He had scaled the heights; he had tasted every sweetness it had to offer. He must have thought deeply of all this in Australia before he made his decision to tour, because so fittingly and without the slightest trace of conceit could he have uttered of his cricketing career the sentiments Keats wrote in 1820:

Now more than ever seems it rich to die,
To cease upon the midnight with no pain . . .

CHAPTER TWO

OFF WE GO TO BLIGHTY

THERE can be no doubting the love of the Cingalese for cricket. Rowing out in all manner of craft, they bustled around the ship the morning the *Strathaird* anchored inside the breakwater and they stood in their admiring hundreds on the wharf as the Australians filed off. Apart from the streets glittering with new cars of all makes and sizes and the whopping prices charged for everything (O'Reilly decided our party would move speedily on after being charged 16s. 6d. for two beers and one gin), it was the same old Colombo with crows wheeling and cawking and car horns tooting and hooting—in short, the honking east.

Such bustle, noise and activity are always bewildering after a quiet spell at sea. So, too, are the narrow squeaks from death the citizenry seem to take in their stride in these narrow Colombo streets. Very proudly, on the way to the cricket ground, did our taxi-driver take a hand off his wheel (still keeping the other on the horn, incidentally) to show us the local gaol. "Full," he said, "full to overflowing." And he seemed very proud of the fact!

It is a thrill for an Australian to play in Colombo. The atmosphere is entirely different from that in Australia. The grounds are English in their score-boards and people squat on the grass, their legs protruding over the boundary. But it is the mass of spectators that makes it so different from Australia. You see thousands of dark, smiling faces against a background of gleaming teeth and the startling white of their dress. The enthusiasm of the Colombo crowd is infectious. They applaud vigorously, chit-chat about every little incident and laugh uproariously at anything which tickles their fancy—and plenty does. Altogether a most interesting place in which to play cricket and the standard, especially the fielding, is quite a fair one. As we walked, perspiringly, to the little room near the score-board where we wrote our despatches, O'Reilly and I were recognised by the spectators—especially O'Reilly. "O'Reilly, O'Reilly," they called out excitedly in their, to us, rather odd, high-pitched voices. The Big Fellow, looking rather like a Cabinet Minister, with his big attaché-case, gave them a wave.

There were a few amusing happenings in this one-day game which was washed out very early by a storm in the afternoon when the home side was batting. Brown was out early and this brought Barnes and Bradman together. At home, Barnes has rather a reputation for being at the other end at the end of an over. So, too, has Bradman. No harm meant by it, of course, and all good fun, if you are the other batsman and you like running and you have a sense of humour, but Syd, in his inimitable manner and with a large grin, began to plan running matters and the Don wasn't having any. There were a few Bradman calls refused by Barnes, and then came the inevitable mid-wicket conference. It was rather unusual to see anybody sending the Don back or calling him for a very short run on the last ball of the over—which call was spurned and had the energetic Barnes bustling back to his crease after setting full sail for the other end. The conference adjusted everything.

The sun dealt with Barnes more effectively than the Ceylon attack and he retired ill. Despite this, Keith Miller came to bat without a cap. This, we thought, surely was tempting Old Sol over much, but Miller thought better of it after lunch and wore a cap. As usual, he turned on some fireworks which the crowd loved.

This Colombo ground is the only one where I have seen a female curator—or should it be curatoress? She supervises the boys and there is no lack of man-power here. The white-attired lads simply swarmed over the pitch to titivate it between innings, under the supervision of Madam, a stately figure. It is, possibly, unchivalrous of me to mention it, but perhaps one of her male assistants measured the pitch, and not she? The Australian batsmen found the going rather tough in the morning. It was hard to get the bowling away, and it was Ian Johnson who discovered largely why. He had his doubts about the pitch, measured it and found it was only twenty yards! From that point onwards the Australians bowled two yards behind the crease and everybody was happy. Such readjustments add a little spice to the game.

Ian Peebles told me at Oxford once that from way down at third man, Len Hutton once decided that the pitch was too long. It was measured and, indeed, found to be twenty-three yards! Peebles says the neatest thing about it was that Bill Bowes, who is certainly a sharp one, had bowled some overs without noticing anything wrong.

This was the first time for many years that an Australian team had called at Bombay on the way to England. The Orient ships sail from Colombo to Aden but, being a P. & O. ship, the *Strathaird* had Bombay on its route and a very interesting call it proved too. At Colombo there had been rumours of smallpox and even bubonic plague at Bombay, and as the team had not been vaccinated, few were anxious to go ashore at Bombay. This was regrettable from the Indian viewpoint but understandable from the Australian angle. C. de Mello, the President of the Indian Board of Control, had flown specially from New Delhi to meet the Australians; P. Gupta, the managerial live-wire of Indian sport, just returned from Australia, had flown across from Madras, quite a considerable hop.

The Indians sent a number of messages to the Australians en route, seeking, at first, a one-day game along the lines of the Colombo game, and then asking whether they would practise at their very famous Brabourne Stadium, the best-appointed cricket ground in the world. The Australians could not see their way clear to accept either invitation, and in the light of what I have written about lack of vaccination, their viewpoint can be appreciated, although, as this was the first modern Australian team to touch at India (I am excluding, of course, the unofficial team which Ryder took there in 1935 and Hassett's Services team in 1946), the Indians were greatly disappointed that only manager Johnson and five of the team were present at the lavish reception which had been arranged at Brabourne Stadium.

The Indians, too, must have wondered why the Australians were so tardy in accepting the most attractive foodstuffs that were passed around. We were told not to eat or drink water on shore. Probably a lot of eyewash is spoken about what one should or should not do on shore in foreign parts, but this is what we had been advised and that was that. I had the best coffee of the whole tour later, though, with an Indian newspaperman, Salivatee.

Vijay Merchant, smallish, dark and dapper, came to meet Ray Robinson and me as we tried to make a dint on this beautiful pitch at Brabourne. And what a beauty it is! I can understand why batsmen play for so long on it. Like a lot of other first-class pitches, it is simply too good, and as I looked at it I could imagine the language dozens of bowlers must have used about it. There's no soft sward, either, to placate the bowler and ease his feet just before he gets to his position of delivery. The hard-rolled pitch runs for some seven or eight yards beyond the stumps. How the bowlers must soothe their toes at the end of a day on this!

Merchant, whose record of 2,385 runs at an average of 74·53 in the wet English season of 1946 will take some beating by an overseas cricketer in England, was originally chosen as captain of the first Indian team to Australia, which returned a few weeks before us. His health, however, was not the best and he had to refuse the trip. He would have made a packet of runs, obviously, on our true pitches. I was very interested to meet this smiling, soft-spoken Indian who has such an admiration for Brabourne. He went to great trouble to show us the Stadium which, as I have said, is the best-appointed cricket ground and general sports area I have seen. The steel-girdered stands (high up in them the vultures have built their nests and, rather giving one the shivers, circle the ground unceasingly) are spacious and airy, but it was the locker-rooms, the baths and showers, the grandstand view from behind the wickets, the squash courts, the swimming bath and the general air of comfort about Brabourne that so impressed us. I'd love to bat on that pitch, especially as the boundary seems not far away. I was glad, though, that O'Reilly was not with us. I know what he would have said of the pitch!

Hassett speaks of the time the Services game was held up there by the intrusion of a rioting crowd. It was rather sticky, but Gupta is the man for such occasions. He told the cricketers to leave it to him and everything would be all right. By some means or other (which would not surprise you if you knew Gupta) he got himself at the head of the procession, and began to lead it round and round the ground. The players almost went dizzy watching the procession. But Gupta eventually led it off the ground and the game went on. It was rather unkind of one of the players (who said it afterwards) to say that perhaps they would have got rid of the unruly ones much earlier had Gupta not come in and taken charge!

Gupta is an energetic soul. I'm sure it was his idea to take the reception down to the ship, and so the scene shifted from the Brabourne Stadium to the for'ard lounge of the *Strathaird*. Bradman and his team were gathered together; Don was presented with an Indian blazer and the rest with ties of the All India Cricket Club, as natty a tie as I've seen and I write this in Oxford, the home of smart ties. (I ask Ron Maudsley who, as a legal Don, is preparing his notes for to-morrow's lecture, if he agrees and he says to watch my step next time I'm in Cambridge.)

Whilst the presentation and speeches were proceeding on board, there was a noisy demonstration on the wharf below. A crowd of university students clamoured unceasingly for Bradman. A well-built lad was the leader. He began with a raucous "We want . . ." and then in came the supports with the roar "Bradman." This went on for a long spell. When the reception was over, Bradman came to the rail of the ship and the welcome he received was loud, spirited and prolonged. Surely no other name has ever been so well known or idolised in the world of sport.

One very popular in Aden was Lindsay Hassett. Uniformed gentlemen, sporting the most luxurious moustaches imaginable, their points almost touching their ears, came aboard to see Hassett. They had played cricket against him when he was with the Australian Services team in the Middle East. One of them, Colonel Swayn, had then performed the rather notable feat of having sight-boards carried all the way from Haifa to Palestine for a game of cricket.

Not only in Aden but in other places along this route there was something basically sad in meeting these Englishmen in such posts abroad. England's financial policy, and otherwise, dictated withdrawal from many places. Recent events have shown the burden a leading nation can carry, with little thanks and often abuse, over a period of years. Even if it is safeguarding the interests of its Empire, it has at heart the well-being of the world and humanity in general, and strives to do what is best in a position of bristling and complex problems. This, possibly, has nought to do with cricket, but we sensed that these Englishmen, with whom we had cricket in common, were doubly pleased at this time to welcome the Australian cricketers. Some of them still bore scars of injuries when trying to quell Arab-Jew riots; others of their type, who would have loved this fraternising, were no longer alive.

I thought of them that sweltering, perspiring day in Aden as I looked out from the European club and saw little naked natives swimming, dog-paddle fashion, to the ship some three-quarters of a mile out in the stream. Every now and then, so they told us, a native is taken by a shark as he swims out to dive for pennies from the ship. As I looked at this scene, with the barren rocks of Aden forming the background, there was more than ever point to the song which we all sang.

> *I saw the old homestead and faces I knew,*
> *I saw England's valleys and dells,*
> *I listened with joy, as I did when a boy*
> *To the sound of the old village bells.*
> *The fire was burning brightly,*
> *'Twas a night to banish all sin,*
> *The bells were ringing the Old Year out*
> *And the New Year in.*

And on to Port Said, where a police strike had preceded us by a mere day, and non-stop through the Mediterranean to Tilbury—a long run of 3,215 miles, lacking the glamour of previous trips with stops at Naples, Nice, Toulon and Gibraltar. Out of Port Said we were challenged by a British destroyer, on the watch to nab illegal migrants into Palestine, to reveal our identity; along the African coast, with Pantelleria to starboard and Cape Bon to port, there was plenty of recent history to occupy thoughts. We were passing over, probably, ships so well known to Australia in the *Awatea*, *Comorin*, *Narkunda* and *Strathallen*, lost in the fighting there of a few years before.

Although we did not stop at Gibraltar, we came in close to put overboard films of the players taken on ship-board. They were flown from Gib. to London and were on view some time before the team arrived by ship. For some miles out, by courtesy of Captain Allen (who one day on his bridge took the most spectacular catch at sea when he caught, one-handed, Lindwall, from the deck below), Bradman, O'Reilly and I followed the course of the ship by radar. We could see, so clearly, the outlines of Europe on one side and Africa on the other, ships in our vicinity, down even to the small launch which came alongside to take delivery of the films. A most interesting morning, begun when General Sir Oliver Leese, who was in charge of the attack on Cassino, in the Italian campaign, told us that he thought the Gib. was still impregnable, even against atomic bombs.

Our first sight of England was at Brixham and Torquay. O'Reilly observed that you could tell the Englishmen that morning from the manner in which they trod the deck with their chests thrown well out. It was a glorious sight, indeed, not ruffled even by the trails of planes high in the sky and naval

2. *Another for Compton. Compton hit by Lindwall in the third Test at Manchester*

3. *Morris misses, but the acrobatic Evans manages to gather the ball at Manchester on the last day*

4. *The author, J. H. Fingleton*

vessels on manœuvres and talk of war again in the air. How similar to 1938!

Whether it was a sign of the times or an indication of order in the bird life, we did observe how well the seagulls queued up for food tossed overboard. They came in splendidly in order from the right, took their morsel while fluttering on the wing, and went away in perfect formation again to the right with never a wing going against the traffic. And all the way along the green coast we had soft, warm sunshine, unusual for England in April, but typical of a spring day on Bondi Beach.

CHAPTER THREE

THE SAME OLD LONDON

I ARRIVED in London on April 19, 1948, wearing a black Homburg hat. Of not much interest, possibly, to anybody other than myself and my travelling companions, but that hat certainly had trouble in its brim. For a beginning, O'Reilly did not like it. He said some very pointed things about it, but my father-in-law had given it to me with the express wish that I should wear it the day I arrived in London.

I did not report O'Reilly's comments. My father-in-law is Mr. Justice Street of the Supreme Court of N.S.W., and though used to most things in court, I saw no reason why he should be given the bald reactions of other Australians to the black Homburg. Such a hat is uncommon in Australia. It raises the eyebrows when seen though it is the common headwear of the City in London. I was delighted to see that my good friend, Toshack, began to sport one (together with a long cigar!) later in the tour, but when we arrived at St. Pancras my press companions, O'Reilly, Ray Robinson (*Sydney Sun*), Brian Feely (*Melbourne Pictorial*), Andy Flanagan (Commercial Broadcaster), Arthur Mailey (*Sydney Telegraph*), Tom Goodman (*Sydney Herald*), Percy Taylor (*Melbourne Argus*) and Bob Maguire (*Sydney Mirror*), were inclined to be stand-offish, though Dudley Leggett (A.B.C.) kept me company in another distinguished Homburg.

The trouble started as soon as we emerged from the boat-train. I had no sooner put foot on London pavement than somebody wished to be directed somewhere. O'Reilly grinned hugely. We walked down to catch a Strand bus and joined our first English queue, gaping at the familiar London sights. We shuffled along the queue. The others joined the bus and just as I was doing so somebody excused themselves and wished to be directed somewhere. It was somewhat flattering to be taken twice so quickly for a man who knows his London, but whilst I was explaining that I didn't know, the bus sailed off and I was stranded in London. I could see O'Reilly waving gaily from the bus so I rose my Homburg to him. When the bus drew out of sight, I doffed my Homburg and carried it the rest of the journey.

I thought, to that stage, I had done a rather fair job by that black hat.

The top deck of a London bus is still a magnificent way of seeing London. This bus wound past St. Paul's, and the sad feelings of one returning to England after ten years as he sees the devastation of the blitz are assuaged somewhat at the miraculous escape of St. Paul's. All the way up from Tilbury we had seen the pitiful remnants of bombed-out buildings and homes. The London dock area had suffered enormously, but here was St. Paul's defiant and magnificent while all around for acres were buildings razed to the ground. On the soil, much of it seeing its first London light for centuries, were growing in great profusion wild flowers and even trees. Wild flowers in the middle of London!

But if, on the first London bus ride for ten years, one was to be saddened by such sights, there was the consolation down Ludgate Hill, up Fleet Street, past the Law Courts and down the Strand of seeing many famous buildings still proudly erect, though their walls showed dints of shrapnel from the blitzing. London still looked magnificently good in April of 1948. It had been battered and purged but it was still pulsating in resilient manner. Down in the streets below were the same puffing, panting taxis, as Cockney as their owners, that squared their way contemptuously past sleek, resplendent automobiles; down in the streets below were the same old London slabs of colour with here a proud Chelsea warrior of the Old Brigade in his scarlet coat and beribboned chest, and there a bank messenger, top-hatted and tail-frocked and as dignified as a duke. Down there, too, were the London bobbies and in the bus were the same old and varied London types—a little frayed in dress, perhaps, a little tired-looking, some of the girls a little prematurely grey but still the same old lovable London types.

"'Old tight, luvs," said the Cockney bus-girl and away we chugged up Fleet Street, the bus driver knowing to half an inch whether he could get his huge charge through without so much as a scrape. "'Old tight, now," said the bus-girl as she pressed the starting button; "'Old tight, gals," said the bus man. It was all very matey, but one wondered whether such cheeriness was not just a little out of court one day when a bus conductor said to a dignified gentleman who boarded just outside the Law Courts. "'Old tight, Pop!" It was the Lord Chief Justice!

Being an Australian cricketer in England, and particularly

London, has its advantages and disadvantages. O'Reilly and I
realised the disadvantages in our very first days in London when,
unhampered by the official welcomes and the "crickety" people
who hem you and your movements in on every side, we pursued
our own free paths and, in consequence, saw more of London
in a few days than we had seen in all the London visits before.

You can't do as you wish when you belong to the Australian
Eleven. Weeks before the team leaves Australia and, indeed,
while it is on the high seas, a round of functions is pruned (a
team could never accept one-twentieth of the hospitality offered
it) and arranged. The players whiz from one to the other in
rapid succession—while the talk is all of cricket.

In our capacity we had nothing like that to bother us this
time, and in three very pleasant days we had taken in the National
Gallery, the Westminster Cathedrals, Hampton Court, Petticoat
Lane on a Sunday morning, the Tower, an opera (*La Traviata*),
possibly the best live show in London in *Edward, My Son*, the
Changing of the Guard, of course, and, just for old time's sake,
a visit to Lord's Cricket Ground.

Edward, My Son, at the Lyric, written by Robert Morley and
Noel Langley, and in which Morley, himself, a superb actor,
plays the principal rôle, provided me with an interesting insight
into the manner in which London accepts things. In one of the
acts there is a very realistic raid during the blitz. There is the
wail of sirens, the drone of planes and the booming of guns.
One would have thought, after their years of travail, that
Londoners would never again wish to hear anything that would
recall such memories. I sensed a tremor through the audience
when it first began but that was all.

It was not until the second act that I settled down to enjoy
Giuseppe Verdi's *La Traviata* at Covent Garden. I went as the
guest of J. R. Jackson, K.C., of Perth, a fellow traveller on the
Strathaird. The opera was tremendously popular and we were
fortunate to get seats at the last moment. They were high up
in the amphitheatre stalls and as we took our seats in the front
row, only a brass rail in front as we leaned over was between us
and a drop of immense height to the floor below. Playing in
front of crowds in a Test never worried me at all; being in a
crowd is for me a different matter. I think it is some boyish
inhibition which grew when I saw a Christmas pantomime and
a bush-fire on the stage scared the wits out of me. At all events,
I sat back tightly during the first act of the opera and clung

tenaciously to the back of the seats. I had an almost unbearable
desire to jump over. Perspiration rolled off me. I will not soon
forget my first opera at Covent Garden.

Lord's had barely changed at all. It was drab and stood in
much need of paint, but then this applied to most of London—
indeed, it did to the cities of Australia. We saw Lord's again in
the soft sunlight of an English spring day. There was freshness
in the trees and on the grass, though the score-board had run
amok in its winter's hibernation. It showed 40 wickets down for
no runs, the last man inconceivably made 82, and the same
bowler had performed the amazing feat of bowling from both
ends. If this were true, then it equalled Warwick Armstrong in
1921 when, after a verbal tussle over the rules in a Test, he ambled
on to the field again and bowled another over after he had just
bowled the last. This, they say, was the only time any bowler
had succeeded in bowling two successive overs in a Test match,
but then Armstrong was big and wilful enough to do most
things on a cricket field.

There were the usual crowds to see the Australians at the
nets, while the war years had produced another generation of
inquisitive schoolboys quite prepared to take their lives in their
hands by poking their noses through the nets. Lord's had
revolutionised itself to the extent of putting down a concrete
pitch and over in the roofed Nursery professionals in grey
trousers, white boots and cricket caps were busy administering
the "do's" and "don'ts" of the game to boys only as big as their
bats while admiring parents looked on.

Behind and in front of the nets and up on the grandstand
behind were the critics and the cynics of the game, noting this
and demonstrating that, already certain in the first five minutes
that A. would be a complete success on tour and B. an utter flop.
There can be no other sound in England to equal the first hit of
a new season at Lord's. With their love of tradition and pageantry,
I wonder that the English don't do something about this. The
Lord Mayor could attend in the robes of office and read a scroll
befitting the historic occasion; there could be a roll of drums
and a blare of trumpets from the band of the Grenadier Guards;
a detachment of Guards could present, just for the occasion, a
row of bats, and the Youngest Member could bowl a ball to the
Oldest Member while free beer was turned on at the Tavern or,
just as momentously, free afternoon tea by the caterers.

But there is no other cricketing place in the world like Lord's, though its pleasant secretary, Colonel Rait-Kerr, once told me that often family parties are very distressed when they take the wrong turning at St. John's Wood Road and come into Lord's in mistake for the Zoo, which is nearby in Regent's Park. The distress is more acute when it is politely said that, under no circumstances, can money be refunded at Lord's once the turn-stile has clicked behind you.

Lord's stands supreme. It is not only historic. It is kind and benevolent. The Pavilion is clouded in antiquity and, in 1948, in peace, too, as the bust of Dr. Grace is back on its pedestal again in the Long Room. Old Father Time swings lazily and understandingly on his weather perch above the scoring-board as if another cricket season, as it is, is just another cricket season to him, and he will, without question, give it his benediction, blessing the centuries and the rich strokes and the clean-bowleds and understanding, with his hoary experience, the discomfiture of the man dismissed at Lord's for nothing.

Lord's does not belong to cricket alone. It belongs to London, and to none more so than the perky sparrows and the strutting doves who take possession of the outfield in late afternoon and wage unceasing battle for worms and scraps. In the warm sun of late August I sat and dozed near the ropes and watched a brood of sparrows feeding their chirping progeny with the worms of Lord's. Almost through their midst, Robins chased a cover-drive by Bradman, but the sparrows did not resent the intrusion; indeed, they barely seemed to notice it. Once, how-ever, a London sparrow did take too much for granted. He flew across the pitch just as Jehangir Khan, the Indian, was bowling a very fast ball to Tom Pearce, of Essex. That sparrow remem-bered nothing more. He was killed instantly and, though it might be an attempt to make a good story even better, they tell that his mute body carried on to Pearce's stumps and took off the bails. I never tried to discover the truth of that. I left the story as it was, but to-day there is that London sparrow still as if in its last flight, stuffed, mounted, glassed-in and on proud display, suitably inscribed, in the sacrosanct sanctum of the Lord's Long Room. He is just across the way from Dr. Grace's bust and I'm not so certain that the sparrows haven't put one across the Lord's committee—to do which, you'll agree, you have to be up with the cock. It might be that this was the chosen sparrow; that he was the martyr sparrow, or the suffragette (one can never be too sure of the sex of a sparrow) chosen to win its way, by hook, by crook or by ball, into the Lord's Long Room to show that Lord's belongs as much to the sparrows of London as the nobility. The sparrow, like Cock Robin, is dead and gone to its case, but not, I feel, in vain, and if ever you gain access to the Long Room, see if you don't agree with me that there is a certain sparkle in its eye.

As Neville Cardus observes, there is only one unpleasant sight to be seen at Lord's . . . the black stack of a huge chimney outside the ground across the way. Cardus once spoke to Sir Pelham Warner about this object. "It's an eyesore, spoiling the picture." Without blinking an eyelid, "Plum" replied: "I agree; but I can't do anything about it. I'm not on the House Committee, you know."

Those who wish to be at peace with the world and themselves can spend a whole afternoon on the prowl at Lord's and love every minute of it, even though there is no cricket match being played. For old time's sake we had a beer in the Tavern and renewed acquaintances. We spoke of Englishmen we would see no more. We spoke of Bill Reeves and an umpire colleague, Denis Hendren, a brother to the inimitable Patsy, told us of Bill, who was a card, if ever there was one. One day Bill gave a young professional out. The decision was a doubtful one, and when Reeves came to lunch he espied the young player sitting very disconsolately in a corner of the dressing-room. Bill knew what the trouble was. Many an umpire would have shied away, seeking another and more appropriate moment to make his peace, but Bill was not like that. He approached the lad.

"You doon't think thou wast out, laad?" said Bill.

"Well, no, Mr. Reeves, as you ask me, I didn't think I were."

"And no more thou wert, m'laad," spoke Bill, "but 'twere mighty cold out yon, as thou knows, and I thought of thy mother and I thought of thee and I thought mother would never forgive me if I kept thee out there in cold wind and thou caught bad cold so I gave thee out."

What could anybody say against that?

Bradman showed in the official functions, most of which precede the first game of the Tour, that he was even a better speaker than in 1938. He had wit and command of words; he uttered pleasing sentiments. London is a shrewd and a hard judge in the matter of public speakers, but Bradman was passed with high honours. His speeches were always a sheer delight and wonderfully received.

The prize for functions was generally awarded to the dinner given by the Cricket Writers' Club. This club was formed in Perth in 1946. The chairman of the dinner was Jim Swanton, of the London *Telegraph*, who performed most nobly, and the speeches, by general accord, reached the highest level of all cricketing time. The B.B.C. broadcast the speeches by the chairman and Bradman and, I believe, did an unprecedented thing by going on longer than the original programme intended and broadcasting the whole of Bradman's speech. Bradman's mail for the next few days was hundreds of letters larger than usual . . . so, too, was the congratulatory mail to the B.B.C.

Bradman quipped at O'Reilly at this dinner in a gentle manner. "He taught our boys to appeal and now, as a critic, he chides them for appealing too much," said Bradman. O'Reilly joined in the general laugh at his expense but, if he had had the chance, he might have replied in biblical terms that one had to ask to receive, even unto Bradman's wicket. Only that week at Lord's I had heard umpire Chester tell O'Reilly that when he first stood behind O'Reilly he had been warned that he over-appealed. "In my opinion," said Chester, "I thought there were times when an appeal was warranted when you didn't." So much for that, but it was interesting to hear Chester tell O'Reilly that he was the greatest bowler he had stood behind as umpire.

The Duke of Edinburgh was present at that dinner and enjoyed it as much as anybody. Bradman said he had seen photographs of the Duke bowling. He accepted him on that evidence and invited him, at any time, to come along and lend a hand against the Australians at the nets. Bradman had a delectable strain of humour in his speeches. At the Savoy he said that he had followed English cricket happenings with great interest because he always liked to know what his side was likely to be up against. For instance, he noticed that a young chap named Allen had been on trial in the West Indies. "Gubby" Allen, at that moment, was limping home from the West Indies with a dishevelled English side. In the middle forties, Allen had allowed himself to go to the West Indies as captain-manager of the M.C.C. side and he had had a soul-shattering experience.

At that Savoy dinner, also, Bradman complimented Bedser. He said the ball with which Bedser bowled him for nothing in the preceding Test series at Adelaide was the best ball ever bowled to him. Though so huge, it is amazing how often one meets people in London. I saw Bedser that afternoon in Piccadilly and told him of Bradman's tribute. He smiled and, I think, blushed. "It was just one of those things that happened," said Bedser; "the ball floated away in the air and turned back. I don't know how I did it."

In a night of brilliant speeches at the Cricket Writers' dinner the honours belonged, we unanimously agreed, to Mr. Justice Norman Birkett, a brilliant member of the British judiciary who had presided at the Nuremburg War Criminal trials. He did not mind, he said at the outset, if people looked at their watches while he was speaking; what did rather hurt him was if they shook them to see if they were still going.

A very distinguished colleague had asked him that afternoon where he was going in the evening. Sir Norman told him it was to a gathering of cricketers, and his colleague told him how he once went to Manchester and was there received with great civic dignity. As the procession was walking off the platform, he saw a trolley loaded with cricket bags, and going over, the distinguished judge looked at the labels and touched one of the bags. "This hand," he told Sir Norman, "can always boast that it has touched the cricketing bag of the famous Johnnie Tyldesley."

I liked particularly the story which Mr. Justice Birkett told of American hospitality. "We English cannot entertain as we would like to do," said the judge. When he was once in America he complimented the gathering on its hospitality, whereupon a gentleman arose, announced himself from Oklahoma, and said this hospitality could not touch that from where he came. "There," he said, "we have drinks between drinks." Which led a gentleman from Arizona to rise and observe: "Gentlemen, in the state from which I come, we know no such intervals." It all reminded him, said the judge, of the film actress who, after a certain period at a cocktail party, said: "Well, folks, I don't know how it is with you, but I feel much more like I do now than when I first came in."

One of the saddest utterances ever made by man, said Sir Norman, was made by Bradman that evening when he said he would never again play first-class cricket after this season. There was infinite sadness in that statement—but life, observed Sir Norman, always gave opportunities for repentance. Another great hit at the dinner was the Rev. Canon Gillingham, who once swam across the Worcester ground to rescue the records of the club when the Severn misbehaved itself. It was rather significant, he observed, that several days before he had seen a news-poster with the following items billed: "Four Murderers Reprieved; Gangsters Charter; Australians Arrive." But he had no reason to talk, said the Canon. The day after his marriage, his photograph appeared in a newspaper alongside that of Crippen, the notorious murderer. His wife wanted to know what Crippen had done!

That first fortnight in London, before the tour proper begins, is always memorable. In spite of apologies for their hospitality, there was about the receptions to the Australian cricketers this time a warmness not equalled, indeed, by those of pre-war years. It was good to be in England again.

CHAPTER FOUR

WORCESTER AND ALL THAT

APART from the two slow bowlers, McCool and Ring, the
Australians were mostly happy after their long spell at the
Lord's nets. It is an unforgettable thrill for an Australian cricketer
to play for the first time on an English pitch. He has read all
about them, has often wondered what they are like, and always
gets a shock when he sees one for the first time. They are not
clearly defined like our Australian ones, nor are they so sub-
stantial under-foot. They look, as indeed they often are, as if
a piece of grass has been selected, the grass cut, rolled a few times
and then marked out.

I remember well the Worcester one in 1938. It didn't look
like a first-class pitch when we got to the middle but its looks
belied it. An English pitch nearly always plays much better
than it looks and, although it is difficult to do at first, the overseas player does well to trust it and not look for funny things
to happen.

I have singled McCool and Ring out particularly for mention
after the first stretch at the nets. One or two of the new batsmen
were still wobbly at the nets, but the two slow leg-break bowlers
showed most reaction. The ball turned too slowly for them.
Ring decided there and then that he would push it through faster
in the air, somewhat after the style of O'Reilly, and I thought
in the weeks ahead that he often tried to bowl too fast. A slow
bowler gets many, indeed, possibly, he gets most of his wickets
in the air because of the batsman making an error in the flight
or pitch of the ball, so it is sometimes better to give the ball
more air and leave it to the batsman to do his worst. Ian Johnson,
with his slow off-spinners, was another who found the pitch at
Lord's too slow for him.

As usual, the photographers were fussing and buzzing as
Press photographers do. They get more snubs in life, bless them,
than a politician. There were stirs when the fast bowlers several
times knocked Bradman's stumps over, but what the photographers wanted most of all was Lindwall at the moment of
bowling. Ambitious news editors, always on the look-out for a

43

story out of the ordinary, wanted to beat up his "drag" which, in films from Australia, had caused such a sensation during the English winter. But Bradman wasn't having any. He warned the photographers out of it.

McCool, who, in his batting, plays somewhat at the pitch of the ball, couldn't get the hang of the English pitch at first. Bradman once repeated the visual lesson he had given Toshack in the middle at Brisbane (this was the day after Toshack had bowled so badly in length against England on a wet pitch). At Lord's, Bradman took up a bat and demonstrated vigorously with feet and bat to McCool. McCool looked puzzled and took it all in.

And so the Australians prepared for their first game at Worcester, observing tradition by choosing what they expected at that time would be their first Test team. The only difference from the team at Worcester and Nottingham for the first Test was that Johnston forced his way in. Harvey was twelfth man and McCool was the one who eventually made way for Johnston. Another pointer at Worcester was that Morris and Barnes opened and Brown came in down the list. This was to be observed, too, in the Test teams.

The beauty of the Worcester ground, I think, is slightly exaggerated. After the first day's play of the opening game against the Australians there is that delectable photograph in *The Times* which shows the Worcester ground to be unbelievably beautiful, but it is always taken from the same angle and shows that glorious Worcester Cathedral in the background. When you look at the ground with the Cathedral at your back, the Worcester ground is no prettier or uglier than most English county grounds though it has a pleasant old pavilion.

But it has atmosphere. The Severn flows between it and the Cathedral, and every now and then gives the ground a flooding. Several huge marquees are erected for the Australian's game, and every tour, as the crowds increase and the ground gorges itself with them until it can stand no more, the playing area becomes smaller and smaller. It was here at Worcester in 1938 that McCormick established that nightmarish record of bowling 35 no-balls and, with the controversy playing about Lindwall, we wondered whether there would be a repetition of history.

Australian cricketers, the evening before their game here, inspect the cathedral. It is a tradition. The tomb of King John, the last of the Angevin kings and the signer of Magna Carta, is the most conspicuous monument in the Cathedral, but the place abounds with general interest. Worcester, which was a Royal port of call in the early ages, was the meeting ground for many conferences with the Welsh or marked the setting-off point of expeditions into Wales. Because we had known the present Earl in London and of his association with Australia, we were interested in the effigies of the first Beauchamps. In 1387 the original Beauchamp was created a baron by patent (the first history knows, I think), but the politics of the time were too much for him and both he and his wife Joan lost their heads. Now they have somewhat quizzical swans at the head and feet of their effigies.

In its depths of wifely love and regard, I liked the tribute on the wall to Richard Saley, of London, who, while travelling on a tour of pleasure with his wife and family "was seized with an inflammation of the intestines which in five days led to his death." I suppose that would be appendicitis to-day and, in the modern way of dealing with it, Richard would have been on his path of pleasure again in a little over five days. But, then, we would never have had his wifely tribute on the wall: "His remains are deposited in a vault near this place where also his wretched widow intends hers shall be placed when it should please the God of mercy and of comfort to remove her from her present state of misery. If the best and most beloved of men, whose aim solely on earth was to promote the happiness of her who now pays this last sad tribute of affection to his memory, could behold her now he would know all she now feels whose every joy and earthly hope centred in himself. May that Divine Saviour in whose presence she trusts he is now rejoicing, vouchsafe to his afflicted widow heavenly faith and patience till through the merits of that same Redeemer she may be united with him in eternal happiness and may he grant that their fatherless infants follow in the footsteps of their much revered and honoured parent and may they share the reward of virtues like his own." What lovely sentiments in an era when divorce and estrangements receive such publicity. They should add to that tablet: Hollywood please copy!

And what a man, after Marco Polo's own heart, must Robert Luddington have been! His tablet tells you that first he was a gentleman, that he had three wives and that he was the first treasurer of the Turkish bank in London in 1625. These were the countries into which his banking business took Luddington: Italy, Greece, Turkey, Syria, Palestine, Egypt, Persia, Arabia, Caldea, Barbary, Brazil, the Moluccas and the East Indies. And, says the tablet, he spoke all these languages with ease! What a man, indeed—the very man to help George Bernard Shaw out in this year of 1948 when he wishes, through the columns of *The Times*, to establish a world-wide political language.

The most interesting person I found in the Cathedral was a woman who pried into the niches of centuries-old statues and tombs with an electric torch. She verified the original colours and then promptly repainted them. This she did in between her household duties, and a splendid job she made of it—the retouching, I mean. I never shall forget the beauty and the magnificence of the Cathedral and its stained windows as I looked down the aisle and saw the westering sun cast them with brilliant daubs of gold. The bombs left Worcester alone with the exception of one small, solitary house. The Cathedral was untouched, which is more than one can say for it during the time of the Reformation.

The history of the Cathedral, as the work of Canon Wilson tells, covers three periods, the first the coming of Monk Bosel, in A.D. 680, to superintend the newly-formed diocese there because Worcester was an important intersection of roads, determined by a ford in the Severn. The Benedictine monks followed and from 1084, which dates the earliest part of the present Cathedral, to 1504 was a period of building and rebuilding. From 1504 to the present time dates a period of vicissitudes, pillage, decay, restoration and use.

I have written at length of the Cathedral because it is of rare vintage and beauty and it seems inseparable from the first match of the Australian tour. The chimes ring out across the Severn and the cricket ground, and there is a fine peal of twelve bells and a carillon. Because of Cromwell's association with Worcester, O'Reilly used to bowl all the harder when he heard the carillon. The cricket ground and the adjacent meadows are open and unbuilt upon, and the ground is let by the Cathedral authorities to the county club.

This was the setting in which Bradman made history in 1930, 1934 and 1938 by making a double century on each occasion. The Royal Worcester firm noted his 1938 feat by presenting Bradman with a lovely piece of work, specially created for the occasion, and everybody was wondering whether Bradman could do it again. Well, as it turned out, he *could* have had another double century if he wanted it but he didn't. He threw his wicket away after gaining his century. Like those gnarled and admirable old men who sit painting little birds on pieces of Royal Worcester, Bradman was another ten years older and behaved himself accordingly.

Palmer, an intellectual-looking person who is a school-teacher with the rounded shoulders of study, played here the finest innings of the season against the Australians by any county man. It was strange that this should have come in the very first match of the tour but, looking back now, this innings by Palmer was the outstanding county one. He had a rich flow of strokes, his footwork was splendid and he had always plenty of time in which to do things. We marked him down immediately as a class player. The Australians would have made him a first choice in England's Test team—particularly as he was more than handy as a medium-paced bowler—but there were the usual difficulties associated with an outstanding amateur player who could not afford to give over-much time to sport. He could fit cricket in only in his holidays, though probably, had the selectors wanted him, his school would have been proud to have had one of its staff a Test player. At least, that would have been the case in Australia.

Lindwall was *not* no-balled here. Unlike in Australia he brought his back foot down somewhat farther back from the line, but I sat opposite his delivery for a time and found that he was still dragging over. But the point was that the English umpires were immediately satisfied that if he brought his back foot down behind the line, that was all that concerned them. Wisely, I thought, they had taken the view that an umpire could not watch foot and hand at the same time, and so in the very first match was blotted out what many thought would give rise to a controversy in no time. In 1938, McCormick didn't drag. He clearly went over the line.

Morris, on the post, took from Bradman the honour of being the first centurion of the tour. Morris was 34 when Bradman came in. Morris was not very comfortable to his first twenty, lacking in confidence, but Bradman, received like royalty with three dozen photographers racing before him to get a snap, knew no hesitancy. We had only one shock. This was when the Worcestershire wicket-keeper let out a roar like a Red Indian. It was a whoop of exultation, and across the field floated what was more like a statement of fact than an appeal to the umpire.

"I've got him," roared the keeper as he tossed the ball up. The umpire didn't think so for a second. He ruled no catch.

Bradman was 74 when Morris was 81. Then Bradman scored two fours while Morris stood still. Bradman raced into the nineties ahead of Morris, but the left-hander caught him, passed him and went to 95 with Bradman still on 91. Bradman hesitated a while before running the third which made Morris 98 and kept him the strike, but Morris could do nothing about it at that time. Bradman sailed into action at the other end and hit two fours in the next over to make him 99 to Morris's 98. It was a tense struggle, but Morris had the strike at the end of the over and from the other end Bradman shook his fist at him in mock disgust.

Morris clinched his century and the honour with it in a few moments; he batted 225 minutes for it with 14 fours. Bradman got his a minute later in the good time of 138 minutes with 14 boundaries also. Then Bradman deliberately played on off Jackson. He did not seek the double century at all. Wisely, he had decided not to take too much out of himself.

Miller came in ninth here and got 50 not out—a very bright innings. Jackson, an off-spinner, had the good figures of 135-6 off 39·4 overs and, in view of the manner in which he faded from view as the tour progressed, it was interesting that slow-bowler McCool had a good match with 67-6 off 36 overs. Johnson had 127-6, but the two fast men, Lindwall and Miller, took things very quietly. They knew they had a long tour ahead, and the fast bowler is very wise who builds up his speed match by match. The Tests, here, were the main considerations.

There were several other features of this game. In the first place, it was played in arctic weather. It was, as the players say, a two-sweater job and there was the usual fire in the pavilion before which players crouched before coming out to bat. This time we shivered in an improvised press-shed that admitted all breezes without question or visa. Those were the coldest days I have spent on a sporting ground, though Leicester and Bradford, particularly the latter, were still looming ahead like icebergs in the Atlantic.

The Australians were vociferous in their appeals. It seemed to be a happy spirit of one in, all in, and give everything a go. Some of the appeals for leg before came from fantastically situated positions, but perhaps the boys wanted to keep warm. Tallon never leaves anybody in doubt that he is appealing, but

5. *A peaceful photograph of the first game of the tour. Worcestershire is seen batting against the Australians at Worcester*

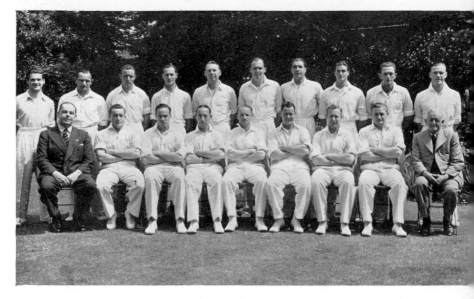

6. *The Australian touring team.* (*Standing*) *N. Harvey, S. G. Barnes, R. R. Lindwall, R. A. Saggers, N. D. Ring, W. A. Johnston, E. R. Toshack, K. R. Miller, D. Tallon, S. Loxton.* (*Sitting*) *K. Johnson* (*Manager*), *R. A. Hammence, I. Johnson, A. L Hassett, D. G. Bradman* (*Captain*), *W. A. Brown, A. R. Morris, C. L. McCool W. Ferguson* (*Scorer*)

7. *Hassett hits a boundary off Jackson on the second day at Worcester*

I think there is character and a certain amount of artistry in Toshack's appeal. Toshack strikes an attitude as he turns and he raises *both* hands on high to the umpire. I like the clarity of his "*'OW Whizz 'E*" which floats across the ground and penetrates every nook. In a few succeeding games when Toshack continued to exercise his vocal cords without stint, I devised the name for him of "The Voice," and Ernie didn't mind a bit. Some cricketers are touchy on these things but not Toshack. He is one of the best-tempered fellows in the game.

The Worcester crowds were record ones. On two succeeding days there were 14,000 present and the gate receipts were £4,000. They were considered highly successful in 1938 with £1,933, but we were to find in this post-war England that the man in the street had more money in his pocket and had developed a bent for sport which exceeded the days of pre-war. But what a strangely silent crowd was this one at Worcester. It was the most unresponsive one I have known.

We met splendid hospitality from the county club. The secretary, Brigadier Mike Green, did everything possible to welcome and entertain the team and the Australian Press. Nothing was too much trouble. It was rather spoiling for us to have this in the first match because we were soon to find that most county clubs, though the game must be heavily indebted to the Press and could barely exist without the publicity given it, were coldly indifferent to the needs of the Press or seemed to be unaware that visiting Australians, some of whom had helped to swell the coffers for county clubs in previous years, were among those present. The hospitality and help we did receive from some of the clubs stood out boldly and we appreciated it. In Australia the Press is always made to feel welcome, and appreciation is shown of the time factor of their jobs by providing them with luncheons—as guests.

It was at Worcester I heard one of the best remarks of the season. It was relayed to me by Bill Brown, who heard it in the outfield. As the groundsman was sprinkling sawdust after rain for the bowlers, one of the spectators grumbled: "'Ere, go easy with yon sawdust. Why, yon man is wasting full month's ration of ruddy sausage meat." You had to taste English sausages of 1948 to appreciate that. One other Worcester memory remains. That was the hotel-keeper who stood at the door and blew a terrific blast on a referee's whistle. That meant time, gents, please!

B.F.D.   D

Most of the opposition at Leicester came from fellow-Australians. Jack Walsh and Victor Jackson are from N.S.W. There are hosts of Australians in the league cricket in the north but these two qualified for Leicester before the war. Jackson, a medium-to-slow off-spinner and cutter, bowled these figures: 37.2—3—91—5. Walsh: 29—0—125—2. Walsh top-scored for Leicester with a hard hit 33 in the first innings, and Jackson made second-top in the second with 31 not out.

Walsh's figures by no means showed the value of his bowling. He is a left-handed twisty bowler after the Fleetwood-Smith style. His googly, which is a leg-break to the right-handed batsman, is the hardest I know to pick, and after I saw Bradman once play for an off-break and miss the ball by a good two feet as it spun the other way, I guessed he might agree too. I had never before seen Bradman so completely beaten. Walsh bowls his googly in three different ways. One is from his palm, the other is through his fingers, and the third in a different manner through his fingers. He makes one very obvious to try and mislead you for the others. No wonder it is hard to pick. The trouble with him, possibly, is that he has too much variety and his length suffers, but he is likely to bowl anybody head, neck and heels. Glamorgan, county champions, shiver whenever his name is mentioned. He spun them out at Swansea and did so again, taking 14 wickets for a little over 80 runs, the match after Glamorgan had won the title. This was a sickening blow for the Welshmen because Walsh had the game over in two days.

Jackson bowled much better here than in Australia. He and I played with Waverley (Sydney) for years and I often felt that the poor type of pitch we had there robbed Waverley of another international in Jackson. He was one of the most brilliant stroke-makers I've seen, but in later years went into a defensive shell. That pitch, crumbling, of many heights and paces, was the bane of our cricketing existence. It could run a batsman out of form in one innings. Jackson admitted that he bowled better in England than Australia. "It's my living here," he explained. "I have a different outlook on the game."

This was the only time on tour that Bradman vacated the number one down batting position. When the first wicket fell, youths, girls, women and men raced in their hundreds towards the entrance and dozens of cameras were cocked ready for the shutter to click on the Great Man. But Miller, smiling hugely, emerged instead and there was a disappointed "Oh!" from the crowd as they scattered back to their seats, the film untaken.

This was recompense for Miller for the lowly position he had occupied at Worcester. He showed his appreciation with a double century and a beauty it was, too. One of his skimming hits bounced into the crowd and sent a lad into the infirmary for the week-end with a bump on his head. Bradman was in good form again, this time for 81, and Barnes, 76, showed there was nothing wrong with his form either, but some of the new men to England were all at sea against the spin of their countrymen. Harvey, Hamence, Ring, Saggers and Ian Johnson could manage only 33 between them, and smiling, angular Bill Johnston had to see Miller through the final twenty runs of his double century.

Miller was not out and so, at this stage, was 252 runs up for no outs. His success was having an interesting reaction. It brought letters and friends of his Air Force fighting days from all over England. They all called him "Dusty." And, wishing to do their former comrade a good turn (or were they?) they invariably gave him names of dogs and horses that were certainties—or so they said!

Leicestershire county club has had to change its ground since 1938. The ground on which we played is now the home of huge electrical retorts. This ground of 1948 is a barn-like one and the record crowd of Saturday, like most cricket crowds in England, watched the game in considerable discomfort. Most of the Saturday crowd stood, some of them yards and yards back from the field on a mound.

We met an interesting personality at Leicester. We dubbed him "Wigan." He had set out to see the Rugby League final in London but got no farther than Leicester, where he did some celebrating. After going through some hectic performances, he produced on Saturday night two dozen eggs from his pockets. The team and the Press had fresh eggs for breakfast on Sunday. Where he got them from was just as much a mystery as why they weren't broken. But they were good eggs.

The station-master at Leicester entertained the Press while we were waiting for our train to Bradford. He looked hard at Maurice Tate and said, very seriously, "You remind me very much of a chap who used to play cricket for England, Maurice Tate." Maurice looked at him hard, and said "Uumph." "Yes," said the station-master, "remarkably like him. I suppose a lot

of people have told you that." "Well," I said, "he *is* Maurice
Tate." The station-master collapsed, but recovered, put on his
top-hat and walked down to put us on the train. The war has
come and gone and the British Railways are nationalised, but
the English station-masters still retain their top-hats, striped
trousers and frock-coats. They always look, to me, like the father
of a bride.

Maurice Tate has two outstanding characteristics, apart from
a sunny nature. He has the biggest feet I've seen (apart from
Tiny, deck-hand of the *Strathaird*, who has his size 15s specially
made for him in Belfast) and he has the smallest voice ever. He
barely whispers. Maurice was three pounds when he was born
and was minus finger-nails and toe-nails. For every cricket season
for twenty-five years he shed the nail of his big toes, so hard did
he pound the turf in delivery. A room attendant said to him one
day in Adelaide (when Tate was in terrible agony) that he could
fix things for him. The attendant left for town with Tate's boot.
He returned with the toe of the boot opened up and the stiffener
removed. Tate played with his boot like that until the end of
his cricketing days. The first ball he ever bowled in Australia,
in Perth, threw him back. The hard pitch, unlike the soft English
ones, would not take his weight. He was very worried and told
Strudwick so, but "Struddy" told him not to worry, that he
would get used to it. He did. Used to shedding his nails!

I think Tate was very hurt when Bradman said that Bedser
was the better bowler. Bedser, though I have never played
against him, and that is the best way to judge a bowler, is a great
trier and, I am told, has always to be watched for the one that
does a little something extra off the pitch, but I have never found
anybody to agree with Bradman regarding the two. Tate was
undoubtedly one of the great bowlers of all time. He showed me
a cutting in which Alan Melville, the South African skipper, who
had played against and with Tate when at the University and
Sussex, and against Bedser the preceding season, plumped solidly
for Tate. Maurice was proud of that cutting.

Tate told me one very interesting thing about his bowling.
For the one he wanted to swing across from the leg, he did not
put his front foot straight down the pitch, as most bowlers do,
but it was thrown out to his right across his body. This meant
that the ball was delivered more than side-on. It was delivered
against his body. He held the ball with two fingers down the
seam as if for a natural swinger but he did not deliver the ball

with the seam full on to the batsman, as a swing bowler does. He rolled his two fingers over the ball towards the batsman . . . the opposite to an off-break . . . so that the ball was delivered with what we might call a leg-break roll. This, with the positioning of his front foot, could well explain how he made the ball run away so well. He was a master in this. He never used the crease, he told me. He always delivered from the same place. The in-swinger, as it was becoming in 1938, is the fetish in English cricket to-day with its fieldsmen packed in on the on-side. I know which is the harder ball to play by miles. I think Jackson, of Derbyshire, was the only one we met, apart from Bedser, who ran the ball away. Tate's methods might repay study.

Pace off the pitch? Was there such a thing or was it merely an optical illusion? I have heard that one argued for hours on end, but Tate thought increased pace off the pitch was certainly possible. "You know, Jack," said Maurice, in a tremulous whisper, looking about and as if on the verge of imparting a secret about the atom bomb, "I got pace off the pitch from these." And he motioned down towards his feet.

"Maurice," I said, "say nothing more."

CHAPTER FIVE

SOME LUCK AT YORKSHIRE

OUR old cobber, George Duckworth, was in a spot of strife as we reached Bradford. George is a keen man on Rugby League (or Northern Union, as it is known in England). He writes on the game and some weeks before our arrival had expressed the view that the "bounce of the ball" had beaten Wigan in a game against Bradford Northern. Though that was weeks ago, the dust still had not settled. There was a leader on the subject in a newspaper the day we arrived which ended, rather splenetically, that both Dolphin and Wood were better wicketkeepers than Duckworth, anyway. Need I add that Dolphin and Wood were Yorkshiremen.

I thought so previously in England, and I was convinced again that there is no other county spirit in England to equal that in Yorkshire. It may be that Glamorgan's championship victory in this year of 1948 will stir the Welsh patriotism to something akin to that of Yorkshire's, but Wales formerly concentrated all its fire and spirit into Rugby.

The interest in cricket in Yorkshire is tremendous. It is vital and one senses it on all three Yorkshire grounds—Headingley in Leeds, Bramall Lane at Sheffield, and at Bradford. Yes, and even in the festival match at Scarborough, too. The Yorkshire skipper is a county figure. I heard of one who was entering a restaurant once on a dark night in Bradford. Two men were entering at the same time and one, grabbing the other by the sleeve, pulled him back and said gruffly, "'Ere, let skipper go fust." And up on the moors, forced to remain for the night in a little pub because of a thick fog, Herbert Sutcliffe once had to stay up half the night to explain how it was he came to get run out at a critical period in a game against Lancashire.

Yorkshire is the sole county in England which puts up with no nonsense in the covering of pitches—not even with an Australian team in action and the record gates at stake. Bradman had his first rest here, and Sellars batted when he won the toss though the pitch was so wet that a start could not be made until 2.30.

The first run of the match, by Hutton, was cheered as lustily as if it were the winning run, though at that stage nobody could sense how close Yorkshire, whose fortunes the previous season were at a very low ebb, were to come to beating Australia. The approaches were so greasy that Miller bowled off-breaks, and Loxton, trying to achieve pace, strained his groin. That first run by Hutton was an eyent. He didn't score another until an hour had passed, and then he was out for five to a swish off Miller.

This was the coldest day, surely, that cricket has ever known. The sunshine came in watery, rationed patches and a chill wind froze us in our open-air seats. I swear I once saw snow. Players jumped up and down on the field and swung their arms and kicked their legs to keep warm, and not even the effort of the civic authorities in playing "Waltzing Matilda" on the carillon could warm the Australians.

Watson, a left-hander, who is a prominent soccer player with Sunderland, looked a class batsman for Yorkshire. He looked as if he knew how to go about his business, but at tea Yorkshire could manage only 38 runs for three. In this first adjournment we saw the keenness of the Yorkshire youths. Every one seemed to own a ball of some description, and as soon as the players began to walk off, the young fry streamed on.

Yorkshire could scrape and scrounge together only 71. Miller took 42—6 and bowled 22.3 overs. The pitch and its approach did not suit Lindwall, and Johnston had 22—4 off a long spell of 24 overs. But the Australians could do little better than Yorkshire and managed only 101, Miller being the hero with 34 and most of the others not liking the turning pitch at all. This was not a ferociously bad pitch but it was bad enough for the Australians. Smailes, an off-spinner, took 51—6, but Yorkshire in the second innings could manage only 89. Johnston took 18—6, giving him the grand match figures of 40—10, and Miller finished the match with 91—9.

Australia wanted only 60 to win, but had it not been for good fortune Yorkshire would certainly have won this game. Hassett might have made an initial mistake in not having the pitch rolled because whenever there was rain about in England the heavy roller seemed to knock any nonsense out of the pitch. It was interesting to see Wardle rub the new ball in the dirt before the innings began to get the gloss off it, and he and Smailes were destined to bowl the whole innings.

Brown was leg before to Smailes again without attempting

a stroke, and Morris was soon out. Australia was 4—1 and 5—2 and Yorkshire tails and the spectators were up in the air. Smailes and 10,000 spectators howled for leg before against Miller, the menace of the first innings, and Hassett, who was facing a "pair," was very dicky. Australia was fighting hard, and then Miller, attempting a six, was caught at long off by Halliday. Australia 13—3. As Hassett awaited Hamence, he anxiously patted down the pitch, and Sellers, good humouredly, bent down and said something to him. Hassett, with a wide smile, threatened Sellers with the bat, but there was no time for laughing when Hamence, slightly slow to get off his mark, was run out and Australia was 20—4. With not another run added, Hassett tried to pull Smailes and hit it high overhead. The wicket-keeper and four fieldsmen could have caught this. Sellers caught it under Hassett's nose with hands opened like a fishing net.

This left Australia in an alarming position. Half the side was out for 20; the remainder had to double that, and the injured Loxton, it was stated, would not bat. Then came the chance which, unaccepted, lost Yorkshire the match. Harvey, at one, turned a ball to Hutton, one of two short legs. Hutton fell forward, got the ball into his hands and, in falling, dropped it. Had that chance been held, Australia must surely have lost this game. Harvey showed his appreciation by sweeping the next ball for four.

In 1902, Yorkshire dismissed the Australians for 23. F. S. Jackson took 12—5 and George Hirst 9—5. Sensing defeat, the innumerable critics pored over the records books and found that Australia (minus the Big Six—Trumper, Armstrong, Carter, Ransford, Hill and Cotter—who had had a row in Australia with officialdom) was beaten by five counties in 1912. These were Lancashire twice, Notts, Surrey and Hampshire. In 1909, Surrey beat Australia by five runs, and in 1905 Essex beat Australia by 19. It was on this latter game that Bradman was bowled out at the Writers' Dinner in London when he stated that Australia had not been beaten by a county for fifty years. One of the speakers to follow had the Essex score-card in his pocket.

Australia still hovered between defeat and victory when McCool hit a very short ball back to the bowler. That made Australia 31—6, three wickets had still to double the score, almost, and Tallon, walking out, wondered whether the small dog that preceded him was to prove a mascot. I shall never forget the chatter of the Yorkshire spectators at this stage. The sun, now, was shining brilliantly. Everybody again roared "How's that" as a ball rapped Tallon on the pads. The atmosphere was full of sparks. Afar off across the field I could see Lindwall in the dressing-room as he swung his bat in preparation or in letting off some nervous tension.

Wardle had bowled some very loose balls and Tallon helped himself to four off one of these. It could be said, in excuse, that this was early in the season for a bowler to be in top form, but I thought that Verity would not have been guilty of shortness at such a time and on a helpful pitch. Tallon played a rash stroke before tea, the ball dropping just short of a sprawling fieldsman amid agonised "Oh's," and at tea we were left to collect our wits with the board showing 47—6.

Out came the balls and the youngsters during the interval, and I loved the manner in which one mite trotted right out to the middle and stood gazing at the pitch in great earnestness until a policeman came and led him away.

So eager were the players to get on with things that they arrived on the ground some minutes too early after tea and there was an anti-climax as they all waited in position for the clock to tick on. But the greater anti-climax was to come. The game was finished in another three overs. The Yorkshire bowling fell into unforgivable poorness in length, and Harvey and Tallon smote the runs off in grand style. Harvey had another life at 12 when he moved yards up the pitch to Smailes to miss, only for Brennan to miss the ball behind. The Australian youth finished the game with a flourish as he hit Smailes for a six into the pavilion and for victory.

As the players were leaving the field, a small youth pleaded in vain for an autograph from the Yorkshire players. Of course, it was not possible. If a player stopped to sign one he would be there for the next two hours, but Tallon took pity on the lad. "Give it to me, son," he said. "I'll sign it for you." "No," said the lad, a true-blue Yorkshireman, even in defeat, "I doon't want Australians. I want Yorkshire players."

This was to prove Australia's closest call on the tour. Defeat for an unbeaten side came almost in the third match of the tour. It would have come, for a certainty, I think, had Hutton been able to retain that ball in his hands just a little longer. Nor, I think, could it have been avoided had the Yorkshire attack been better. There were far too many loose balls for such a state of affairs and such a pitch.

From cold Bradford, cold only in weather because the people
there are the warmest in spirit and hospitality, the Australians
returned to Surrey, London and sunshine. The last time an
Australian team had played at Kennington Oval, Surrey's home
ground, it had been a tragic affair. England had scored nearly
a thousand, Hutton had made 364, taking Bradman's record from
him, Bradman had broken a bone in his ankle when bowling,
and with me snapping a muscle in my leg when fielding, Australia
had to bat two short. No wonder Bradman told his audience at
the Surrey dinner that he had a little of his own to get back at
the Oval.

The war gave the Oval a hammering. Bowlers, the world
wide, would have given three cheers had a bomb hit the som-
nolent pitch area and dug it up, but fires had badly damaged the
pavilion and surrounding buildings, and as he entered the
dressing-room a player had to watch his flannels from brushing
against the black, burnt sides of the woodwork. They have had
to work hard to get the Oval going for cricket again.

The Oval was a P.O.W. internment camp during the war. It
has had a varied sporting history. Dr. Grace once won a hurdle
race here; the first Soccer Cup Final was played about sixty years
before, drawing a crowd of 1,000 (that at Wembley a few days
before had drawn 93,000); the women have played a Test here,
and Jim Swanton, who is an authority on such matters, declares
there was not a dry eye in the whole pavilion once when an
English woman player failed by a few runs to make a century
here against the Australian ladies.

Almost every English ground has some outstanding characteristic. What the Cathedral is to Worcester, so are the gas-
ometers to the Oval. Up in the air they tower with their stored
gas on Saturdays, father, mother and baby gasometer, and
deflated down to the earth are they on Mondays after cooking
the Sunday roast or joint—or whatever passes for a roast or joint
in 1948. The atmosphere surrounding the Oval is a cricket one.
The rebuilt flats, after the war, are named after famous cricketers
of other days, and just outside the ground is a new-looking
pub, resplendent in the Australian national colours of green and
gold.

The Oval is a flat and rather drab ground, and is not an
inspiring one on which to play purely because, I think, the
spectators are too far away. The Oval will always be associated
with Jack Hobbs. A grand pair of gates memorise his name at

the entrance. The Prime Minister, Mr. Attlee, is an inveterate Ovalite. A Putney man, he faithfully followed the deeds of Hayward, Abel, Hitch, Hobbs and Sandham, and in hours of national trouble and duty is always somewhat comforted if Surrey has a good day. His first love after Surrey is Glamorgan. He is a keen Rugby man also, and because of that was happy when Wilf Wooller, a former Rugby international, captained Glamorgan to the championship honours of this year.

Queues at the Oval are invariable. The Tube disgorges nearby; trams run past it, giving a good look in at the ground for some several hundred yards, and the buses are also nearby. Perhaps the best look of the game is to be obtained from one of the hundreds of surrounding windows that overlook the game.

Australia gave Surrey a depressing defeat. Bradman won the toss and, though the game began at 11.30, it was not until 12.40 that a ball, intentionally, got past the bats of Morris and Barnes. Barnes looked full of business. With chin on chest after he had made the stroke, he peered hard at the ball and called "Yip" for his runs. Few Australians call "Yes" for a run. Bradman's "Right" floats over the field; Hassett is slightly different to Barnes in that he says "Yep." Openers who associate long together usually dispense with calling altogether. That was so with Brown and myself. Each knew what was in the other's mind.

I liked the look of Barnes this day. He was full of runs. He hit the first four of the day away into the never-never of the Oval, and the chasing fieldsman looked small and distant indeed. Then Barnes crashed Bedser for a jet-propelled four, so fast did it speed, and as he reached the other end he smiled hugely at Bedser and gave him a smack on the rear with his bat.

Morris had a neat 65, and when Bradman came I thought I had never seen him so jaunty or confident. McMahon, an Australian left-handed spinner, beat the bat now and then, but Surridge, trying to bounce them short at Bradman with medium pace, took severe treatment from the Bradman pull. A small boy in front of the Press-box was determined to miss nothing. He had a telescope as big as himself trained on the play. He saw two beautiful centuries, Barnes 176 and Bradman 146.

Bradman enjoyed himself immensely. Once he rushed through for a quick two, grabbed slip and did a turn around him, laughed, turned back smartly, tapped the pitch, hit the ball five yards and sped off for another short run. Once he tried to force Surridge off his toes, miscued badly and the ball veered down past the slips.

A billiardist would have shaken his head and called for the chalk. Bradman called for a run instead. A languid Australian voice called out "Have a go" when Bradman reached 50 in eighty minutes, and there was barracking for a "bobby" who ignored the ball at his feet on the boundary while a fieldsman ran eighty yards to retrieve it. The whole Surrey side converged on Bradman when he wanted a single for his century in 155 minutes, but this time he did not sacrifice his innings. Bedser clean-bowled him as he played back defensively. It looked rather similar to the ball Bedser got past him at Adelaide.

Hassett had his first century of the tour here and Tallon got a half century. They both played neatly but the Surrey attack, apart from Bedser and McMahon, was poor stuff. Bedser clean-bowled his three victims, Bradman, Hassett and Lindwall. McMahon gave Bradman some very anxious moments with his twisty ones. In two successive overs, McMahon had Bradman edge the ball very close to slip, and in the next over he beat him completely with the bosie. As against Walsh, it seemed that Bradman did not detect the bosie as in pre-war.

On the Sunday of this game, O'Reilly and I had a grand day out at Gravesend. We played against the Kent county side, and O'Reilly, though he had not played for a long stretch, gave as good a piece of spin bowling as I was to see in the whole summer. This Gravesend ground is a famous one. It was here that Dr. Grace was once on the field for the entire game. He made 257 and 73 not out. Gravesend is right in the centre of the Dickens country. It is generally thought that the All Muggletonian Cricket Club's doings in *Pickwick Papers* were just a farcical caricature of the Gravesend Cricket Club of that day.

The workhouse still stands where our own Australian, George Bonnor, landed the ball on the roof in 1886. This remains the record Gravesend hit. The ball was never found. George was once asked in England whom he thought were the world's best three batsmen. "Well," said George, knitting his brow, "you can't get away from W.G. and Murdoch is not far behind. I would rather you did not ask me the name of the third." •

On our day out at Gravesend (it was a benefit game to aid the Leslie Ames Fund) I saw something I had never seen before. Brian Valentine, the Kent skipper, hit a six over point. This was a grand day in every way, greatly helped by the local Mayor, who had made his business name, locally, in the fish business. "Now then," said this grand character, as he was selling tickets in a raffle for a bat, "you'd better be in this. There's nothing fishy about this."

Laurie Fishlock was the hero of Surrey's innings, batting right through for 81 not out. I wonder why Fishlock has never been a power in Test cricket? He has all the strokes and has splendid footwork. He might have been a good choice for England in the final Test when Washbrook dropped out, especially as Fishlock would have been playing on his home pitch. Lindwall bowled in this match his fastest in England. He once sent the ball at least three feet over Squires' head—and that is no mean feat on an Oval pitch, even if Lindwall had to pitch the ball half-way to do it. Johnson was the main wicket-taker, and in three games had cleared away from the rest of the Australian bowling field with 23 wickets.

No finer amusement was given in the match, though, than that provided by a little tan and white London mongrel which suddenly took the field and refused to vacate it. Johnson took it off first but back it came. Bradman threw the ball at it but it chased the ball. On came a dignified policeman but the dog knew his policemen and gave him a wide berth. Barnes trapped it with the ball as bait and then marched it up to umpire Skelding, who got in a great flurry. Skelding refused to take the dog, backed away and, with Barnes persisting in his offer, took the bails off and made for the pavilion.

The groundsman got the dog eventually and a few minutes later, during tea, a tired voice on the amplifying system asked would the owner of a tan and white dog please call to the secretary's office and collect him. The Oval had had enough of the foxie.

Behind Barnes's offering of the dog to umpire Skelding is a delectable story. At Leicester, Skelding, who is a keen humorist, knocked back many appeals by the Australians. Barnes made immediate friends with Skelding and then told him he wasn't a bad chap but all he needed as an umpire was a dog. "You know," said Barnes, "you must need a dog. You're blind when you give those decisions not out." And at the Oval the dog turned up! Hence the Barnes offering but the lovely part about it is that Skelding has a horror of dogs.

Barnes is always good for a laugh. Those who went through the Brisbane storm of 1946 will never forget it. It was a terrifying experience and in no time the Cricket Ground was a sheet of ice. The dressing-room there is next to the Members' Pavilion, the scene of so many rows in the cricket world and as hard to enter as Paradise. This is fenced off with barbed wire and once led an English Pressman to term it Belsen. Drinks in the dressing-room are contained in a large tub which has a block of ice in its middle. Barnes struggled out with this block of ice in the middle of the storm and tipped it over the fence into the "Sacred Pavilion." Down it slithered on the grass among all the hailstones. The eyes of the members bulged. They think to this day that it came down from above—and had you known that storm, you might have believed it too!

Surrey put up a very dismal showing. Harvey distinguished himself with two sensational catches, flying high in the air with his hands stretched above his head. The Oval habitues said they had never seen the like of them before. The Surrey skipper, Errol Holmes, had a bad match. He made a blob in his first innings which made three in a row. A friend promptly sent him a telegram: "Best wishes for your thousand in May."

From London the team went to Cambridge—and there's no lovelier place to visit in the whole of England nor a more pleasant cricket field on which to play. If there is a more tranquil hour than paddling down the Cam, underneath the bridges of the various colleges and past their green meadows, I have yet to know it in England. One night from outside I heard the massed University choirs sing Verdi's *Requiem* in King's Chapel. The graceful spires were etched against the crescent of a new moon and life, at that moment, was full of good things.

We did have some sun at Cambridge. On the second day of the match I sat on the open seats atop of the pavilion and basked in warm May sunlight. The field itself is the most beautiful in England, and purely because of the way it is cut. The grounds-man puts down his pegs and by a most intricate system weaves up and down with his cutting machine so that he leaves broad sweeps of grass, the nap running this way in one width and that in the next. It looked at its best this lovely spring day. Around the ground were dotted the most colourful trees. A red May peeped over the sight-board, and just to the left of that is the corner residence where Ken Farnes, rest his soul, hit a six as beautiful and as chivalrous as himself into the back garden. The stentorian call of Pepper, one of the Cambridge men, hit the red-bricked Teachers College, where girls lolled in the windows, and floated back over the field in a queer echo with redoubled volume. There were green oaks, the red and green of the walnut trees, the white of the horse chestnut trees and the yellow of the laburnum. An exquisite cricketing field, indeed, is this Cambridge one, though our thoughts on its radiant beauty were suddenly interrupted when the groundsman appeared with a pail of water to ditch a fire smouldering in the rafters.

Once, on a tour here, an undergraduate bowled Bradman for none, but I refused to believe that this doughty deed helped him greatly in his examinations. Bradman stood down here. He did not play against either University but there was still a record crowd of 20,000 for two days. And, judging by the cycles on Parker's Piece outside, every one came ariding.

Parker's Piece is a famous sward on which Hobbs learnt the game. It is one of the cricketing sights of England after business hours as hundreds and hundreds of men and boys play cricket. The pitch is merely cut. It doesn't look as if it is rolled, and some of the bowlers we noticed there looked about as dangerous as Lindwall.

Doggart took my eye at Cambridge. He has a lovely, upright stance and his cover drive off Lindwall for four was the best stroke of the tour we had seen against pace. If his back-play were as good as his forward stuff, Doggart would be making many runs in English cricket. Dewes, who later was to play in the final Test, took the field like a ball.

I asked about this and was told by an undergraduate that when playing against Miller in a Victory Test, Dewes was hit three times in the same place and so, this time, he was taking no risks. He had several towels wrapped about him beneath his flannels. He wasn't hit but his leg stump was. Miller yorked him as he did in the Victory Test.

"You know," said the undergraduate, explaining the towel plan, "that ball hurts if it hits you."

"Does it really!" I said. Shades of Larwood, the Great. Had I not been able to move myself on a Sunday in Sydney after taking a drubbing from him in a Test!

It was Brown's turn to hit the highlights here, and this he did with 200 in a total of 414—4, declared. It was Brown's turn as his four previous innings had been 25, 26, 13 and 2. Any innings by Brown is good. The students could have done a post-graduate course on cricket after seeing it. Hassett, as in 1938, was not out, this time with 61, so that he had made 281 runs at Cambridge without dismissal. Hamence, as was to happen late in the tour at Somerset, got so near and yet so far from his century. He made 92.

Cambridge is my favourite place in England. It differs from Oxford because it is untramelled by industry which threatens to crowd Oxford in. Each University has its own particular characteristics, but I never tired of wandering around Cambridge's narrow and beautiful streets. Life there is very different to the pre-war period when the students enjoyed themselves in many hectic ways. Many of the present students are ex-Service men, many married with their domestic shopping carried into the lecture rooms with them, and time is very valuable. With the years missed at the war, they can't afford to fail in their exams. A new generation and justifiably a more serious one, too, you think, as you see many an undergraduate come stumping down the road with an artificial leg.

CHAPTER SIX

FROM SOUTHEND TO TEST

NOT many county teams entered the field against this Australian side with confidence. It would be near the mark to say that Yorkshire alone, with that spirit of never-say-die that is so typical of their history, stuck out their chins from the first ball against the tourists. Yorkshire played and, as I have written, almost defeated Australia in the third match of the tour, and although Hampshire did head the Australians on the first innings, it seemed in most of the other county games that the tale of invincibility had travelled ahead of Bradman's men with telling effect.

Some critics were writing of invincibility before the tour even began, but I think what happened at Southend on Saturday, the 15th of May, jolted many a county side. This was against Essex. In 350 minutes, Australia made 721, and such a score in a day had never before been made in England. Surrey held the previous best for a team when it scored 645—4 against Hampshire in 1909, and Surrey was also concerned with the previous best aggregate for a day when, in 1920, the innings was declared at 619—5, and in the time left for play in that same day Northants had 59—2. The Australian total of 721, in ten minutes under the day's time, thus far outstripped the previous best and did much to depress the counties generally in their hopes against the Australians.

This is how the scoring rate ran at Southend:

100 in 74 minutes		500 in 247 minutes	
200 in 118	„	600 in 286	„
300 in 170	„	650 in 297	„
351 in 189	„	700 in 338	„
451 in 220	„	721 in 350	„

The way to the cricket ground at Southend is along a front which possesses an individuality all its own in England. To be true, Southend has much in common with Blackpool, Scarborough and other seaside resorts, but Southend (as it fronts to the Thames it really is, technically, not a seaside resort) is the closest such holiday place to London and thus is predominately Cockney. There were, I think, almost as many different smells along the front that day as the Australians made runs. The crowd throngs the front slowly amid varied yells and smells as the innumerable shops emit the odour of their eating wares and attendants advertise them. In quick succession one sniffs curried eels, elks, whelks, mussels, cockles, oysters and the like, and even early in the morning the sounds of community singing float out from the pubs. The Whitsun holidays in Southend are something to remember, and these of 1948 were crowned with unceasing hours of sunlight.

The officials of the Australian team had a few qualms before this game. Even so early in the tour, there was a kick-back from Bradman's claim on landing that this was the fittest Australian team ever. Lindwall was suffering from a strain; Tallon had injured hands, and McCool, though cracking hardy, was at a severe disadvantage with the skin breaking over his spinning fingers.

It was Bradman who set the tempo for the Southend slaughter. He came to bat after Brown and Barnes had put on 145 for the first wicket, this passing the previous best for the tour of 136 at the Oval. Barnes was in his perkiest mood. A terrific round of applause from the packed ground greeted his off-drive for four in the first over. The Southend spectators, too, were out to enjoy themselves, but the afternoon sun was not long on its downward path before boundaries were being received in complete silence. The spectators had had too much of a good thing, and no wonder, because 87 boundaries were hit in the day on a field of average size.

Bailey, of Cambridge, was again playing. He was a late selection. The day before at the University it was not thought he would be playing, but his late selection coupled with his making of 66 not out in the second innings at Cambridge rather suggested he was being included at Southend in the guise of a Test trial. Bailey is slight, hardly the build for a fast bowler. He is very dark and runs up with his left hand splayed out in front. He is not very fast, barely above medium-fast, and it was soon apparent that he would not trouble the Australians on what was a perfect pitch—vastly different from the hills-and-dales one of 1938 here where Essex, with Farnes, Nichols and Stephenson, twice dismissed Australia for low scores though Australia won the game.

Barnes scored his 79 runs in 97 minutes and Brown made his 50 in 90 minutes, but in 20 minutes left to him before lunch Bradman hit 42 runs. This set off the massacre proper. Bradman hit Price for five fours in the one over and the 200 was up before lunch. The attack was beaten completely in that pre-lunch session, and with superb stroke-making, Bradman went on to his century in 74 minutes. When Brown was 153 he threw his innings away. As this followed upon his 200 at Cambridge, Brown had thus effaced the four small scores with which he had begun the tour.

This situation had no appeal whatsoever for Miller. He showed his boredom as he walked to the wickets. He took guard indifferently and to the very first ball bowled walked across the pitch and missed it intentionally. He flung his hair back and left, still looking bored.

Bradman was out at 187, making a furious cross swing to leg and being bowled. He made the 87 runs after his century in 48 minutes and that tells its own story. He hit 32 fours. Then came Loxton and Saggers to make each his first century in England, and it was done, particularly by Loxton, in exceedingly quick time. He drove and hooked vigorously and, as always, enjoyed every minute of it. Saggers was more deft. He reminded me at times of Alan Kippax in his artistry. He plays all the strokes but, like Tallon, was not to receive many batting chances on this tour.

That first day whipped the Essex bowlers who, a few days before, had routed Derbyshire for 32. It also took the heart out of the batsmen, and no less spirited display of batting was seen on the tour than the county's first innings. It was simply deplorable and that on a pitch with still hundreds of runs left in it. There was an omen before play began with the Essex flag flying upside down. Most of the Essex men could have shaped no worse had they batted that way! The board showed 9 for three wickets; 19 for four and in an hour it was 30 for five. The whole side was out for 83 with Ray Smith making the few full-blooded strokes of the innings.

It was a better second innings. The skipper, Tom Pearce, batted in fine style for 71, and Peter Smith, whose bowling figures were 193 for four off 36 overs, got some of his own back with the bat and 54. Tom Pearce, a bluff fellow, continued to have a grand season, finishing higher in the averages than any other amateur, but his stocks were low at Lord's. He failed even to get a place in the Gentlemen against Australia. Barnes finished this game off with a catch at short leg and, in typical manner, threw the stumps down for good measure, but Essex gave poor return for the crowds which paid £3,482 over two days. Ian Johnson, Miller and Toshack enjoyed themselves with good figures, but the game, as the scores show, lacked spirit and technique.

From Southend to Oxford was a vivid contrast. Oxford, because of its Rhodes scholars, is more "Dominiony" than Cambridge. Each has its own interesting individuality as a University city, though I thought Cambridge, which is without the busy industrial traffic that crams its way through Oxford, more serene and beautiful.

As in other years, the game with the Australians could not be played on the glorious Parks, Oxford's home ground, because admittance money cannot be charged there, but the Christ Church ground was a worthy deputy. There is untold difference in the Australian games between the counties and the Universities. There is atmosphere in the 'Varsity games, first of all culturally and secondly in the ground itself because no ugly tenements or factory chimneys crowd the grounds. On this beautiful spring day at Oxford there was a country-house atmosphere about the flat and sleepy pavilion and the deck-chairs sprawled in the sun. A military band played tunes that made one's feet tap (a band is as much in keeping with a cricket match, I think, as the two umpires), around the ground were lovely multi-coloured trees as at Cambridge, over to the right was a tower, and farther right again was a church with a tall steeple that topped itself with a weather-vane and every quarter chimed the time across the fields. From the Isis also came the cheering and urging of the bumping races, a rowing event of repute.

Oxford played almost a Dominion side. Jika Travers, the Rugby international, hailed from our own Sydney University; van Rynveld from South Africa; Hafeez Kardar from India, and, strangely, a Canadian in Robinson. The tour was just a year too late for Martin Donnelly, the brilliant New Zealander, who captained Oxford and finished there in 1947, but even with the others Oxford turned out a pretty representative side.

Bradman stood down here and Hassett took the leadership again. There was keen interest to see how Philip Whitcombe would fare against the Australians. Just the week before he had twice clean-bowled Len Hutton. He reminded me very much of

Ken Farnes in looks and delivery. He is six feet six inches (I was told he accompanies a six feet five inches girl undergraduate to Oxford parties) and he uses all his height in delivery. Brown and Morris played him with caution but the pitch was on the slow side.

Somebody told me that Robinson was the first Canadian ever to win a cricket blue at Oxford. He is, undoubtedly, the first Canadian ever to play against an Australian team in England. He bowls slow off-breaks, round the stumps, but his first over was a poor one and Morris helped himself to three fours off it. Kardar, who had toured England with the Indian team, bowled left-handed round the stumps, and it was not long before we were convinced that in him we had seen the best left-hander of the tour to that stage.

Kardar has a loose, flowing run to the crease and spins and flights the ball nicely. I smiled when I saw Bill Brown's first reaction when Kardar was given the ball. Bill looked hard at him and then immediately drew out the crease line with his foot to make certain that he did not leave the crease before the ball was bowled. A fellow countryman in Vinoo Mankad had twice dismissed Brown in this fashion in Australia the preceding summer, after giving him copious warnings, so that my one-time opening partner was taking no chances again with an Indian.

Off 13 overs from Kardar, the Australians could manage only 31. It was a splendid piece of length bowling. Webb, fielding in the gay colours of the Harlequins (shades of Douglas Jardine!), brilliantly ran out Morris from the boundary with a throw over the stumps, but that cap gave him away. The Australians never again took a risk with him. The cap meant immediate identification.

Whitcombe got the only ball of the match to pop and Hassett was the recipient—which meant a "blob" for Hassett, and Harvey also was not too happy about things. The young left-hander was playing very much at the pitch of the ball at this stage and did not think too highly of English pitches. This game saw Brown's third successive century—in eight days he had made 461 runs, whereas in the preceding fortnight he had managed only 66. This burst took Brown six runs ahead of Bradman in the aggregate but the skipper had played only four innings compared to Brown's seven.

Loxton again batted well here, and Ring and McCool each had a half century apiece. I was asking an Oxford undergraduate what Kardar was doing at the 'Varsity when the Indian chased a ball right to our feet.

"What are you doing here, Abdul?" asked the Oxford man as Kardar swooped on the ball.

"P—E—P," answered Kardar, who was as quick in gathering what we wanted as he was in returning the ball.

"That means Politics, Economics and Philosophy," said the Oxford man. We had got our information from the most reliable source.

The Oxford people treated the Australian Press most hospitably. We were their guests for lunch each day and they appointed a steward, Ron Tillett, to look after us. I had known Geoffrey Keighley, the Oxford opening batsman, for some years. In 1938, I had taken him to the Oval to see the final Test and he reciprocated next morning with Tillett, taking O'Reilly and me on a tour of the colleges.

Beneath the beautifully timbered cloisters of New College, we were inspecting a 1760 fire engine when an undergraduate approached us and said, "I've played cricket against you chaps in Sydney." It was Don Hughes, who had come on from Sydney University. Those Oxford lads gave us a grand morning and it didn't stop at that. The nights also were good fun. In New College we saw the old wall of the City. I liked the story Tillett told us of how it was ordained that the gate of the wall should never be opened again until a Stuart came to the throne of England. That is still observed. The undergraduates of Trinity have to go on a long walkabout to get to the Parks. If the gate were opened, the short cut would get them there in a few minutes, but a hoary old custom is faithfully observed.

Keighley, Kardar, who top-scored in both innings and who would have been a leading member of the Indian team in Australia had he not come to Oxford, and van Ryneveld did well with the bat for Oxford, but the University was badly outplayed. Van Ryneveld was to distinguish himself later as a slow bowler in the University match but he was not known at this stage as a bowler.

Like that at Cambridge, the game at Oxford is always a great success and is much enjoyed by the Australians. The Oxford skipper, Tony Pawson, was very popular with the tourists. When the pitch was to be rolled at one stage, Pawson asked Hassett what type of roller he would like. Hassett has a splendid poker-face.

"What have you got?" he asked Pawson.

"There is the heavy, the medium and the light," answered Pawson.

"Haven't you got a spiked one?" asked Hassett, without a glimmer in his eyes.

Pawson looked hard. "I don't think so," he answered very seriously, "but I'll make sure." And he went away to ask. Tony was known as "Spike" Pawson after that.

I returned to Oxford later to spend several nights in Brasenose. The Oxford legal Don, Ron Maudsley, who captained Warwickshire for part of the season, was my host. I had the quarters of Dr. R. A. Hull, M.A., and the atmosphere of Boutry's "Les Phenomenes Photoelectriques et lenis applications," Kennard's "Kinetic theory on Gas," Gamow's "Atomic Nuclei and nuclear transformation" and the like. I settled, hopefully, for a pre-nap read on "The Mechanical Properties of Fluid," but was surprised to find that Oxford, or Dr. Hull, does not believe that study should be done in bed. There were no bed-lights. During the night I was awakened by a carousal in the quadrangle (brightened up a week before with red geraniums for the visit of Princess Elizabeth). A window was flung open above and an authoritative voice called down, "Be out of it, you cads." It seemed almost like Greyfriars. I certainly enjoyed my several days and nights at Brasenose, once meeting in the quadrangle the Oxford Vice-Chancellor, and world-famous legal authority, Mr. Stallybrass, who also knows his cricket.

Just before the Australians began their first game of the tour at Lord's, against M.C.C., the gates were closed. There seemed to be more people outside the ground than in. Lord's made a gallant sight, though for the Australians it seemed incongruous to have the pitch so far over towards the tavern. With thousands sitting on the grass here, it looked to me the shortest boundary I had ever seen in first-class cricket.

Morris had not decided by this time that English pitches were to suit him. Indeed, he seemed to have serious doubts of them and did not last long in this innings. Bradman received an uproarious welcome, and as in he walked Yardley, who had taken his wicket thrice in Australia, grinned and swung his bowling arm. There was some excellent length bowling on this first day by Young and Cranston, but Bradman, though he began shakily, looked all over a century-maker. He was snapped up by Edrich off the Army player, Deighton, when he was 98. Bradman seemed very

disappointed and lingered momentarily at the pitch as if dis-
believing that such a thing could happen to him when so close
to a century. So far as I could tell, it was the closest he had ever
been to a first-class century. Four times in Australia he had been
dismissed in the nineties. They were 97, b. Lee (Sydney), 1932-33;
92, b. Ebeling (Sydney), 1934; 91, c. O'Brien, b. O'Reilly (Adelaide),
1937; 97, c. Tallon, b. Cook (Brisbane), 1939.

That same afternoon Hassett played the prettiest half century
we saw in the whole summer. There was no effort in his play.
The ball sped quietly and quickly in all directions. Hassett is a
most gifted stroke-player but he rarely allows himself scope.
Barnes had a good 81. Once, for the whole of an over by Yardley,
a pigeon quietly cropped at point—and no man hits the ball
harder there than Barnes.

The Australians had batted brightly enough on this first day,
but the morning of the second was undoubtedly the most hectic
Lord's has ever seen. Miller had hit one huge six off Laker on
the Saturday and he twice repeated the dose on Monday, batting
most brilliantly for 163, but it was Ian Johnson and Lindwall
who covered themselves in hitting glory. Johnson hit three off
Laker; Lindwall hit three also off the same bowler, and added
one against Young, and Tallon also helped himself to one six
off Laker. The Australian innings lasted only 82 minutes that
morning but it brought ten sixes, nine off Laker.

It seemed that the boys had something personal to settle with
the tavern. Most of the sixes floated in that direction.

When M.C.C. came to bat, Barnes, at short leg, fielded almost
in the batsman's pocket. This was the closest I have ever seen
any fieldsman on the leg side. I have seen Richardson field two
yards behind point to Grimmett but the risk on the leg side is
considerable. I wrote in my little note-book there and then that
some day Barnes would collect something in that position he
wouldn't like and that came true in earnest at Manchester when
Pollard laid him low. I had fielded in that same position for
years and "collected" mine one day at Birmingham when Santall
swung on to a short ball from Waite. A fieldsman who spends
much time in that unhealthy position takes a great risk. Luckily,
at Birmingham, I sensed the hit coming and was dropping to
the ground when the ball made contact. Had I not, I would have
had my skull split wide open. As it was, I had a headache for
weeks. O'Reilly, unkindly, thinks I've never been the same since!

Other people thought, too, that Barnes was too close. In the

Daily Express, Brian Chapman wrote an open letter to Bradman and suggested that in fielding so close, indeed with a foot sometimes on the pitch, Barnes was taking an advantage over the batsman. We had much the same said of us in South Africa when Richardson and I fielded up close to O'Reilly but the matter is entirely in the batsman's hands. It is the fieldsman who takes all the risks and if there is any suggestion of improper tactics the umpires are there to take action.

If the batsman allows it, such a fieldsman does have an intimidatory effect, and I think Barnes, in this position, was of great value in a nuisance capacity throughout the tour. He missed several catches there. I think he stood too close to sight them. He missed one this Monday at Lord's and, in mock disgust, motioned Hassett in to take his place. When Hassett made a movement, Barnes hasted him away and the crowd laughed. Barnes provided plenty of amusement on this tour.

Apart from Hutton, the M.C.C. batsmen shaped very poorly in this innings, and none more so than Edrich and Compton. These two had broken Tom Hayward's long-standing aggregate record the previous season, but the standard of some of the county sides we had seen took some gloss off that achievement and I thought, at the time, that making easy runs against poor bowling had run these two star Englishmen very much out of form against the good stuff.

Hutton had 52 and 64, so this match was a splendid one for him. Robertson, a Test prospect, had 6 and 0; Edrich 4 and 25; Compton 26 and 20; and Yardley, who probably had never before been in such poor form, 17 and 24. Toshack, with 94—7, had a good first match at Lord's, and Miller, Johnson and McCool also had good figures. This game did much to depress England's chances for the Tests. Lindwall had taken only two wickets for 68 runs so that it was not pace, on this occasion, which beat the home men. It was Toshack, with his bowling at the leg stump. It is interesting that the Englishmen consider the Voice (and he used it very plentifully on his debut at Lord's!) is purely a negative bowler. His attack is at the leg stump and outside it, but he is generally so close to the stumps that nearly every ball has to be played.

The next game at Old Trafford against Lancashire provided the outstanding personal highlight of the season. It was here that the 19-year-old, Malcolm Hilton, took Bradman's wicket in both innings. This was a feat which sent Hilton's photograph,

with his family history, on to the front page of all English
newspapers.

That evening, the Western Brothers broke into song on the
B.B.C. about Hilton to the tune of " Uncle Tom Cobley." In the
Sunday Despatch Lester Wilson broke out to this effect

After days of high excitement we are left to contemplate
Events that cause misgivings to awaken,
For the African election
Proved but one of two directions
In which ties that bind the Empire have been broken.

Yes, my native North put further strain on commonwealth accord
And diplomacy was helpless to forbid it.
As by hard, unsocial cricket,
Someone twice *took Bradman's wicket!*
(Yet I hail the co-Lancastrian who did it).

Cranston won the toss here and sent the Australians in on a
pitch somewhat affected by rain, but Cranston spoilt much of
the effect of his decision by playing a customary, dry-day field.
Cranston had a very poor grip on the game at this stage and I
once noticed Harry Makepeace, the former English player and
now Lancashire coach, almost fall off the balcony as he waved
a whole set of stumps to Lawton. This, plainly, was to tell
Lawton to bowl at the stumps. Morris and Barnes were being
called upon to play barely a single ball in the over.

Bradman did not bring his customary confidence when he
came to bat. This was another instance of a pitch with some
nastiness in it causing him concern above the ordinary, and I
noticed that he did not seem at all keen to get down to Pollard's
end. He played forward to Hilton, probably got just a tickle off
a ball which came in with the young bowler's arm and it found
his stumps. What gave added point to Hilton's success was the
fact that he was included in the Lancashire team at the last
moment and, I was told, with a feeling of desperation. In previous
matches, Lancashire could not get the opposition out. Bradman
had made 11.

Loxton, especially, and Harvey batted nicely in this first
innings, but such was the publicity given Hilton's performance
in getting Bradman out that we sensed there would be trouble
waiting for him in Australia's second innings. Lancashire's

batting fell away and the side could manage only 182 against Australia's 204. Hilton had taken four for 81 off 19 overs, and Bill Johnston (who had hit three soaring sixes) had a splendid match with five wickets for 49 off 29 overs.

Bradman has never allowed any bowler to think for long that he enjoys mastery. In all his years, he has gone out of his way to give particular attention to any bowler who has had temporary success with him, and I felt rather sorry for Hilton when I saw Bradman walk out to bat. The pitch this second time was of a peaceful nature. When Hilton took the ball, Loxton rushed at him like a bull at a gate. It was to be a double-barrelled offensive. The Australians were out to "kill" this fair-haired lad in double-quick time but he had the last say again with Bradman.

Bradman was the victim of his own eagerness. Over-impetuously, he wanted to drive Hilton into the ground in one over. Cranston had a strongly packed off-side field for Hilton, but Bradman, who was in the forties when Hilton came to bowl, made a terrific swing to the on. He missed, was almost clean-bowled the next ball, and then the next one rushed wildly down the pitch, swung furiously to leg with a cross-bat, missed, swung about and fell flat on the pitch with the momentum. He was quietly stumped by Edrich, well down the pitch. This was, I think, with the exception of the bodyline days, the only time I have seen Bradman behave in such a manner. Usually, when he sets out to "kill" a bowler, he does it with calm intent. This was clearly a case of over-anxiety. I think he took Hilton too cheaply, and I admired the spirited manner in which the lad did not quail but continued to give the ball air. It was fine bowling on his part.

Hilton received world praise overnight for this outstanding feat but I think he was wisely handled by the Lancashire officials. He did not become a fixture in the side but was played off and on, and did not play in the return game against the Australians at Old Trafford. He is a neat bowler of the usual left-handed variety in England, round the stumps and with reliance placed on the field. This game faded away, as so many games do in England, into a draw on the third day, Harvey and Hamence making runs in the second try.

As usual, thousands turned out at the Nottingham railway station to greet the Australians. There were some cheerful calls as the players walked down a long line of "Look out, here comes Larwood." On the morning of the match I went for a haircut and heard the whole saloon enthusiastically going all over the bodyline and Larwood affair. I sat tight and said nothing. It would have been mere folly to have told them that I was in the middle of that cricket donnybrook, but his home townsmen will never forget Harold Larwood.

The game at Trent Bridge against hapless Notts saw some outstanding individual feats. Joe Hardstaff, with 107, made the first century against the tourists; Simpson, a former policeman who is a pretty authentic edition of Hardstaff, had a good double with 74 and 70, and a grand crowd of 26,800 saw Lindwall deliver some in the real Larwood manner in the first innings. He took six wickets for 14 runs off 15 overs and absolutely paralysed the Notts men, apart from Hardstaff and Simpson. The batsmen could score off only ten of the 91 balls which Lindwall delivered and not a single run was scored off his final 30 balls. Bradman had a good game with 86, and Brown had another century with a sterling 122. His Test stocks should have been very high and as an opening batsman. Ring had a long spell of 43 overs (104—4) and this rather suggested that he was working his way in for the Test here.

Simpson impressed me very much. He is taller than Hardstaff and has the same flowing action. It is said of him (as it is of Hardstaff) that they don't do themselves justice away from Trent Bridge, and I must admit that Simpson's figures at the end of the season of 1,255 runs for 44 innings were not as good as his form against the Australians would lead us to expect. I think the bats used by Hardstaff and Simpson that day were the sweetest-sounding I have ever heard. They came from the Nottingham factory of Gunn & Moore, and these two Notts favourites evidently had been given first choice. The Nottinghamshire score of 299 for 8 in the second innings was the best to that stage against the Australians. Sime, the local captain, is a barrister. His best record is six undefended divorce suits and 36 not out before lunch!

From Nottingham, O'Reilly and I called on Jack de Philps and his family at Dunchurch. They live in the original home, called The Forge, outside which grew the tree made famous by Longfellow in "The Village Blacksmith"—"Under the spreading chestnut tree." The tree itself has gone but in its place is one of its progeny. O'Reilly, we found by measurements on the wall, is the tallest ever to have been inside The Forge. He left not only his mark on the wall. He gave himself a terrible whack also on one of the centuries-old wooden beams. He thinks they must have been very small men in Longfellow's day, despite the tribute to the physical bulk of the smith.

Dunchurch was the place where Guy Fawkes had to make a rendezvous with his followers after blowing up the Houses of Parliament. It was arranged that the church bells would be rung to drown the sound of his horse's hooves as he sped through the night. They give the bells a good ringing now every Guy Fawkes's Day and they drink the gentleman's health with gusto in the "local," outside which, in the village square, are remains of the stocks.

While the Australians went to Southampton to play Hampshire, Mailey and I went to watch the English Trial game at Birmingham. It was spoilt almost completely by the rain and must have left the English selectors about as confused as a cab-driver in Birmingham's one-way streets for the first time. There was some tension in the game at Southampton when Australia could manage only 117 against 195. Knott had the splendid figures of 57—5 and Bailey 27—4. In view of his trials at Bradford, Mailey sent a telegram to Hassett which ran: "Good luck but why must you always be carrying the baby when it's wet." This, I thought, in its reference to a wet pitch, was rather neat.

With the Test looming, there was some solid planking for Robins as the English captain. Yardley did not look well and was not in form though he made some runs at Birmingham which promised better things. Robins, remembering the bitter fate of Allen in the West Indies, said he was not interested in the Test captaincy, but I often thought he was tempted by it. Over the years, he has been a very close friend and a keen sporting rival of Bradman's and, I thought, might have liked a Test tilt at him before the end. One could sense strong London and Lord's backing for Robins, but his captaincy never struck me as being of the genius type. He is very keen on the field. He bustles about and barks out orders like a sergeant-major, but at Lord's, later, and at Scarborough he was not impressive as a skipper, nor was he ever a capable Test performer in the few games he had against Australia before the war.

Thanks to good bowling by Miller and Johnston, good batting again by Brown and a star batting turn by Ian Johnson, Australia put Hampshire away by eight wickets at the finish so that Hassett, in his captaincy, emerged with honours again after a fright on the opening day. This was the second tight corner Hassett had been in with the side.

The game with Sussex, the last before the first Test, did not provide the Australians with much of a challenge. Sussex crumpled completely against Lindwall in as depressing a batting performance as the tour knew—and they were plenty. Lindwall took 11 wickets for only 59 runs off 34 overs. He bundled the stumps over in all directions and Toshack had the unusual experience of bowling 17 overs for only six runs. Only three scoring strokes were made off him. Bradman, fortunate early in being missed at two and escaping stumping at 25, batted in his best manner, making 109 in 124 minutes with 12 fours. Morris ran into his best form with 184, including 26 fours, and Harvey made a brilliant last-minute try for Test inclusion with a superb century, rich in youthful daring and stroke production.

And so the Australians emerged from their programme of twelve matches before the first Test with ten wins and two draws. It was a convincing experience. The frights had been at Bradford and Southampton but, generally, this part of the tour showed that the Australians held a commanding reputation, were considerably feared by most of the players against them, and, in all ways, apart from wet pitches, were a Test side above the ordinary. And, apart from Yorkshire, there was little fear—in fact, no fear—of a wet pitch. The money to be had in the gates saw to it that the pitches were covered.

CHAPTER SEVEN

IN KNOTS AT NOTTS

BECAUSE of events preceding the first Test at Trent Bridge, Nottingham, it was only natural that the Australians should have come here with much more confidence than the Englishmen, who must have felt about as apprehensive of the future as did the gay Roger Mortimer, when caught by Edward III.[1] Bradman was in his best form by the first week in June, and though he began curiously out of form in the preceding game against Sussex at Brighton, he finished in a blaze of glory, scoring at the rate of a run a minute and making 109.

He gave a few chances early against Sussex, and from this he had gained the reputation of being a somewhat doubtful starter, though I disagreed with what we saw in the columns of some English newspapers that he was always a doubtful starter. It was obvious at this stage that had Bradman played in an average number of games he would again have scored a thousand runs in May—a feat accomplished by him in 1930 and again in 1938. But, wisely, he conserved his energy, not playing against Yorkshire, Cambridge or Oxford in May, and, further, it is to be noted that in all the games in which he played in May, only once did he have two innings in a match. That was at Manchester against Lancashire, where a pitch affected by rain saw the Australians out for 204 in the first innings, by far their lowest score in this month if we except the 101 at Bradford, where the pitch was not a good one.

Lindwall and Morris also had a good match at Brighton. Morris, a pleasant lad, was beginning to fidget about his trip and was not entirely reconciled when told that the cricketer has never toured who hasn't had his "trot," or run of small scores,

---

[1] Mortimer, Earl of March, was the paramour of Queen Isabella. In Ye Olde Trip to Jerusalem Inn at Nottingham, so called because the Crusaders were said to have one 'for the road and success' there on the way to the wars, is still to be seen Mortimer's hole through which the Earl crawled to the Fortress above for his nocturnal visits to the Queen. Edward and his followers surprised him there in the Queen's Chamber and despite the Queen's entreaties that the 'Gentle Mortimer' might be spared, he was executed at Tyburn in November of that same year, 1330. Ye Olde Trip Inn, with all its memories and atmosphere, was a favourite haunt of a number of us for a yarn after each Test day.

in England. After his splendid beginning at Worcester of 138, Morris had scored 17, 3, 65, 26, 64, 5, 22, 5 and 16, so that he had some reason to be perturbed. This, too, had an interesting effect upon his cricket. He was concentrating so much upon not snicking the ball to the slips that he was taking an initial move in defence across the pitch and was then adding some peculiar shuffles so that he was actually on the move when playing the ball. How easy it is to make runs when you are making them; how impossible it seems when you are not! A little cricket philosophy appreciated by all who have played the game.

Anyway, Morris. threw off his shackles and his cares at Brighton and made a superb 184. Lindwall had his best match there by far and received from Bradman his greatest amount of work. Very cleverly, I thought, Bradman was conserving Lindwall. He knew the hard work ahead of Lindwall in the Tests and so the fast bowler did not play in four of the eleven games preceding the match at Brighton, and in most of the others did very light work. At Brighton, he bowled 34 overs in the two innings, his greatest number of overs then in a match, and took 11 wickets for 59 runs. The Sussex batsmen did not have much idea of what it was all about. Lindwall had had one devastating burst similar to this, and it was of interest that this was at Trent Bridge where, in 15.1 overs, he revived for the local gentry memories of their own Larwood by taking six wickets for 14, somersaulting stumps in all directions. Lindwall was destined to break down in this first Test, and it was galling for Australia that, because of Lindwall's absence, Miller had to bowl 44 overs in the second innings, busting himself in the process.

It is a moot point whether the big victories the Australians were having in the games preceding the Test fitted them for the big occasion. Poor cricket is not of much use to a good cricketer. We saw the evidence of that in the M.C.C. game at Lord's, where Compton and Edrich, who had performed so brilliantly in 1947 that some were speaking of another Golden Age, were very much out of form against the Australian bowling. This, undoubtedly, was due to their many innings against poor county stuff. Their technique was too loose and needed tightening against the capable Australian bowling and fielding—and captaincy.

Before it was covered for the night I had a look at this Trent Bridge pitch. It was a beauty. The only point about it was whether it would last, with Sunday counted, the six days of the Test, but I remembered looking at it after the Nottinghamshire-

8. *Fenners appeared to the author the most pleasant ground in England. This photograph looks towards the pavilion as the undergraduates bat against Australia*

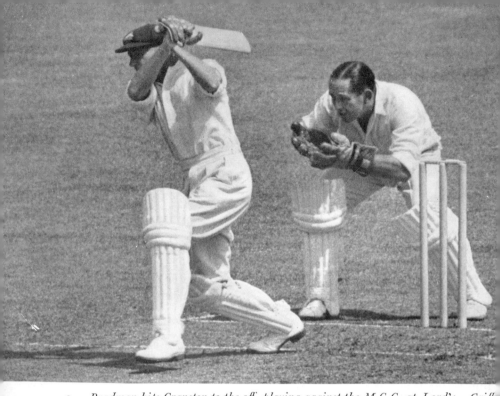

9. *Bradman hits Cranston to the off, playing against the M.C.C. at Lord's. Griff is the wicketkeeper*

Australia game of a fortnight before and the only marks on it then were caused by the footmarks of bowlers. There was no other wear. During that previous game I was chatting to Bill Voce, who is doing much good for the young generation of Nottingham with his coaching, and Bill's conversation was very pleasant until we mentioned the subject of the pitch. The voice of my old adversary took on a decided bitterness. I won't repeat his words but he didn't think much of his home pitch for bowlers —except in the first hour, when it has some life. I was to remember that when England got into such dire trouble in this first hour of this first Test.

It was decided the evening before that Douglas Wright, one of the English bowling hopes, would not play. I saw him two matches before in the Test trial at Birmingham and he looked far from well. The weather there did not help him either, and he spent much of his time off the field under the attention of the masseur. Douglas had the fashionable cricketer's complaint— lumbago—so the night before the selectors sent for George Pope, from the next county of Derbyshire. He was not to play and the feature of the first innings of each side was the success of two men included at the last minute—Laker (England) and Smiling Big Bill Johnston (Australia).

Thursday, June 10, was a grey, depressing day. It was not until 11.25 that Bradman and Yardley, overcoated, muffled and escorted by a horde of photographers, made their way to the centre. They looked and departed. No announcement of their decision was made over the amplifying system, which was dispensing some canned music to a very large and silent crowd, but at twenty to noon a sombre individual appeared with some stumps and five minutes later the covers were removed. Action at last in England's first post-war Test against Australia. The pitch had changed colour overnight from brown to light green. It looked somewhat after the style of a "green-top." The man who produced the stumps then appeared with a can of sawdust, which he solemnly heaped in a pile at each end. All in all, rather a sad ritual.

At ten to noon the captains came again, this time in flannels. Each poked the pitch. Alongside of me, Bill Bowes muttered: "Thou needn't try to fracture finger doing that, laad. Pitch will be all ruddy right." Like Voce, Bill evidently had no pleasant memories of this pitch.

They tossed, and a few yards on the way back Bradman

B.F.D.   F

10.   *Barnes hits Deighton for four runs to leg against
the M.C.C.*

slipped his blazer down over his shoulders. It was the sign to his watching countrymen in the pavilion that they were in the field. First blood to England!

It is interesting, afterwards, to reflect on what might have happened had certain circumstances been different even though the "might haves" count as little in cricket as in other things. This pitch did have some life in it. At close of that day's play there were some who wondered whether Yardley was right in batting when he won the toss. He had no option. He just had to bat as Bradman would have done had he won the toss, and, in that event, the Australian openers would have been concerned, as the English were, by the life in the pitch. Then, too, the Englishmen had to face a frightfully bad light, and on a dull day I cannot imagine a worse background than the Members' Pavilion at Trent Bridge. I could imagine Hutton and Washbrook straining their eyes to pick up Miller's deliveries against this background. The light was so poor at the beginning that an immediate appeal against it might have been upheld.

Lindwall began to bowl between half and three-quarter pace; Miller was at his fastest. Like Kenneth Farnes, Lindwall, who touches his toes, swings his arms and does loosening exercises before he bowls a ball, prefers to come to his top gradually. Miller, throwing back his shock of brown hair as he begins his run, is at his top almost from the first ball. A nasty pair of opening customers to face as they differ so much, Miller bringing his arm over high above his head and Lindwall with a slightly round-arm action. This gives each a varying height off the pitch. Miller lifts higher off a good length ball, swinging the ball away late or bringing it in from the off, whilst Lindwall, who scoots off the pitch at a great rate (he might even be said to skid), brings the ball in mostly from the off.

Washbrook was soon in the direst trouble against Miller and one snick went luckily to earth, but it was Hutton who went first. Miller bowled him with the first ball of his second over. Hutton was three, the total nine and the start a most depressing one. Hutton played forward, seemed to play outside the ball, and it seemed to me at the time that I had seen Hutton go on occasions like this before. To the end of the second Test, I met many Englishmen who criticised their players for not playing forward enough against our fast bowlers. I disagree. To the ball that knocks the stumps kicking, surely the best defence is back and behind the line of flight to watch it all the better, to give yourself more time in which to watch the ball and to play it when its change of direction off the pitch is expended. I, too, often heard these Englishmen criticise the Australians for playing back too much, but they found it hard to fault the defence of my countrymen and the number of runs they made. An interesting point, this, and one which marked a vital difference in the methods of players of both countries.

There was rain soon after this, and at lunch England was 1—13. Lindwall was at his fastest after lunch, and Edrich, at four, was dropped by Ian Johnson at first slip. Johnson is a good slip field, but the Australian specialist at first slip is Colin McCool, watching all this from the pavilion. This was a high catch, not an easy one, but Johnson got both hands to it. The next Lindwall ball got Washbrook. It was short and Washbrook hooked it powerfully and cleanly. It sailed through the murky atmosphere, looking somewhat like a six in flight, but down on the fine-leg boundary, looking eerie in the gloom, Brown set off at top pace and caught the ball brilliantly on the edge of the white line.

Probably some said this was bad luck for Washbrook. It was a thrilling stroke and to be caught so near to a six does suggest ill fortune, but a Test opening batsman usually denies himself the hook or pull in the early part of an innings. Washbrook had been most uncomfortable against Miller. Probably he thought, as he saw this short ball coming along, that if he "clocked" it and succeeded, his horrors would disappear. This dismissal was strangely like that which sometimes befell Herbert Sutcliffe against Australia.

England's start was as dismal as the weather—two for 15, as the Australians say, or 15 for two, as it's put in England. This was the first stage when tongues began to wag and ask whether Yardley had not made a mistake. They recalled what English cricketing history has termed the "calamitous" decision and even the "offensive gesture" of A. W. Carr (epitaphs applied in the wise knowledge of after events) when he asked Australia to bat at Leeds in 1926 after winning the toss. From the easeful depths of their club chairs, the pundits are always on pretty safe ground in shooting at a captain who must make a decision on the spot, but again I repeat that Yardley could have done nothing but bat when he won the toss. The pitch was plumb and true, and winning the toss gave England the weather and the wearing of the pitch. It was not Yardley's fault that his openers should have failed so lamentably, but it was true that with two wickets gone so cheaply England, at this stage, had already lost the advantage of the toss if, indeed, it had not lost the match.

Compton began like the Prince of Cricket he is. He played that glorious square drive of his in front of point off Miller. The ball speeded to the boundary, and the roar of relief and pleasure that greeted this challenging sight was as if it were the winning run. Now, with the possible exception of O'Reilly, I have not known a bowler who dislikes being hit for four as much as Miller. Miller is the most modest bowler I've known—also one of the very greatest. He decries his bowling ability and doesn't like doing the job, but a four hit off him brings his dander to the surface and the batsman can generally expect something pretty lively the next ball. And so Miller bent his head to the ground, tossed back his mane and bowled a hostile bumper to Compton. "Eh, eh," called out the crowd in censure of Miller as Compton ducked. A flicker of their own Harold!

The fight was now intense, Test stuff of sterling character. Compton was splendidly defiant; Edrich, though not in form, was fighting hard; Lindwall and Miller bowled very fast indeed, and Brown made several sensational one-handed saves in the field. At one part of the adjacent railway line, a glimpse can be had from the train of the cricket field, and craning passengers seemed to be in imminent danger of a tumble on the line below as they strained to catch just a glimpse of the flannelled figures.

In quick time the English score had been doubled. Bradman rang a double change with the left-handers Johnston and Toshack. It is an unusual sight to see left-handers having charge of a Test attack, but these Australians are dissimilar in style and technique.

Toshack rolls his hand over the ball (somewhat after the O'Reilly style) and works it in from the off, attacking the leg-stump or to the on of this objective with a leg field. Johnston can move the new ball both ways at fast-medium and he can then settle down as an Australian stock left-hander.[1] A more than useful man to have in a side.

Johnston soon had Edrich. He moved one off the pitch and Edrich played off the line of flight, his off-stump toppling. Here,

[1] Ironmonger and Hornibrook were Australian stock left-handers. Away from the new ball, Johnston follows this style of bowling over the stumps with medium pace and leg spin. This seems not popular in England. Nearly every county has a slow left-hander who bowls round the stumps with slow stuff to an off-side field. For example, Young (M'sex), Hilton and Roberts (Lancs.), Wardle (Yorks) and so on.

again, was an Englishman bowled in playing forward to pace. Edrich has a reputation in England of not playing straight up and down the line of flight but sometimes across it. He never seemed comfortable but fought on as he so often did in Australia in the previous series.

Young Joe Hardstaff was next. He will always be Young Joe, even if he lives (as I hope he does) to 90. His father, a pleasant character whom I met as an umpire in 1938 in England, was Old Joe, and the two share family honours with the Tates of being the only sons and fathers to represent England. Some thought Hardstaff's inclusion in this side was on the principle of horses for courses. Young Joe has had many successes on his home ground of Trent Bridge, but his Test inclusion, surely, was certain when he became the first Englishman to make a century against this Australian Eleven, and at Trent Bridge.

But Young Joe, though blessed with great natural talents, seems too airy for the grim Test stuff. The welcoming cheers from his ain folk were still fluttering in the air when Joe was trudging a forlorn path back to the pavilion. Off the second ball he received (the second ball, mark you, and with England in such a position!) Joe tried to cut, and the tumbling and effervescent Miller at second slip dived, balanced himself on his vertebræ, and held the ball. The critics thought Joe might have denied himself such a "naughty" stroke at such a tragic moment in English cricketing history, and the critics, moreover, were right. But what a grand English Test debut this over was for Johnston, who smiled in his embarrassment, shy fellow that he is, at taking two wickets for no runs.

Two runs later came the greatest blow of all. Compton was clean-bowled by Miller, switched for Toshack, and England was 5—48. Denis moved over to force Miller, missed and left his leg stump open and over it went. Compton looked hard at the pitch, but it was himself, and Miller, not the pitch, to blame.

I wonder if England has known a more sickening ten minutes in Test history as this! It followed upon much pessimism in the country before this Test, and this frightful catastrophe justified all the pessimism. But Yardley could still sport a grin as he came to the middle. As so often happens when a side is up against it, nothing would go right. For some time Yardley and Barnett played attractive, attacking strokes, but they all went straight to a fieldsman and England's score stood still. But not so Barnett's stumps soon afterwards when he played on to Johnston—again, be it noted, in playing forward.

It was an ironic cheer that greeted Evans. The spectators felt sick in the stomach at this frightful batting. England's lowest score ever at Trent Bridge was 112 in 1921, but this seemed bound not to reach the hundred mark. Hereabouts, however, the English "tail," as it often did in Australia the previous series, made the efforts of the top batsmen look even more pathetic. Evans played a splendid forward shot in front of point for four. He is full of courage and vitality, Evans, but then he twice saw Bradman drop him at cover off Johnston. The first was hard and went on for four; the second got through Bradman's hands and hit him in the tummy. Then Morris caught him brilliantly at forward short leg, a hard-hit stroke, but Evans had batted with more dash than any of his predecessors.

But it was Laker's 63 which should have made the talented batsmen hide their heads in the pavilion. He played the Australian attack as if it had no terrors at all. His driving was splendid; his temperament as good. The previous season Laker had batted 21 times for Surrey, his top score being 60. Lindwall was not back after tea, due to a strain, and the chink in the Australian attack was shown when Morris came on to bowl his doubtful left-handed slows. Laker made 50 in 60 minutes, and Bedser, who is a much better batsman than credited, gave him grand support in a partnership of 89. If, one might ask, Laker, Bedser and Evans, why not Washbrook, Hutton, Edrich, Compton and others?

The only answer is that the splendid batting of the tail made all the more ignominious the failure of the head—though full marks must be given Bill Johnston for a grand bowling effort. His figures were 25—11—36—5—and those are pretty good figures for a bowler on his first Test appearance in England. There's no better-tempered or better-dispositioned man in the cricketing world than Johnston. He's always smiling. He displaced Ring at the last moment because of weather, but as he can bowl with speed or spin, Johnston's place should never again rest upon the weather. Miller played resonantly at second fiddle; the others merely strummed along, Lindwall not being outstanding.

Barnes and Morris came out that evening to open for Australia. Edrich bowled the first ball, which was a wide, and then Barnes walked down the pitch and said, "Eh, the light!" The remark was addressed to Chester and surely must be the only time ever that an appeal against the light has been framed in such a fashion. I was told later by those on the spot that Chester almost had a stroke. It is worth mentioning that this appeal was refused, and it is certainly worth mentioning that the incessant appeals by my friend Barnes against the light in the Sydney Test of 1946 had much to do with the rule operative in this game—that after one appeal, the light is left in the hands of the umpires.

For those who like action, there was not much to sing about on the second day, but there was plenty to observe for the student of the game.

It was again an overcast day, and Cooke, the umpire, gave Barnes and Morris to understand early that he was on the field as an umpire, not a clothes-horse, and so the discarded sweaters were despatched to the pavilion when Barnes and Morris warmed up.

Barnes was full of confidence, as ever; Morris was again hesitant and had reintroduced the double-shuffle. The Press had its usual sweepstake on the score, the highest being 904 and the lowest 302. The only incident of note for a long time was when Chester, with his foot, stopped a ball from Morris's bat from disturbing the stumps at his end, so Barnes then picked the ball up for the bowler. Chester wagged his finger at Barnes, so Barnes wagged back again at Chester for committing the first breach. Barnes is not easily kept down.

The Australians, with the toss well reversed by now, were out to rub it into England. The bowlers were to be worn into the ground for the assault later, and so it was soon obvious that there was much more method about the opening partnership of the Australians than the English. The duty of a Test opener is not so much to score runs but to take the sting out of the attack, and this Barnes and Morris were doing. Barnes, the brilliant stroke-maker, had turned himself into a Test opening batsman with all his solidity and caution, but even thus Barnes scored runs much faster than Morris, who, at one stage, had scored seven runs in 55 minutes. Morris brightened later, but was out in trying to force Laker and Australia had lost its first wicket for 73. Then came the Don.

CHAPTER EIGHT

PEGGED ON THE LEG-SIDE

THE responsibility of being a champion is that the champion
is never expected to be anything else—come weather, come
age and all the ills and little upsets that champions must suffer.
I thought of this at Trent Bridge after the second day's play when
Bradman was being widely criticised for slow play.

If one is to judge by the time factor (and this is generally
misleading because it does not take into consideration theories
of negation, fall of wickets or apportioning of the strike between
the batsmen) then the Australians were decidedly slow on the
second day in Nottingham, but I, for one, never found the game
dull. There was a very shrewd battle of tactics going on in the
middle, and at the end of the day Bradman was on top by virtue
of the facts that his side was well ahead of England, his own
score was 130 and he was also unconquered.

Now this is what took place when Bradman came to bat.
Yardley ordered and led a full-scale attack against the Australian
champion. He brought on Bedser immediately and he fringed
Bradman with men on his leg-side with Bedser concentrating
on Bradman's leg-stump. The second ball from Bedser, Bradman
almost played into his stumps. England was fighting hard to get
Bradman's scalp and the champion did not look at all confident.
I sensed some unusual wavering in his bat as if it were not altogether certain as it went forward to meet Bedser. Then, too,
Laker bowled solidly from the other end, and when twenty
minutes had passed Bradman was only four runs. The English
bowling had the Australians pegged down securely at this stage.

Yardley switched Edrich on for Bedser and the intention of
this was soon made obvious. Edrich swung his arms round and
round before delivering the ball and then he bowled a bumper.
His second, too, was a bumper, but Bradman hooked this
viciously. So it can be taken, then, that if England possessed a
Miller and a Lindwall, Bradman would get more than a share
of the bouncers, but Edrich, short in build and not now possessed
of very much pace, was a poor bouncing proposition against the
two virile Australians.

88

Barnes made his half century after being 135 minutes in the middle. It was a splendid innings. "He's a reight good cricketer, is this laad," said Bowes as Barnes swung Barnett for four, and Bradman, with 29, was more like himself as lunch approached. After that we saw some stirring happenings. Evans dived back like a Rugby winger going for the line in an international to catch Barnes, who had chopped the ball down on to Evans's pads, and Miller was out for *nil* to a very intelligent piece of bowling by Laker. Miller's big reach gives him a good cover up the pitch to a good-length ball. Thrice did he play forward to Laker this way, but from the back I saw Laker bring his arm over next ball and, instead of spinning, his hand straightened up the ball. It went straight through, Miller played forward, allowed for the off-break, and the ball clipped the outside edge of his bat to go on to Edrich at first slip.

This made Australia 3—121 and Laker had taken all three at a cost of 22 runs off 12 overs. As he had top-scored, Laker, the last-minute selection, who had not been played in the Test trial at Birmingham, was sitting on top of the Test world.

Brown looked uncomfortable at No. 5, as well he might after his long career as an opener. Yardley, who had taken Bradman's Test wicket three times running the preceding series in Australia, came on to try his luck again but he got the wrong "B." He trapped Brown leg before with one that came in from the off, and Australia was 4—185—a good fight back by England. As Hassett came in, I started to think of Wright and how much England might miss him at this stage. He had given Hassett unceasing worry in Australia.

A flight of Hurricanes over the ground seemed to upset Hassett's concentration and he made a hectic swish off Bedser which spooned up and landed safely behind the keeper. Then, at this stage, Yardley showed his defensive hand. He had Barnett, principally, and himself bowl outside Bradman's leg stump to a leg-side field. Now there's not much a batsman can do about this stuff. It is thrown up to him for two purposes: (a) of slowing down the game and (b) of inviting the batsman to commit suicide. Some Englishmen argue that Toshack's bowling is of this negative nature but I do not agree. Toshack nags at the leg-stump and is never very far from it.

These English tactics did not seem to impress Bradman. He watched one whole over go by without attempting a stroke, and at the end of the over crossed his legs and stood with a hand on his hip, ruminating, no doubt, on just how much cricket there was in such bowling. After having played against a lot of this stuff in England, I could well imagine Bradman's thoughts. It is, without doubt, the most unsatisfactory type of bowling in the game. It is soulless, but I could see eye to eye with Yardley in his use of it. At this stage Bradman was over his poor start and was rapidly gaining the ascendancy. This was the period, in the innings of his career, when Bradman commenced his onslaught and rapidly changed the whole nature of the game, and Yardley was simply determined to have none of that.

So Yardley closed down the game and awaited only the periods just before and after the adjournments and a new ball to attack Bradman again. At tea, Bradman was 78. In the 15 minutes prior to tea he did not score a single run and, strangely for him, was being barracked for slow scoring, but Bradman probably reasoned, and rightly so, that he had plenty of time on his hands to play Yardley at the same game. At 5.25, Bradman played a delicious cover-drive off Bedser to gain his century in 218 minutes. This was his eighteenth century in Tests against England. The next Australians to him are Trumper and Woodfull with six; Hobbs leads the Englishmen with twelve, and thus Bradman leads them all. From the viewpoint of stroke-play, this was probably Bradman's most colourless Test century, but I have given the circumstances of it.

Hassett also played the waiting game. He stayed on 30 for 20 minutes and the game that evening went to its close with restless schoolboys (it is expecting a miracle of them to keep still for six hours) indulging in clap-clap-clapping. It was not a great Test day but it was a vitally interesting one to the students of the game.

Bradman overnight was 130. That evening we mixed with English past and present players, and O'Reilly gave Bedser some advice he will not soon forget. O'Reilly, as one bowler to another (and doped pitches the world over give bowlers an affinity that surpasses all batsmen and sides) complimented Bedser on his bowling. Bedser thanked him. "But," said O'Reilly, "I can't say that I agree with the placing of your leg-side field." Bedser was very interested and the pair got down to pencil and paper. O'Reilly has had a cricket lifetime of attacking the leg-stump and he told Bedser how he would arrange his field if he were "having a pop," as he put it, at the Don.

Next morning Bedser moved Hutton, vide the O'Reilly plan,

from leg slip to fine-leg, some twelve yards from the bat and in position for the leg-glance. He also added mid-on to the short legs. In the first over Bradman scored two, and that stroke also gave him 1,000 for the season—beating Robertson, of Middlesex, for the honour, by the matter of minutes. Bradman did not seem to know what all the clapping was about. He asked Evans, who told him, and then he raised his cap.

This was a beautiful day of sunshine, with the ground crammed full, and the stroke Bradman played off Bedser for four through the covers next over was worthy of the day and the occasion. But next ball, Bradman leg-glanced, and there was Hutton waiting for it. Hutton did not have to move an inch— and how the crowd roared! Bedser, grinning hugely, gave a wave of appreciation to O'Reilly in the far-off Press-box, and even three minutes later this momentous cricketing news had gained the outside world because a passing engine-driver exultantly whooped a cock-a-doodle-do on the whistle. The crowd, naturally, which had settled down to some fireworks by Bradman, was more than pleased to see the back of him at 138.

Was O'Reilly false to his country in discussing fielding positions with Bedser? Some of the queasy-minded might think he was but I don't for a minute. I wrote this story later for "Peterborough" of the *Daily Telegraph*, and he, in an unthinking moment, gave it the sub-title of "Fifth Columnist," but it was certainly not that. Arthur Mailey was once hauled over the embers in England by a rather pompous manager for discussing with Ian Peebles before a Test the grip for a bosie. Arthur's reply was a good one. "Cricket," he said, "is like art. It is international." And he then showed Peebles his grip for his leg-break also!

Any bowler is fully entitled, in the interests of the game, to tell a fellow-slave what he thinks of things. English players and officials were very pleasant to us in England and we often discussed matters generally. We were often invited, as a mark of honour, which we appreciated, to visit the dressing-rooms of the county sides and meet the players. Those who have been through the mill appreciate such courtesies. If there should still be doubts as to whether a bowler "should tell," I remember that Bradman, at Manchester, told an English selector before the first Test that Pollard had given him more trouble than any other English bowler and should be in the Tests—advice not taken!

To return to the Test. I noticed that Yardley often conferred with Hutton—two Yorkshire heads better than one! Ian Johnson came and snicked one high over slips, and at this stage it was announced that the ground was full and the gates closed. Laker was somewhat lucky when Johnson hit the ball to his foot and it rebounded to the stumps. Australia was now 6—338.

Hassett was being kept very subdued by the English attack and tactics. Yardley set precisely the same fields which he did to Bradman, and Hassett found them very hard to pierce—as would anybody. These fields were aptly described as the "wheel" fields because to Laker and Young the fieldsmen spread from the stumps like so many spokes from a wheel. Laker's field differed in that he had a slip, but Young's field comprised a perfect circle, close enough in to stop strokes from being singles and yet far enough out to cut off boundaries.

At this stage the Test was almost half-way played. Since play began, Hassett had added 30 in 75 minutes, but suddenly he opened out and swept Laker with a bat hitting across the ball, and soon afterwards he opened his shoulders and played a pull-drive for six, the first six of the match. Tallon was not too comfortable and was, well caught and bowled by Young, but before lunch on this day Young bowled 11 successive maidens—a remarkable feat, credit being due to the bowler for length and direction, and the whole significant of how the Australians, with two days and four hours to play, were still inclined to play Yardley and his bowlers at their own game. Hassett made 53 in the 120 minutes' play before lunch.

Hassett's century, his first in a Test in England, came after five hours and five minutes. He sparkled after passing his hundred; Lindwall batted nicely, and even Toshack and Johnston took themselves seriously with the bat, so that when Australia's innings finished soon after four the total was 509 and the lead was 344 with two days two hours and ten minutes to play. England's only chance was a draw, to play out time. A clear picture of the steadiness of the play is shown by the bowling figures:

	O.	M.	R.	W.
Edrich	18	1	72	0
Bedser	44.2	12	113	3
Barnett	17	5	36	0
Young	60	28	79	1
Laker	55	14	138	4
Compton	5	0	24	0
Yardley	17	6	32	2

This works out at approximately 2 1-3 runs an over, which is a modest rate in a big score, but the failure of the English first innings presented Australia with almost a day of time and so there was no necessity to take risks against the English attack and its methods. Yardley's tactics were thus at a disadvantage. Had the time been more equally shared, Australia would have had to do something about the "wheel" fields in order to force a win within the allotted time, and it did seem a challenge had presented itself for Australian decision in the matches ahead—if the English batsmen did their job!

Yardley's captaincy emerged from this first innings with high honours. He kept always a reasonable grip on affairs and I liked his field placing, though I would not have liked to cope with it as a batsman. When one thought, however, of the profligate manner in which England played with runs in the series in Australia, it was a welcome sight to see Yardley challenging batting supremacy. Bedser, particularly, Laker, who might have had some good fortune in several of his dismissals, Young, the length bowler, and Yardley himself (who is far from being the world's worst Test bowler, incidentally) bowled manfully for England, and as good as a bowler was Godfrey Evans behind the stumps. He's more energetic than any keeper I know. Nothing is too much trouble for him to do or attempt. His red-covered gloves, most conspicuous, were on the move unceasingly.

When the Australians came to field there was no Lindwall. Instead there was young Harvey, by far the most brilliant fieldsman of both sides, who was to save many runs in the field. Harvey was the Australian twelfth man, a position always filled by the best available fieldsman, but surely one was justified in thinking that if Lindwall an hour or so before could make 42 runs, take sharp singles and even run a three, then he was fit enough to take *some* position in the field. Lindwall did not come out to field after tea on the first day. He was then incapacitated during play, and, under the rules, there was no necessity for Bradman to ask Yardley's permission to field a substitute although a captain would, of course, pay the opposing captain the compliment of telling him that he required a substitute fieldsman as a particular player had been incapacitated.

Bradman, I understand, did inform Yardley of the position in the first innings but not, I believe, in the second. Possibly Yardley was at fault in not approaching Bradman in the matter, because a Test match is precisely a Test match and not, as O'Reilly pointed out in an article the next day, a Sunday school affair. He, too, took the view that Lindwall should have fielded. It was noticed that several times during his innings Lindwall did clutch at his strained groin, but he made, as I have stated, 42, and figured with Hassett in a hundred partnership. He was, therefore, in a degree of fitness to fill some position in the field, and if restrained from getting to a catch because of his ailment, then England was entitled to that advantage. Many Test captains I have known would hade demurred at the situation. Once in Sydney the then captain of Victoria, Ebeling, told an inquiring player he could leave the field if he wished but as he, this particular fieldsman, had batted with an injury, Victoria would play a man short and not ask for a substitute.

It was another wretched start for England. Washbrook was out for one, caught behind on the leg-side, and went his discontented way to the pavilion. Judging by his demeanour, Washbrook is either very unlucky or often displeased. I was told that there was red on his shirt from the hit of the ball, and from the distance I could see Cyril showing other players his shirt mark. This rather reminded me of that time in Melbourne when the bright English journalist came out with the memorable story that Edrich was out to a bad leg before decision and quoted the mark on the edge of his bat to support his story. Chester gave Washbrook out, but, whether the decision was correct or not, the point is that Washbrook was out in trying to hook. England didn't want runs at this stage; England wanted time and, most of all, a good start.

Edrich, still out of form, struggled hard.   Where lack of success or a succession of misplaced strokes would often lead a player to turn it in, Edrich battles on always in the hope that things will turn. It was a ball, however, that didn't turn that got him, much in the same manner as Laker trapped Miller. Ian Johnson sent through a straight one, Edrich just tickled it and England was 39—2 with Tallon jubilant behind the stumps. In came Compton, again, to play the waiting game, a game foreign to his nature and his parts.

Compton almost turned everybody's hair white by marching up the pitch to the first ball before it was bowled. I must ask him some day just why he does this. One of the funniest sights I've seen on a cricket field was a Compton idolator who imitated this walk-down and was promptly stranded by yards. Compton scrambled out of his dilemma by blocking the ball very hurriedly.

He placed the next prettily to leg for two, but when eight there was a terrific Australian appeal for leg before against Compton. Chester answered "No," but surprise was written all over the faces of Ian Johnson and Tallon. Compton gave the impression that he was ready to walk.

At this stage Australia was missing Lindwall. There was a suggestion of paucity about the attack when Miller came at six o'clock to bowl off-breaks around the wicket. Barnes, too, was called in, and the suggestion forced itself on one at this stage that England would make many runs against this Australian attack if ever the openers gave a hundred partnership.

Despite the bad start, England had 50 up in 65 minutes, and hereabouts we saw a delicious five minutes of stroke-play from Hutton. He leg-glanced Miller like a flash to the pavilion. This is the type of stroke which makes me think one field is not enough to display it. The follow-through is barely completed ere the ball is bouncing back off the fence, so fast does it go. This day had seen three of the most perfect leg-glances imaginable. One was by Hassett, another by Edrich and then this by Hutton—all strokes to linger in memory. Then Hutton crashed Miller through the covers for four to make him 50 in 110 minutes, and then in this same over, with Miller bowling faster, he back-cut one like Kippax. Here we saw Hutton in his most superb moments. Three of the loveliest strokes ever to grace a cricket field!

I have written in another place of the strange effect being hit for a boundary has upon Miller. He simply cannot forgive it, and to those who know him it was obvious what would come next over. Miller is highly excitable. He motioned his field back, cast down his head, threw it back like a charging bull and there came a bouncer to Compton, which he played on tiptoes. The crowd roared "Bodyline" at that. Walking back to bowl, Miller, by actions, showed the crowd what he would have done with that particular ball. He showed that he would have pulled it with disdain for four. Well, probably . . .

The next ball was an out and out bumper, and this time the crowd roared louder. Miller charged down the pitch to field the next ball and finished up by running around behind point, back to bowl. At this stage there was plenty of hooting . . . and advice. The next Miller over was the last of the day, and with the fourth ball Hutton was hit a nasty blow on the shoulder. This further incensed the crowd, but Hutton had the last say of the day by gloriously leg-glancing another boundary and that ended the day's play, England 121—2: Hutton 63 and Compton 36. Miller, walking slowly off the field in last position, was roundly hooted by the members, but this was nothing new for an Australian at Trent Bridge.

There's something magnificent in Miller's spirit. He keeps it not far beneath the surface and it's easily pricked. There's much magnificence in the manner in which he readily accepts a challenge but I did not care over much for these bouncers at this particular time and at a place of such memories. Miller was a schoolboy (as George Duckworth would put it, "nobbut a laad") when the bodyline series happened. I thought it might have been wise of Bradman at this stage of looming bouncers to have a quiet word with Miller and calm him, but Bradman, though he holds more field conferences than any captain I've known, had remarkably few with Miller throughout the tour.

There were some rather strange developments before play next day. Sir Douglas McCraith, chairman of the Notts committee, was reported as having personally apologised to Bradman for the behaviour of the crowd on the Saturday and particularly a section of the members' reserve. "Old members are furious," said Sir Douglas to Bradman. "I believe trouble was started by colliers from Larwood's former district who, when they arrived at the ground, asked a policeman, ' Can we barrack here?' The policeman replied, ' You will have nothing to barrack.'

Before play recommenced, Captain Brown, secretary of the county club, made this appeal over the amplifying system at the ground: "Let us keep Nottingham a place where Test matches can continue to be played. On Saturday the Australian, Miller, was booed and there was much subsequent publicity in the press. These Australians are great sportsmen. They stood by the Empire in the war and we should always be pleased to greet them. Let us show them how really pleased we are and give them a warm-hearted greeting this morning."

That announcement was applauded and so were the Australians when they came out. Miller again had to carry the yoke of Lindwall's absence, but he did not bowl until the fifth over, when he took the new ball. There were no bumpers so it was to be a two-way peace—which was as it should have been.

Hutton and Compton began in great form. The day was oppressive and the light grew very bad around noon when thunder rolled. Most of the crowd got thoroughly drenched in

11. Top. —*and Edrich looks anguished as his middle stump is sent flying at Lord's. He seems to have played across the ball*

12. Bottom. *Lindwall gathers himself for a destructive delivery*

13. *Bradman makes a typical shot to the leg boundary off Yardley in the second Test at Lord's*

14. *A beautiful photograph of Bradman as he makes a late cut in the second Test at Lord's*

a sharp five minutes' shower, but the delay was only a short one, and then came the hundred partnership between these two gifted batsman—and this partnership was as valuable to England at this stage as a large splash of Marshall aid.

The cricket was tense, full of drama. Even hardened, cynical men of the old brigade in the Test-box were on edge as Compton and Hutton measured up the Australian attack. This hour, I thought, would be one of the most vital in English Test history. If this pair could see it through, there was no telling what England would achieve in this and following Tests, because that final hour of Saturday had shown some telling weaknesses in the Australian attack.

Hutton did not see it through. The rain made the ball skid, and seven minutes after the resumption Hutton was clean bowled by Miller, who delivered what seemed to be an off-break. Hutton played forward with his typical half-cock defensive stroke and the ball, skidding but not turning, got past him to the stumps. As I saw this happen, it seemed that I was watching something I had often seen with Hutton before. The English critics condemn their batsmen for not playing forward to the Australian bowling, but as Hutton walked back I made a note that at the end of the series I must work out just how many times English batsmen are out *in* playing forward to balls which the average Australian would play off the back foot. All in all, this was a beautiful Hutton innings. No man playing the game possesses more artistic strokes.

Enter Young Joe, to give the usual palpitations. In mockery, perhaps, of those who criticised him in the first innings, Hardstaff flashed at the third ball with a cut—as if his first innings escapade had been already forgiven or forgotten or, indeed, had never happened—and Morris dropped him low at second slip. It went for four and the ground breathed again, but, at that, I thought Young Joe should have been served with an immediate summons to appear at the Old Bailey on the morrow on the charge of wilful, unthinking, aiding and abetting of national sabotage. Probably, I thought, he would be acquitted with a severe caution, but cautions mean nothing to Joe, and lo, in the same over, he flicked at another and missed, played one into the top of his pads and then snicked the last ball for two through the slips. Phew, what an over! Joe flicks his bat like a magician his wand, but 'tis his nature and naught will change it.

Bad light stopped the play at 12.35, and after that Chester and

Cooke made two mufti inspections. An interesting point to this stage was that Miller, bowling beautifully, had not bowled a single bouncer in seven overs. Like Palestine at that moment, it was to be a two-way truce with both Jew and Arab observing the cease-fire order. Nearing one, play began again with the waggish Hassett hiding the ball in the sawdust before he went out to the boundary, and it took some moments for Miller to dig it out.

Hardstaff began to bat as if he knew he had only a limited time to live. With lovely wrist-work, he forced Miller wide for three, hit Johnston superbly through the covers for four, did the same to Miller and, when Miller threw a slow off-break for variety, hit it amid the tumult of his countymen straight for four. How the crowd hummed at this! Joe had scored 23 to Compton's four and he was again on his Nottingham throne—though he then flicked one uppishly through the slips as if to test fully the loyalty of his subjects.

Deciding to be in the boundary business, Compton majestically swept Toshack for four, and in the final over before lunch Joe gave us all a succulent *hors d'œuvre* by stepping back almost to his stumps and forcing Johnston off his tiptoes square to the boundary. What a sight this was for cricketing eyes, and at lunch England was 191 for three, Compton 63, Hardstaff 31. England, with one day and four hours left for play, was still 153 behind Australia.

This was Test-match cricket of the best vintage. It was lovely stuff, and so eager were the players to get on with it that they were out some minutes too early after lunch. The Australians whiled away the time with catching while the bare-headed Englishmen "nattered." The light was burked by a thundery haze. I wondered why the Englishmen did not appeal immediately but then I began to work it out. It looked obvious that rain would come. Probably Yardley had reasoned that it would be preferable to play on in bad light on a good pitch than be caught on a sticky one with a deficit of a hundred runs. What was Bradman's reply to this? As there was a faint suggestion that England would control the Australian attack in this session, he did not want to be caught on a sticky pitch with a hundred or so to get, and so he brought on Toshack and Ian Johnson to bowl good-length stuff to a run-saving field. This was bitter, calculating Test cricket to gladden the heart of the most fastidious with every now and then a stroke of the utmost beauty.

Barnes's head was almost the sacrificial offering for England's 200. A savage hook by Hardstaff almost took Barnes along with it, and, as one who had collected "it" in that position, I again thought that Barnes would some day receive like medicine. It's too risky up there to anybody but an O'Reilly. Compton picked one off his toes to the boundary against Toshack, and Bradman retaliated by bringing across slip to make two leg-side slips with four other men on the on-side—playing England at its own game.

Toshack bowled extremely well at this stage. He had good length and every ball was so naggingly close to the leg-stump that it had to be played. There was an awesome hush among the thousands and thousands of bare-headed English spectators who followed every move most intently. I saw a nearby train pass and every window was crammed with craning passengers to catch a quick glimpse of this place where English cricket was fighting so valiantly for recovery.

But I must not dwell too long on the descriptive part of the game. There were more comings and goings because of rain, and it was at half-past four that Compton reached his century. The whole ground rose in acclamation. It was, indeed, a lovely century of stroke-play and patience. He is the Prince Charming of Cricket, is Compton. He let his concentration drag after his hundred (227 minutes, 12 fours), and Johnson dropped him in the slips off Miller. Had that catch been taken England's sun would have been close to setting because Hardstaff had gone, lofting Toshack to the on, Barnett had been brilliantly caught by Miller in the slips and only Yardley remained of the proven batsmen. One could not expect miracles from Laker again.

Compton drove Miller like a flash with that favourite square drive of his that cleaves the space between point and cover, and again did the Miller blood surge. Miller answered with a bouncer. This was his first of the day and it happened in the nineteenth over. Compton played a typical short-arm jab for two and the next ball slipped out of Miller's hand, careering high over Compton's head amid isolated jeers. Miller was looking very, very tired. He had bowled himself into the ground, but he had the satisfaction of knowing that he had answered every call by Bradman in the absence of Lindwall.

Yardley began badly but improved with time. Once Barnes, at silly silly-leg, fielded and threw the stumps down in a flash. Yardley scrambled back and then machine-gunned Barnes with his bat. What a terrific nuisance value Barnes has in that position. Once Toshack appealed for l.b.w. against Yardley and the umpire and 20,000 spectators said "No," the latter screaming vigorously.

At stumps that night, England had a rare chance of saving the game. Yardley was gone but Evans was hanging on nobly with Compton. The score was 345—6, Compton 154 and Evans 10. The toast that night in Merrie England—and England's day of success did lift national morale in many places—was broad-shouldered, black-haired Denis Compton. He had been 347 minutes at the wickets and he had passed Bradman as top-scorer for the Test, and though the game seemed to be well in Australia's grip, while there was Compton there was hope for England.

This was one of the grandest Test days I have known. Apart from Compton's superb innings, there was a constant battle of wits going on between Bradman and the Englishmen, and whilst the game was proceeding in the utmost gloom in which batsmen and fieldsmen had intense difficulty in sighting the ball, I always sensed that Yardley was making a brave attempt to pass Australia's total that night so that he might have a little up his sleeve if the weather broke that night. If this was Yardley's intention . . . and the doggedness of the Englishmen in batting on in the pitiable light for such a long time suggested it . . . he was to be commended, and even the most cynical admitted that night that England had won back much of its cricket glory.

England, that evening, was one run ahead with four wickets in hand. A storm was predicted that night and I often saw Bradman cock an eye at the sky. His job that day was to see that England did not scamper away with runs, as a storm that night, with England a hundred ahead, could set the stage for an Australian defeat on a "sticky." All day long the battle revolved around these points, with Compton, amid it all, playing his noble century. He is as noble in his cricket as in his character. They use to say that of Victor Trumper and no sportsman can be paid higher praise. The scenes that day were unforgettable. The tension could be sensed in the morning. In the almost impenetrable gloom, people sat with bated breath as England fought back from the hopeless position. Then came the unprecedented scenes of enthusiasm as first Compton made his century, beat Bradman's score and then reached his 150. I can see Compton again as he tilts his trousers with his left hand and waves his bat overhead to the crowd in tribute to their tributes. Another hero was

Miller. He had almost broken his back in trying to do his job and that of Lindwall's also.

Neville Cardus later told me that when the game was at its tensest he saw George Gunn walking around the pavilion with a measuring tape, checking on the many historic bats that are in the pavilion. "There's one of the 'Old Man's' upstairs. Come on up and we'll have a look at that," chortled Gunn, who is one of the greatest characters the game has known. I liked, too, the story of Evans as he came to the middle that day. Compton met him and asked him if he had a preference for any particular end or whether he wished to be kept away from any particular bowler. And Evans made this reply: "Denis, I couldn't care less!"

It was poor light again next day. A light appeal was dismissed, but rain drove the players in at a few minutes to twelve. With storm clouds wheeling, it seemed that weather would save England, and not even an Australian would deny that Compton's truly great innings merited some such reward. There was a delay of half an hour and then Evans began to bat like Compton, so much so that the score-board put up two of his sparkling fours to Denis. With left elbow well forward to the ball, he drove beautifully, and England's score, amid tremendous enthusiasm, passed 400. What a grand effort this was after the first-inning debacle, but soon afterwards Compton was out and England's gesture was practically completed.

Compton was out to a Miller bouncer. The ball pitched the bowler's side of half-way and Compton at first tried his inimitable short-arm jab to leg, but he forsook the stroke as he saw the ball near his head, overbalanced, fell backwards and, throwing his legs apart, made a desperate effort to straddle the stumps. He went into them. Chester said "Out" at square-leg. This was a most depressing end to an innings that will live always. Compton told me later that he found the ball hard to sight against the dark pavilion background; Tallon told him that this was the fastest ball Miller had then bowled on the tour. So the bouncer had again been Australia's greatest shock weapon in this game.

Evans tried valiantly but England was all out at 2.40 p.m. Australia had three hours in which to make 98 for victory. The Australian bowling figures made interesting reading. Johnston, who had had a most successful Test and fully deserved the rewards that came his way, bowled the enormous number of 59 overs,

and next to him was Miller with 44. Miller's heart is as pronounced as his spirit, but it was to prove that this huge amount
of work was to be his undoing for a long spell so far as bowling
was concerned.

Barnes began Australia's innings as if he had an urgent
appointment immediately after tea. The runs simply flowed on
the board with 13 off the first over from Bedser. England had
two successes, both to Bedser. Morris was again uncomfortable,
but Bedser's great success was the dismissal of Bradman for none
—his first Test score of *nil* in a Test in England. The amazing
part was that Bradman went as in the first innings, caught
Hutton in the short leg-glance position, bowled by Bedser and
aided by O'Reilly.

Hassett shook things along, with one eye on the English
bowling and another on the very dark clouds, and with Barnes
batting in his brightest manner, Australia had won at 4.20 by
eight wickets. The end was delectable. Everybody on the field
miscalculated the runs needed, putting it down at 97. Barnes
achieved that number with a sweep to leg, and almost before the
bat had finished its arc he had grabbed two stumps as souvenirs
and sprinted to the pavilion. Scorers and pressmen shouted to
the middle, the players returned, Barnes from the depths of the
pavilion, and the stumps were set up again. This time Barnes
failed to get a single stump, not even a bail. He threw his bat
on the pitch in mock disgust.

Thus did Australia win the first post-war Test in England.
Bradman, Barnes, Compton, Hassett, Laker, Johnston, Bedser
and Evans (whose work behind was as good, I think, as I have
seen) were the individual heroes. In the post-mortem it was
obvious that England lost the game on the first day, with its
pathetic batting collapse. The bad light then provided the only
extenuating circumstances. Compton almost saved them the
draw but the task was a colossal one. Many complained against
the slow scoring, but to the student of cricket, I thought, the
game never dragged. It was constantly a battle of tactics and its
ending left the countries with the following problems: *England*
(a) the necessity for the opening batsmen to give the side a good
start; (b) the enormity of the task in tackling Bradman without
an express bowler; (c) the need to withstand bouncers and not
allow them to demoralise a person's technique. *Australia* (a) the
desperate position Australia would be in if Lindwall were to
suffer a complete breakdown; (b) the toll the second innings

bowling took of Miller and the bad effect bowling was having upon his brilliant batting; (c) the necessity to overcome the "wheel" field because such a lavish presentation of time could not again be expected; (d) the arduous stock work the fast bowlers had to perform because of the failure of the slow leg-break bowlers and their inability to make the Test side.

One should not leave this Nottingham Test without comment on the bouncers and the apology by Sir Douglas McCraith and the statement by Captain Brown. Bouncers, especially if they are unlimited and the other side has not the means of retaliation, will always bring feeling into the game, and in showing their displeasure the Nottingham spectators were doing only what the Australian crowds had done in the Jardine-Larwood tour. I think they were fully entitled to show their displeasure and should not have been coerced from so doing by the threat of Nottingham losing a Test or by introducing the Australian war effort. If both sides take and give bouncers, there can be no complaint. Often, when I was writing Hammond's 1946-47 M.C.C. tour of Australia, I drew attention to the Australian method of attacking Hutton, particularly, and drew the obvious parallel. Most of the Australian batsmen in the Jardine-Larwood tour took exception to the principle of turning the other cheek and wanted retaliation ... but Woodfull stood firm. In cricket, as in all things, one side must compete against the other on equal terms and methods must be adopted to meet a particular state of affairs. Finally, on the barracking angle, one should observe that the principle of freedom of expression must hold good in all places.

CHAPTER NINE

GLOOM AT LORD'S

THE English selectors altered the side considerably for the second Test at Lord's. Although his feats against Australia at Bramall Lane did not suggest that he would be a severe Test proposition, Coxon received a position and Dollery, who had been making most of his runs on the doubtful Edgbaston pitch at Birmingham, came in to bolster the batting. Wright was fit again and was an obvious choice. A poisoned toe saved the selectors a decision with Hardstaff; Barnett was obviously past Test cricket at Nottingham and he and Young were omitted. The Australians kept the same team, Lindwall proving his fitness at the Lord's nets the day before the game started.

Lord's is always a lovely sight for a Test between England and Australia. The historic ground takes on its atmosphere from dawn of the big day, but this time it began the evening before when the inevitable queue formed at ten o'clock. Heading it was sixty-year-old Bill Davies. When the Test was played there in 1938, Davies was next man to enter the ground when the order came out to close the gates. This time he took no risks.

At 11.15, as I walked from the bus to the ground, the queues outside were terrific. It was obvious there were more people who would be unable to get in than there were inside, and so it proved, the gates being closed before play started. There had been a storm to the south of London at eight o'clock and the weather, as Bradman and Yardley walked to the pitch, looked about as troubled as England's cricketing thoughts. But the setting was there. Hats and coats were off in the popular stands, flags were flying, the trees looked very green and clean, and people were squatting contentedly on the grass behind the white line and in front of the pavilion.

As we looked down on the ground from the Press-box, the playing area seemed very small. It would be interesting to know when this habit of marking off much of the ground with a circle first was accepted. On some grounds it is necessary but not, I think, at Lord's. In the game against the M.C.C. here, a ball had only to pass a fieldsman on the Tavern side to become four.

Under such circumstances, a century score would not compare with one such when the ground was not circled off. It seems wrong to me, though I admit the anxiety to allow as many people as possible to see a Test. It does not allow a bowler to angle much for catches in the deep, and I was surprised when I put this to O'Reilly and he disagreed. He wanted to know what did it matter . . . but I think he would have thought differently had he been in the middle as a bowler and saw shots earn boundaries which did not merit them.

As Bradman and Yardley and the inevitable swarm of photographers made their way to the middle, there was that delightful hum of expectancy which envelops all grounds just as a Test is to begin. Bradman won the toss this time and tapped his legs to the pavilion . . . the sign for the batsmen to put on their pads. But this time it was the Australians who made a bad start. Barnes played a stroke altogether out of character off a poor-length ball from Coxon, was caught on the leg side and Australia was one for three. It was noticeable in his very first over that Coxon, as at Bramall Lane, was taking toll of the pitch in his marks after delivery. He bowls directly over the stumps, and his marks for two paces are along the pitch, just wide of the leg stump from the other end. I think it was owing to these marks that Evans twice failed to stump Barnes in the second innings.

Bradman had a spirited reception in this his last Test at Lord's and one could sense in the reception deep feelings of regard and admiration. He was fated to play one of his least-inspiring Test innings. He played a wind-and-water stroke between his legs and the stumps off the first ball from Coxon, he was beaten by the third and appealed against for l.b.w., and at the other end Bedser beat him completely off the pitch, just shaving the stumps. Bradman was struggling and here there was plenty of justification for the English claim that he was a bad starter.

In twenty minutes Bradman scored three runs and Australia was only 14 after thirty minutes play. Again I noticed that Yardley frequently conferred with Hutton, and after one of these Edrich relieved Coxon, whose first spell of Test bowling showed 7—3—10—1. Again Edrich tried to bounce the ball and Bradman made a very wild swing to leg, mistiming, the ball curling up to land behind point. This was a streaky stroke, and then, at 13, Bradman was almost out in the "Hutton" position at fine-leg, the ball off Bedser just going a little wide. I don't think I have ever seen Bradman so uncomfortable. His 14 runs had taken him an hour of extreme discomfort, but Australia began to make runs when Wright came on. There was the usual no-ball, which Morris hit for six to the on, and again, soon afterwards, Morris, who was very sound, hit another for four.

Bedser, after seventy minutes straight of great-hearted bowling, was eventually handed his sweater and a large round of applause from the appreciative audience. There is some finality with which an umpire hands a bowler his sweater which tells that his spell of bowling is finished for the time being, and so the crowd claps accordingly. Bedser deserved his particular applause this morning. His figures were 11—4—19—0 and his experiences were of an unlucky nature.

Bradman settled down against Coxon and Wright, and at lunch was looking more like his true self. He was 35 and Morris, who had batted extremely well, was 45. Australia was 82 for one and the real looseness in the English attack had sprung from Wright, whose figures were 24—0.

Bradman was out in the third over after lunch, and again in a similar manner to his two innings at Nottingham. He put a leg-glance straight into Hutton's hands off Bedser. Nobody had ever seen the like of this before. Bradman out three Test times running in a leg-side trap and, counting the occasion in Yorkshire where Hutton was also the villain of the piece, caught four times by Hutton ! This gave Lord's plenty to talk about as Hassett came in with 87—2, but Morris now began to play glorious cricket. He drove through the covers with grace, giving the ball great speed, and he forced prettily to the on. In all ways this innings by Morris was stamping itself with the insignia of Lord's, a pretty Test century in the grandest of all cricket settings. His century came with two successive fours off Coxon, and it was made with Australia's total only 160.

Morris is a confusing cricketer. I have always been a keen admirer of him and, indeed, before he had played in a Test, wrote that he would leave a bigger impression in the game than the other left-hander, Warren Bardsley. Last summer in Australia, a polite but spirited gentleman telephoned with a complaint because I had placed Morris in the same category as Hill. Thus it will be seen that I have always admired Morris, but several times on this tour he gave me qualms with his footwork.

Like Badcock in 1938, Morris seemed to be playing back without altering the length of the ball. His step was across the pitch . . . not back . . . and at Nottingham, where his batting caused him to be despondent, he had added that peculiar little shuffle to his first step. He seemed to be in mental trouble, but there was not the faintest suggestion of this at Lord's. His century was a century, century all the way . . . from the very first ball bowled to him, and it was accomplished, as I have said, with a rich variety of classical strokes.

Morris was out at 105 and then Australia encountered a pickle of trouble. Miller was out leg before to a ball he ignored with the bat; Hassett had slices of luck with misses at 37 and 42, only to be yorked by Yardley at 47 (175 minutes), and Brown, again playing out of character at number five, was, as at Nottingham, again l.b.w. to Yardley, this time for 24 (85 minutes). Tallon batted grandly in the last hour, but Australia, at stumps, was 258—7. This was England's day without any doubt. The English fielding in the last hour was really brilliant, with Washbrook outstanding. Bedser, as usual, was the side's grandest bowler, and so complete was the spirit of elation at England's success that people, on leaving the ground, immediately queued up for the next day. Poor queue-happy England!

But Friday was a sad, dismal day. It began with the Australian tail clouting runs in all directions and with many strokes unknown to the science of the game. Tallon was batting perfection in a half-century innings, but both Johnston and Toshack, often aiming in one direction with the ball going in another, must have sickened the Englishmen. Treatment such as this from the tail after subjecting the head ! Two overs from Edrich cost 28, the ball sailing over the heads of slip or cover. Yardley purposely kept off Wright because he didn't want the Australians to score easy runs, and, though a captain is powerless to prevent runs from unorthodoxy, I did think the bowlers might have concentrated more upon yorkers.

In 66 minutes during the morning, Australia added 92 runs. This was a staggering blow for England after its grand play of the day before, but there were blows almost unlimited soon to be delivered. Washbrook and Hutton opened, and there was a stir when Bradman handed Miller the ball to bowl the second opening over. Miller handed it back. He considered himself not fit and so, as Miller had to carry the burden at Nottingham, it was the job for Lindwall here. Lindwall anxiously felt his groin after each ball but it was to be a big day for him.

Washbrook was out for ten . . . caught behind again, and again looking not pleased. I don't think I have ever seen an

opener caught behind so often and as often look dissatisfied with
the decision, though off the field Washbrook is of a very pleasant
disposition. Lindwall's figures pre-lunch were 6—4—7—1. He
had come through his first physical test.

Hutton was batting brightly, but soon after lunch he came
forward again with that half-cock stroke of his to a good length
off-break and back went his stumps. This made England 2—32,
and again the openers had failed the side. It became 46—3 soon
afterwards when Edrich, after 70 minutes of fruitless endeavour
that yielded only three, played right across the line of flight of
one from Lindwall and was bowled. Dollery, in his first Test
against Australia, played one with his pads and was bowled the
next, and England was 46—4 . . . and the atmosphere hereabouts
at Lord's was in keeping with this, one of the saddest moments
in English cricket, all the more so because it followed on the
successes of yesterday.

Lindwall was the demon. In six overs since lunch he had
taken 2—11 and his complete figures at this stage were 3—18.
He was bowling beautifully, lithe athlete that he is, his loose
limbs ambling over the ground until the final four yards, when
he gathers himself up and stretches taut every muscle. The
English batsmen seemed mesmerised by his pace. It seemed that
they had not struck fast bowling before in their careers. Lindwall
yielded up his position soon after three, his figures being 14—6—
28—3. He had done his job nobly for Australia. He had broken
the English back.

"Yorkshire Annie," a figure in black and well known on all
cricketing grounds, could be seen far off in the Mound stand.
Her quips were the only cheerful thing of the moment for spectators, and floating across the ground came her strident "Cum
on, England. Play oop." Yardley and Compton set about
retrieving this dismal position and for an hour they played
brightly, defensive stuff blossoming out later into rich strokes,
but the failure of the men higher up had left them with an
impossible task. The true value of a Test opener is never realised
until he begins to fail, so one should pause to honour the memory
of Hobbs and Sutcliffe, Collins and Bardsley, Woodfull and
Ponsford, to name a few famous partnerships.

At tea, England was 129—4, a grand recovery, with Compton
51 and Yardley 42, but, alas, the stop for tea was the undoing
again of England. Miller caught Compton at slip off Johnston,
and Lindwall clean bowled Yardley. Lindwall then had 4—42

off 18 overs. Evans had a fly at one outside the off-stump, Miller took another brilliant catch in slips and England was 145—7, a hopeless position. Laker was twice dropped in the slips but made a spirited 28, but at stumps England had lost the position irretrievably with 207—9. Just before that, the follow-on was saved. What a horrible reversal after the first day.

Wright and Bedser defied the Australian attack next morning for 20 minutes, but I could see no necessity at all for Lindwall to bowl bumpers at Bedser. This was something Larwood never did and I was sorry to see Lindwall so lacking, for the nonce, in a fellow spirit for bowlers.

And so England took the field again at five minutes past twelve. Bedser, after his great feat of the first day, was not even to have a full day's rest from his labours, and he took up his burden in a worse position than where he left off. Barnes escaped his "pair" off the second ball and came down the pitch with a huge grin. His great pal of 1938, Badcock, made a "pair" here on that occasion. It was agreed in the room that nobody would speak to Badcock, as a lark, when he entered the dressing-room, but Badcock stole the show by entering the room with a spontaneous peal of laughter. He is the first batsman I have known to see the humour of a "pair."

Coxon did his preliminary canter before he took the ball at the other end. This consists of an imaginary bowl before the real thing and usually induces the batsman at the other end to play an imaginary stroke. The origin of this is interesting. Bill Bowes said that Wilfred Rhodes told him one day to make his first ball of the day to Arthur Carr a yorker. Bowes did, bowled Carr but wrenched a muscle. Since then, it has always been a Yorkshire tradition that the bowler warms up with one or two imaginary balls before beginning the real stuff. "What a lark," said the irrepressible Robertson-Glasgow, "if the bowler strained himself in his preliminary ball."

The Australian openers saw through the new ball, but Morris might have been out first ball of the change had Laker been quicker on his feet. Laker was very slow to move to a caught and bowled, and then Laker had further misfortune when Evans failed to stump Barnes at 18. The ball came high off the pitch and, I think, pitched in Coxon's marks with Barnes well down the pitch. One did pitch in Coxon's marks the other end the next over from Wright and bounced high away for four byes.

Yardley certainly called out his bowling men in the first

hour of this innings. This is how they ran: Bedser, Coxon, Yardley, Bedser, Coxon, Edrich, Wright and Laker. Wright again had his customary no-ball, and again Morris helped himself to six.

Wright has a most unusual run for a bowler of his type. It is long enough for any fast bowler and in the middle of it he stretches out into an elongated step. His action always caused great merriment in Australia. He told me once that he thinks he bowls no-balls because he is so anxious to get at the batsman. This is a great pity, because I think it often has upset his length and makes him concentrate upon his feet and their positioning when he should be immersed in hostility.

From the Australian angle, there were two interesting points in the play. Morris had completely lost that hesitant shuffle. His batting was pure poetry and it seemed only a matter of time before he scored another century. This would have made him the first ever to notch two centuries in two Tests in this series, as he recorded the double in Adelaide in 1946-47. The other point was that Barnes was playing down the pitch to Laker. This seemed premeditated. In previous innings, I had noticed Barnes being either bowled or l.b.w. to bowlers delivering from round the stumps. He had been playing across the flight in trying to force the ball to the on, but here he had decided on a different technique and almost every Laker ball found him playing forward. He had one superb straight drive off Laker to the pavilion, and lunch was taken with Australia 73 for one, Morris 40 and Barnes 25.

This was the Saturday of the Lord's Test and this particular day always seems to me to be *the* day of the cricketing calendar. During the adjournment I wandered into the Members' Pavilion with J. R. Mason, the former English player, and on all sides were reunions and greetings with innumerable "do you remembers."

But Lord's, I thought, had lost much of its colour and glamour by closing the playing area to the public during an adjournment. In previous years the public always paraded the ground whilst the players were at lunch, and Lord's always looked typically Lord's to me as one saw the parade from the dressing-room balcony, the colours of the frocks making a moving picture in all ways. It added spice, too, in leaving the field, as a horde of groundsmen rushed *en masse* on-field with spikes rampant to rope off the playing pitch area. One was never too certain that a player or a spectator wouldn't be spiked before the pitch was pegged, but on this Saturday, alas, there was no parade and the tolling bell, which customarily returned all to their seats, was meaningless ! We had instead a terrific crush at the back of the pavilion, where bright frocks, tall hats and lurid ties were lost in the maze.

I liked, too, in those pre-war days to see the knowledgeable ones as they stood pointing over the rope to some spot on the pitch where A's off-break nipped to take B's leg-stump. No! Lord's delivered up one of its loveliest traditions when it sacrificed the Grand Parade. Begging the pardon of the ladies and the gentlemen, it used to remind me of the Grand Parade at the Royal Sydney Agricultural Show as the lines threaded in and out.

It seemed to me, also (especially when I was wanting to concentrate upon some writing!), that Lord's lost some of its rusticity and charm when it introduced the loud-speakers. If one is so inclined, it is always interesting to wonder what stark tragedy lies beyond the urgent call of Mr. X to Bow Street Police Station; why in heaven's name is the Rev. Mr. Y needed at home at once . . . has his suspicious wife pried into his study, found him not there and, to avenge herself, sent an urgent and unspecified message to where she suspects he is? And one is left wondering whether Dr. BMA is wanted because a child is entering life sooner than expected or one departing it, or whether an operation, performed in the morning, has gone phut. All this is interesting in its way, but most go to the cricket to forget such troubles and don't wish to be reminded of them.

Over the Adelaide loud-speaker (they seem to install these now before putting down the pitch) dulcet tones ask for the owner of car number so-and-so to report to the office. He is a doctor, you see, and it is a nicety that there's no publicity for his name— unlike the unnamed war correspondent who used to pay the bell-boy 5s. weekly to parade the hotel lounge in Adelaide paging him "Mr. A, the (with emphasis on the ' the ') War Correspondent, please." In Sydney, Dr. W has his name blazoned on the scoring-board if he is wanted urgently.

But at Lord's on the Saturday one does seem to see everybody. In five minutes I saw Douglas Jardine, weightier than in his cricketing days and smiling happily, Hobbs, Hendren, Tate, Bowes, Parker, Abe Waddington, George Duckworth, Buster Nupen of South Africa, Martin Donnelly of New Zealand, Nigel Haig, J. C. White, seemingly unchanged from the days he spun us all out in Australia, G. T. S. Stevens, Ian Peebles, and so on and on as they all passed along behind the stand.

In lovely sunshine, Lord's looked resplendent after lunch. Over the score-board, Father Time, scythe over his shoulder, and attending to the bails on the three stumps, had turned his back on the game as he faced to the south-west. Beneath him sat thousands in the sunshine, and lower down the Union Jack fluttered gaily in the breeze. At the nursery end were the line of varying greens with sycamore, lime and plane trees, and at their back, in the distance, standing like so many Guards on parade, were the chimney pots of London. Over on the right continued the open stand, thousands on the grass, and it was a memorable sight to see the pin-heads of faces. The only blot on the scene was that ugly huge chimney-stack on the left of St. John's Wood Road.

In this setting, Lord's did not have long to wait for an English success. Morris tried to sweep a short ball from Wright too fine to leg, missed, his stumps were open and he was bowled. Morris had engraven his name in Lord's history because of his two lovely innings. I was standing in the Long Room with a group as Bradman came to bat for the last Test time at Lord's. The Long Room is world famous. As a player, one enters it from the stairways down from the dressing-room on the first floor and you pick your way through the scrutinising members as you walk to the door, which is securely shut after each exit and opened only for entry. Along the room are two sizes of stools, suitably backed. The smaller ones are in front, the longer-legged ones at their rear, and from these two rows of stools the members watch proceedings through the glass windows. There is no atmosphere in all the cricketing world to equal this one at Lord's, and as Bradman passed us by and walked slowly along the linoleum floor I sensed that I was watching something I would never see again. Bradman's last Test innings at Lord's and the only fitting end would, of course, be a century in his own individual style.

There now ensued a period of quiet cricket. Yardley crowded Bradman again and Laker gave the Australian a very trouble-some time, beating him three times in the one over. Bedser came on immediately and we saw Bradman's answer to the leg-trap. He refused to play the ball with his bat but pushed his left leg at the ball. It was an answer that Bradman would have spurned in the 1930s—or is it conceivable that bowlers in the forties found a weakness that bowlers did not know of in the thirties? I don't

15. *Lord's can take it! Spectators sit through a sudden squall in the second Test*

16. *Yardley sweeps Ring for four in the match between the Gentlemen of England and the Australians*

17. *Morris makes a powerful drive off Sims in his century against Middlesex at Lord's*

think so. I think the passage of time had wrought its changes.

Barnes was dealing only in defence, and there was ironic clapping when at last he hit Laker for four through the covers. Barnes is never lost for an answer. He placed his hand on his chest and bowed to the ground—the lowest bow possible. A character is Barnes!

This took Barnes from 69 to 73, and Bradman, hereabouts, was more like his real self. I was watching him at this period with "Buster" Nupen, the former South African Test player, who had flown from Johannesburg purely to see Bradman. He had never seen him bat before, and whilst I was telling him that it was most unfortunate he had never seen Bradman in his hey-day, Bradman began to play some of his inimitable strokes, particularly that terrific crash of his that pulls the ball in front of square, and Nupen began to like it immensely. Bradman took two successive fours off Wright, whose length was again astray, probably because of his lack of play, and at five on this lovely sunny afternoon, Australia's score was 222 for one, Barnes 96, Bradman 52, and their partnership worth a hundred. Alongside the pavilion, on the grassy mound, at least two dozen people slept soundly in the warm sun.

It took Barnes ten minutes to find the ball he wanted for his century. He straight drove Laker, a lovely stroke, and his century had come in 255 minutes with ten fours. Almost immediately, Evans missed him behind. Barnes jumped into Laker again but missed, when several feet up the pitch, but the ball spun away on the leg-side and Evans's hands did not go near it. It might have jumped again off Coxon's marks.

Barnes understood the portents. It was his day, and so he opened out on Laker and swung him for two successive sixes over long-on, glorious strokes that had Bradman, with a big smile, shrugging his shoulders to the Australian pavilion. Barnes had two other fours in this over, too, so that it cost 21 runs. As the Australians showed so often against Laker, his even-spinning off-break lends itself to big hitting. The two hits by Barnes now made the Australian tally of sixes twelve against Laker at Lord's. This big hitting by Barnes even induced old Father Time to swing lazily on his weathervane perch above the score-board to cast a hoary eye on things. He swung from the south-west to south-east, and as the evening was advancing I noticed now for the first time of this season that, unlike all other pitches I have noticed, the Lord's pitch does not run true north and south. It runs north-east by south-west, and thus in the late afternoon a batsman's shadow at the pavilion end is apt to get in his way. Apropos of this lovely old weathervane, I believe it withstood all the troubles of the war years only to topple over after peace was declared. I could never discover, however, whether Father T. was putting on or taking the bails off the stumps as he leaned over to catch the wind. He is one of the loveliest things in the whole of Lord's.

Compton came on for the first time of the match now, and Yardley also took a turn, but Barnes continued with his heavy smiting until Washbrook, on the very edge of the boundary, with lemonade bottles at his feet, made no mistake in catching Barnes from a huge, soaring hit. This was a grand catch, with the eyes of Lord's upon him, but Washbrook injured a finger in the taking and left the field momentarily.

Then we saw some rapid comings and goings. Hassett walked in and out first ball. He snicked Yardley on to his stumps. The most remarkable thing about this was that Hassett never heard the ball hit the stumps. He knew he snicked it, but when he saw the ball lying on the ground he thought that Evans had dropped the catch. He walked out in a dazed manner . . . I always feel sorry for the batsman who has to wait hours and hours in the pavilion with his pads. I looked across at Hassett once during the Barnes-Bradman partnership. The Australian balcony is just a few aerial yards away from the Press-box and Hassett was having a quiet little doze to while away the time. Just before he went to bat, Hassett, who is a very proficient tennis player himself, was watching Bromwich play at Wimbledon on the television set in the Australian dressing-room. He observed, as he returned, that, anyway, he had missed little of the tennis.

These two quick wickets had put Lord's on good terms with the world again. Even the slumberers on the mound awakened and took a new interest and it was most thrilling as Miller, tossing back his hair as usual and casting his eyes about to see what was in the sky, came out to defeat Yardley's hat-trick. The first ball rapped him on the pads and there was a roar for l.b.w. from Yardley, Evans, some of the English team and, by the sound of it, the whole of the spectators. It must have been a close thing. The umpire said "No," and then the spectators laughed at themselves because of their enthusiasm. Lord's was certainly wide awake now, and then, in a few moments, Miller hit one of those huge sixes of his behind square that landed half-way into the grandstand there.

This is a beautiful stroke of Miller's. As all know who have tried it, such a stroke requires the very essence of split-timing as, unlike a stroke down the pitch, the bat must pick the ball up at one very precise spot. Miller hits across the ball and up at the same time to get elevation. I saw him hit two of these in succession against Phadkar, the Indian, in Melbourne one Test day, and in England he seems to hit at least one every second match.

So far as we could see, no one was hurt in the stand. This is always most remarkable to me . . . a ball skimming into a massed crowd and everybody ducking to time. Of course it is not always so. A lad got hit on the knob from a Miller hit in Leicester and ambulance officers were to lead away a blonde girl in green at Leeds who was hit by another Miller six. No one should ever go and watch Miller without an insurance policy in his or her pocket.

During this commotion, Jim Kilburn, of the *Yorkshire Post*, who sat alongside me at Lord's, told me that one day Wally Hammond, now, also, a scribbler for the Press, hit a six that bounced on the iron ledge of the Press-box just in front of us and careered on through a door just as it was being opened. Jim told me, also, that when Horace Cameron, the South African, hit his three sixes and three fours off Hedley Verity in the one over at Bramall Lane, they found one of the balls the following winter. A pavilion guttering-pipe was overflowing, so a workman went aloft to investigate. He found it stuffed with a ball that had last left Verity's left hand. The biggest six Kilburn saw was that hit by the Australian, Cecil Pepper, at Scarborough. It cleared five-storied buildings outside the ground to land out in Trafalgar Square.

Whilst we were talking of sixes, Bradman was dismissed. He seemed to be concentrating upon Bedser's leg-trap all the time, but the Surrey bowler, who is one of the few men in England who can do this nowadays, it seems, made a ball go away and Bradman snicked it. Edrich dived in the slips and brilliantly caught it with his right hand, a lovely catch. This made the fourth time in succession Bedser had dismissed Bradman in a Test . . . a highly distinguished and quite unparalleled feat. Bradman had made 89. There was not, I'll vouch, a single onlooker there that Lord's day who would have begrudged

Bradman a century. It would have been the perfect finish to his grand Test career at the cricket holy of holies, and, after his hesitant start, he batted well enough to merit it. Nupen was satisfied. He considered his trip from South Africa worth it. I thought Bradman looked sad as he walked back from the sinking sunlight into the shadow of the Long Pavilion. This was a moment to live in the memory . . . Bradman's last Test walk at Lord's and, again, he was cheered all the way into disappearance.

Australia had the game won that night. Miller and Brown were still there, the score was 343 for four and this made Australia 478 runs ahead with two days left for play. That day Yardley had taken 36—2 off 13 overs; Bedser had, as usual, bowled well for 51—1 off 21 overs; Coxon had 47—0 off 19 overs; Wright 69—1 off 19 overs and Laker 96—0 off 28 overs.

The gates were closed on Monday at eleven o'clock after 22,000 non-ticket-holders had been admitted. There came this M.C.C. communique over the loud-speaker: "Owing to the grass being wet, a falling barometer and an extraordinary doubtful [sic] weather forecast, spectators are not being permitted to sit on the grass to-day." As the players walked out, Yardley looked at the sky as if to suggest he was relying on it and, indeed, the weather was England's only chance.

There was heavy rain at twenty to twelve and a long interruption, but Miller, batting beautifully with one of the sweetest cuts ever seen at Lord's and driving powerfully, was 63 at lunch, and Brown 32. I always like the way Miller plays the game. Once he made a terrific lunge at Laker and missed. Evans had no idea where the ball was, so Miller pointed up in the air with the ball behind Evans on the ground. Once, too, Dollery had the misfortune to be underneath a Miller stroke that went so high it seemed it would never come down. With thousands of eyes watching, these are the hardest catches in a Test. There's too much time in which to think, and so everybody on the field and many off understood and felt sorry for Dollery when he missed it. Australia had passed the 400 mark at lunch and, with 600 minutes left for play, was 544 runs ahead. Though there was every chance that the weather would cut short the 600 minutes, Bradman still batted on.

Bradman closed at last, soon after three, but the Englishmen were on the field for only a minute before rain drove them off. My friend, Sydney Goldsack, cynically noted that this was the first period of play in this series in which the English openers had not been separated. Off the field for 15 minutes, the players returned just as heavy, black clouds were rolling in from the west . . . somebody suggested it might turn out to be some additional Marshall aid, as it was coming from that quarter. At ten to four there was an appeal against the light, which was disallowed, but there was rain a minute later and the players were off until 4.30, taking tea in the meantime. Bradman, at this stage, must have been very worried about the weather; just as Yardley had his hopes pinned in it.

But England's back was to be broken that night. Washbrook pulled a four off Lindwall that almost took Barnes's nose with it (coming events casting their shadows!) and Washbrook scored all of England's first 16 runs. Hutton was missed before scoring. Lindwall dropped him in slips off Johnston (again Miller did not bowl) off a stroke of poor texture and conception. Hutton played some really bad strokes off Lindwall before he was caught at 13 by Johnson off Lindwall. This was probably Hutton's worst effort in a Test, but I felt sorry for him in trying to sight Lindwall's thunderbolts against the pavilion in this bad light. Hutton returned to the pavilion in cold silence. The chopper was about to fall for him and the silence, presaging it, indicated the general disapproval of Lord's at his showing.

Edrich was splendidly caught low down in slips by Ian Johnson off Toshack, and Tallon brilliantly caught Washbrook, whose aim was attack, and with 65—3 the bottom had again fallen out of the English batting. Compton, however, was full of faith and ability, and Dollery, too, batted nicely.

The Test crumpled up with the second ball of the next day. England's hope was another repeat performance of Compton on the Nottingham lines, but he tried that favourite square drive of his against Johnston, and Miller, at first slip, diving, hit the ball up and caught it on his back. Though he hadn't bowled a ball, Miller was more than pulling his weight in the field. What a vital cricketer he is!

Dollery's batting was the best of a bad lot this day. He was out in a peculiar manner. He ducked to what he thought was going to be a bouncer, but it came through at normal height and bowled him. Evans was valiant to the last, but at 22 minutes past two the game was over, with Miller and Hassett putting more spirit into a rough-and-tumble on this Lord's pitch for stumps as souvenirs than England had put into his batting. Toshack was the chief destroying medium in this innings, but it was Lindwall, in the first innings, who had demoralised the Englishmen.

England had now reached the satirical stage regarding its cricketers. London newspapers were publishing letters advising the selectors to drop or scrap the whole of the English eleven or even play Glamorgan, the Welsh county and leaders then of the competition, as the English team against the Australians.

This was all very humorous, if one's humour inclined that way, but the truth was a sad one and it was that English cricket, at this time, was very, very sick. England held the advantage at the end of this first Lord's day, but the further the game went the greater the mess England got into.

The trouble with English cricket in this game was largely in the mind. Physically, the Englishmen who played in this game were of a more robust type than the Australians. If we compared the bulk and the strength of the opposing parties, we could not excuse England on this score. The chief trouble was in outlook to the game and technique. It was pretty obvious, I thought, that county cricket was not a mettlesome, proving ground for Tests. The English selectors must have been greatly embarrassed in trying to assess county feats in a Test light, and Edrich had not yet been able to forget his record-breaking feats of the season before and get accustomed again to sound, steady bowling.

It was a rare blessing for England that Miller, who sometimes seems to me to be a nastier proposition than Lindwall, because he gets the ball up off a good length, could not bowl in this game, but Hutton and Washbrook were incapable of the job of making the most of this and nobbling Lindwall. Of course, Lindwall is not the easiest of bowlers to nobble, but in Sydney, of a Saturday afternoon, I have seen immature youngsters take runs off Lindwall when he has been bowling at his fastest. Hutton's batting in the second innings was very poor, but I feel one should always use the soft pedal of criticism with Hutton against pace. To be true, he never did shape confidently against bouncers, and his war injury has made him like them even less. Should the Australians, in the circumstances, have spared him the bouncers? If they did, then Hutton, as he showed at Nottingham, was quite capable of taking the Australian attack where he wished . . . and Test cricket is Test cricket. Though I have not liked seeing a profusion of bouncers against Hutton, the Australians could argue that if a man is not physically fit for Test cricket he should not be chosen.

The Lord's Test gave us innumerable disappointments. The game, in retrospect, failed dismally to live up to its reputation and the colossal amount of money, £43,000, paid for admission. This was a record cricket gate, but, in all the disappointments, one thing was well worthy of the Test match at Lord's. That was the batting of Arthur Morris. I doubt whether I have ever seen a more pleasing innings than his century in the first innings. It contained everything which a truly great player shows in an innings—style, variety of strokes and a generally pleasing manner in the middle.

CHAPTER TEN

SOME SUN AT OLD TRAFFORD

ONE morning, in the county of Yorkshire, a dour business man sat down to breakfast, opened his newspaper, blinked his eyes and said: "Wife, doon't speak to me. Tha've drooped Hooton!"

That same morning Surrey was playing Yorkshire at Bramall Lane. The captain of Surrey is Errol Holmes and the selector on the English committee is A. J. Holmes, of Sussex. But Hutton had been dropped, a man named Holmes was on the selection committee and, rankling under a slight to their county, the stout Yorkshire supporters were in no mood to worry about initials. Errol Holmes was hooted all the way to the wickets and he was hooted all the way back. In this particular game he made a "pair of spectacles" and the Yorkshire supporters thought that, in this, some justice had been done.

Why was Hutton dropped? That was the question all cricketing England was asking on the night of Sunday, July 4, when the team was announced by the B.B.C., and next morning, when it appeared in the newspapers. Hutton, himself, first heard the news over the wireless and it must have come as a shock to him, particularly when both Washbrook and Edrich had again been included. Much as it shocked Hutton, however, it shocked the Australian cricketers more, who were spending that week-end at Bristol. It suited them because they have a pretty high opinion of Hutton. Why, then, was Hutton dropped?

Probably it was because of Hutton's second innings at Lord's. He made 13, which rather held its own in England's score in that innings, but he was missed at *nil* by Lindwall in the slip off Johnston; he never looked comfortable and made some wild slashes at balls, which if hit, could only have gone to the slips. Finally, he was caught in the slips by Ian Johnson off Lindwall. From all of which it will be gathered that Hutton played a streaky innings. It was indeed, and he brought down much criticism on his head at critical Lord's, but I am always inclined to spare Hutton criticism because of his war-injured arm. It is true that Hutton did not care much for bouncers before the war, but,

120

having seen this badly injured arm of his, I can understand how
he must feel when a bouncer comes along. That arm must surely
be in the back of his mind. He had two operations on it. It is
noticeably shorter than the other, has had forty-five stitches in
it and carries pieces of grafted bone from Hutton's legs.

Hutton is such a fine batsman that he would make packets of
runs in Tests under ordinary conditions, but the bouncers do
unsettle him. The point, then, is whether Test captains and fast
bowlers, knowing all the above, should spare Hutton the bouncers
and promptly chase hundreds of runs from him. It is not a
problem which should altogether be solved by opposing bowlers
and captains. English officials, perfectly aware of the bouncing
position in Australia in 1946-47 and knowing Hutton's great
ability, should have discovered somebody in the intervening
period to protect Hutton by offensive action. Not a single bouncer
was bowled in the decisive Melbourne Test of 1936-37, despite
the fact that the teams included most capable bouncers in Allen,
Voce, Farnes, McCormick and Nash. The absence of bouncers in
this game was not because of accident. It was a policy, bi-lateral,
agreed upon before the teams took the field.

Bradman was not a great lover of the bouncer even in his
halcyon days. I once saw Voce bust himself in the process by
trying to bowl bouncers at Bradman in Melbourne in 1947. Voce
retired with a strained groin, but Bradman did not look very
happy against the bouncers, even though Voce was then 38 and
was only 24 when first he bowled bouncers in Australia. Hutton,
obviously, should have been protected by retaliatory action and
more particularly because he is such a batting power when
unworried by intimidation. It was no excuse to say England
had no fast bowlers. That is merely an indictment of the English
people controlling cricket.

In mitigation of Hutton's failure at Lord's in the second
innings and the manner of it, it must be stated that the light was
far from good. It is no easy matter to sight the ball on such days
against the crowded pavilion, where there is no sight-board. On
the other hand, Old Trafford sports two sight-boards, and one
thought that Hutton, if rested from the opening position, should
certainly have been played lower down. But the selectors thought
differently. Hutton was dropped completely and that was precisely that . . . a bad selecting mistake in the minds of most
people.

This made Emmett certain of his position and, with an average of 132 against the Australians at Bristol, Crapp could hardly be left out.   Laker was omitted, and Wardle, surprisingly, was brought across from Yorkshire to be twelfth man.   Laker's omission left England very short of bowlers and increased the gamble of winning the toss. It looked like tough days ahead for those willing horses, Bedser and Pollard, with Yardley, Young and Edrich to carry on until the new ball came every 55 overs.

Old Trafford was resplendent for this game.   The grass was very green and the ground looked spick and span, much work having been done since the Australians were last in Manchester. This ground had a very bad doing during the war, stands being blasted and a bomb hurling up the middle. Of a morning after raids, the groundsman, Harry Martin, used to wheel his barrow along to pick up hundreds of incendiaries that hadn't gone off. Though Manchester had a very bad time during the war, the Lancastrians will tell you that they had some grand friends on the Continent who, working in munition factories, left out vital parts in bombs so that many that fell were duds.

The Manchester weather, too, was on its best behaviour, atoning for 1938 when our Test never had a ball bowled. The ground was packed as the skippers tossed, whilst from outside came the strident tones of a traffic policeman directing, over an amplifier, hundreds of cars into parking spaces. Yardley won the toss. The first gamble had succeeded, but, as at Nottingham, the value of the toss had been lost by lunch-time. Washbrook, very careful this time, was moving along nicely, but just as the last clanging of the noon-day Angelus was fading, Washbrook played all over a ball from Johnston which he tried to drive.   Over went his stumps.   Washbrook retired to the pregnant silence of an unsympathetic pavilion, even though this was his home ground.

Fifteen minutes later Emmett had gone.   Only a small man, Emmett was very surprised when Lindwall bowled his first bouncer. It almost seemed that Emmett had never before seen a bouncer. He turned his head away, pushed his bat forward with one hand and up went a sickly easy chance to Barnes at short-leg. England was two for 28 and once again, as at Nottingham and Lord's, did a silent pall of gloom envelop the ground. This was a horrible beginning, but, considering the part he had played in previous Tests, worse was to follow with Compton's accident.

Just before Compton was hit, there was an announcement

over the amplifier (these intruding amplifiers!) that pirates, who were selling score-cards outside the ground, had got into the ground. "Wait a little while longer," said the voice, "the official score-card will soon be on sale."

Lindwall's second ball to Compton was a bouncer. Compton stood high on his toes and brought it safely down to earth. "Play the game," sang out a sad spectator. As the tones of the policeman outside the ground came floating in about parking, Edrich was making batting look the most difficult of all arts. His bat was waving in all directions. It was coming in suddenly with hectic dashes to get at the ball or, just as hectically, being pulled away at the last second. There is seemingly nothing more difficult than batsmanship when one is out of form and luck. Edrich, who seems to have a flaw in his back-swing, was showing us all that.

Then Compton was struck by a no-ball. The ball came off his bat. It was a short bouncer and, with the call, Compton fell into a position to hit, but he did not have enough time to do the stroke correctly and the ball glanced up into his face. Just previously, Lindwall had hit Compton on the elbow with another short ball. Compton reeled from the wickets and was obviously in a bad way. He was escorted off the field and England, with the board showing 32—2, was literally 32—3. It was Black Thursday indeed, and an awful moment for Crapp to enter his first Test match after play had been delayed for ten minutes.

Edrich received a blow on the fingers from Lindwall and there were angry cries of "What about Larwood?" England batted painfully on to lunch, Edrich being 14 (90 minutes) and Crapp 11 (an hour), with the total 57—2. During lunch, we learned that two stitches had been put into Compton's wound, that he was resting and that he would bat again, if needed, after first having a net. That was a nice way of putting it, *if* needed. Compton was needed much sooner than expected.

Crapp showed us some splendid cricket after lunch, batting, indeed, as we had not suspected at Bristol that he could. He hit a no-ball from Ian Johnson soaringly over the sight-board for six, and he played three delightful off-side drives for fours. It was as well Crapp did make these runs because, otherwise, the first new ball would have come at a ridiculously low score. As it was, it came at 87, and with it, as usual, trouble for England. Crapp was leg before to Lindwall without playing at the ball and, a run later, Dollery played all over a yorker from Johnston.

Then came the safest-looking batting I had seen on tour from an Englishman against pace. It was by Yardley and he looked perfectly at ease. Then, suddenly, I realised why. He was playing pace off the back-foot—an object lesson to those innumerable Englishmen who are obsessed with the conviction that the way to play pace is to push up the pitch. I can't accept that belief at all. I believe strongly that if in doubt, one should play back. Yardley took his pace back quickly and had plenty of time in which to sight and play the ball.

Poor Edrich! At this time, I thought, he typified the gentleman whom Rudyard Kipling advises in "If." Edrich had lost everything but the will to hold on. He fell to the ground once in attempting a pull and was hit on the hand. No batsman could have been in more trouble, but Edrich is always a grim fighter, though, at this time, there seemed reason for the doleful voice on the amplifier that announced, officially this time, that Compton would bat "if needed." This seemed to sum up the general Edrich position at that moment, but it was Yardley who was almost first out. He was almost caught by Miller in the slips, that worthy shaking his head as he scooped the ball up on the half-volley. Then Yardley snicked a four, but he followed this with a superb on-drive for four off Lindwall. No one plays the on-drive as well as Yardley. It is, by far, his most graceful stroke. He is strong on the on-side but it was an indecisive hit that got him out at 22, caught by Ian Johnson off Toshack, half-way to the fence. Yardley shook his head and left wondering—obviously thinking that if only he had let fly at that ball it would have been a different story.

England lost Edrich at 119, caught by Tallon after batting 190 minutes for his 32, and Yardley went at 141. Compton, his head bandaged, took Edrich's place and received a grand ovation. But after Yardley's dismissal, the bottom seemed to fall out of the game. It was dull, apathetic and pathetic, strangely unlike a Test. Despite his injury, which must have given his nerves a shock also, Compton batted on quietly and confidently and reached his 50 at twenty to six. Evans gave him support but the light, now, was not good. Tallon missed Compton from a one-handed catch behind while he was still 50, and then, just when he was well on top of the Australian bowling, Evans permitted himself the indiscretion of a very wild swing against Lindwall and was easily caught by Johnston.

While Bedser was walking in, R. H. Spooner, the famous

English batsman of other days, told me that he admired the slow off-spin bowling of Ian Johnson. Johnson does not thrive against Australian batsmen, who move to him much quicker than Englishmen, and Australians, too, do not seem to be worried as much by his flight. Johnson is an old-style off-spinner. He cups the ball and delivers with a twisted elbow. His length is always splendid until, I sometimes noticed, he is attacked.

It is sometimes the custom to say of a tail-end batsman that he is "not the worst batsman in the world." Bedser is too good a batsman to be classed a tail-ender. He showed that in Australia in the preceding series when, usually at number ten, he showed much more command of the general position than a number above him in the batting order. Bedser is a big chap. He stands well over six feet and he uses his reach and feet. He plays a very steady straight bat, and thus it was not surprising that he was still with Compton overnight. Compton had another life from Tallon, this time at 64, and off the last ball of the day, from Johnston. Tallon was feeling the effects of tender hands. I noticed him flinching often from the ball.

The second day was dull. It looked like rain. Compton was reported to have had a fair night but there was nothing fair underneath one of his eyes. It was blue-purple from his injury. Down on the grass, thousands of people were kneeling and squatting in trying to look at the play. There must have been many stiff necks in Manchester that night, and one never stops to wonder at the inconvenience with which the majority of English spectators watch the game compared to their Australian brethren.

In that morning's newspapers were reports of criticism by Falkenburg, the American tennis player, and American golfers, who had played in the British Open, that the English spectators were most unfair in their applause and lack of it. Falkenburg claimed that none of his good play against the Australian, Bromwich, had been appreciated in the Wimbledon final, and Bulla, of the golfers, was just as deprecatory, but the Australian cricketers certainly never had any cause to complain about the spectators. They were always most generous to the Australians.

Tallon was to continue his run of misfortunes. He again dropped Compton and again off Johnston, this time on the leg-side. Compton was then 73. Lindwall was not very fast this morning. He bowled little above half pace, with every now and then his fast one. He conceals his pace very well, so that even when he is reserving himself the batsman finds it difficult to tell when his fast ball is coming along.

Bradman gave his pace-men plenty of work this spell. Lindwall bowled for 40 minutes and Johnston for 53. Miller, who had broken down at Sheffield, had not bowled at all and, whilst we were noting this, Arthur Mailey announced that he was watching his ninetieth Test. This also included the ones in which he played. I like the story Mailey tells of the first time he played against Victor Trumper. It was at Redfern Oval, in Sydney, and Mailey was up at dawn to iron his cream trousers for the occasion. He remembers a terrific hub-dub by the milkman, because the jug had not been put out. Mailey says he wondered then why the milkman should have made such a fuss about a forgotten milk jug when he, Mailey, that day had to bowl against Trumper. He clean-bowled Trumper with a "bosie," which the champion did not detect, but Mailey said he was not let off lightly in the second innings.

Bedser defended valiantly during this spell with every now and then a stroke of class, and it was soon after one that Compton sweetly on-drove Toshack for four to make his century—his second of the series—in 235 minutes with nine fours. Had he not suffered his accident, it would still have been a grand feat. Compton, however, survived a lot of mental agony just before lunch when Lindwall morally bowled him three times, once in each of his last three overs. This was a memorable morning's play as England went fighting through without losing a wicket. The English position had been greatly strengthened at 323—7, Compton being 113 and Bedser an invaluable 37. Before lunch, too, the pair had hoisted their hundred partnership.

Before lunch came a delightful interruption to the game. The dirtiest little cur in Manchester obtruded itself on the field and held up play for almost five minutes. Loxton tried to tackle it in Rugby fashion; Bradman threw his cap at it, innumerable policemen tried to arrest it and fieldsmen chased it vainly. The little cur had a grand five minutes fun and completely demoralised the game. This recalled the lovely occasion at the Oval, too, so that the interest of dogs in cricket this season was also on the up-and-up.

The period of play after lunch, an hour all but five minutes, was one of the most dramatic of the series. Compton took two fours in the first over by Lindwall, one a choice on-drive, and he had another boundary in Johnston's over, but with Bedser not adding to his pre-lunch score, the big chap was run out through a bad Compton call.

Compton played one to cover, and Bradman and Loxton, rushing in to save the single, collided. The ball went past them and Compton called Bedser for a horribly short run. Loxton recovered quickly, turned about and had the ball quickly back, with Bedser out by a long way. This was, indeed, a bad Compton call. For such a great batsman, he is sometimes deficient in judgment in calling for runs and often has his partners jumpy. Loxton and Bradman were so thrilled at doing something which had so far been above the bowlers, that they put on an act. Loxton hoisted Bradman aloft and then Bradman reciprocated.

In came Pollard and out went Barnes a few minutes later. It was only to be expected that Barnes, fielding up close, would some day receive his medicine at silly leg, though on this occasion he was not as close as usual. He was of immense nuisance value to bowlers but, fielding so close, a person simply has no chance of evading a hard hit. If a yard or two farther back, he has a chance to duck. Pollard played a typical tail-ender's swish and Barnes could neither duck nor cover up. He received a sickening blow above the left ribs and dropped like a fallen tree. He was obviously in a very bad way. There was, in the circumstances, a long delay before four policeman walked on-field and carried Barnes off. One wondered why there was no stretcher for such an accident.

This accident cast a spell over the game. Compton was first to cast it off. He swept one in his grand manner for four, then cut one to the boundary, and there was a repetition of the Adelaide game of two years before, when Bradman strung the field out to Compton and in to the others. Tallon looked very lonely. Standing back behind the stumps, his nearest fielding neighbour was at least 70 yards away.

Pollard and Young, however, are not very gifted with the bat, and England's innings finished at ten past three for 363—a really magnificent total when one remembers that the first six wickets had fallen for only 141. Compton was again the batting hero and this time again in difficult circumstances. One wondered what would have happened had he not been hurt and made his runs at second wicket down instead of much lower down when he came to bat after being injured. In the previous Tests, however, the other English batsmen, the acknowledged ones, had not done anything to suggest that things would have been different for them had Compton been at the other end. As in other innings, the tail had again given the head a convincing lesson in defence and technique. Compton's 145 not out covered five hours and forty minutes and included 16 fours.

This splendid English recovery had put Old Trafford spectators in a "reight" good humour but better was to come. Ian Johnson was the stop-gap opening batsman for Barnes but he was out for one, brilliantly caught off the inside edge by Evans off a ball from Bedser which hurried off the pitch and rose high. That made the total three, and ten runs later Bradman was out and, to the tumultuous delight of Old Trafford, to their very own Dick Pollard.

This was a scene one will not soon forget. Bradman played back and across the pitch and missed. Pollard beat him off the pitch with one that evidently hurried or turned in. There was a whoop from Pollard like a Red Indian (or, rather, as one would imagine a Red Indian to whoop for l.b.w. if he played cricket) and up went the finger of umpire Davies. Old Trafford went delirious. Thousands of cloth caps were tossed high in the air, schoolboys threw their colourful caps even higher and everybody shouted, laughed and talked at once. What bedlam it was, and in the midst of it Bradman, the centre of it, walked out very slowly. What a tribute to a cricketer that his dismissal should cause such a scene.

I wonder, on his way back, if Bradman thought of the talk he had had at Old Trafford during the Lancashire match with Robins, the English selector. Though Hilton had then twice taken Bradman's wicket in the match, it was Pollard, I noticed, who gave Bradman much more concern and, for once, the Australian did not appear eager to get to the business end. At the end of that game, Bradman recalled to Robins the trouble Pollard had once given him in Adelaide. Despite this, Pollard was not chosen in a single Test in Australia. "I don't know," Bradman is stated to have said to Robins, "why you don't pick Pollard in a Test. He worries me more than any other Englishman."

Over the years, Bradman and Robins have been very close friends. They are alike in many things, looks, build and, in many ways, temperament. As soon as the Australians arrived in England this tour, there began between Bradman and Robins keenly contested games at squash rackets and golf, and I think Robins would not have taken amiss, though he stated that he

18. *Edrich gets one through the slips to the boundary off Miller when playing for the Gentlemen of England*

19. *Barnes badly hurt from a shot by Pollard in the second Test Match. He was fielding in his usual silly mid-on position*

20.   *Exit from Leeds. The game and rubber won, Don Bradman, preceded by policeman, leaves his favourite ground for the last time*

was too old for the post, a chance to tilt his Test captaincy against Bradman. They indulged in much leg-pulling and, obviously, Robins must have thought that Bradman was teasing him about Pollard. The Australians have long had a reputation in England for trying to force inferior people into Tests, to the advantage of the Australians, and, no doubt, Robins thought Bradman was up to an alleged Australian trick. At all events, I think it was rather a smart piece of psychology on Bradman's part to plead Pollard's cause to Robins if he, Bradman, did not want Pollard in England's Test team.

The loss of two quick wickets, and Bradman's in particular, put Australia very much on the defensive. We saw some grand bowling by Pollard and Bedser. Pollard, who is known in Lancashire as the Chain Horse because of all the work he does, day after day, bowled 17 overs straight. There was a huge crowd of 30,203 to spur him on, and when Pollard began his long run he seemed to be within earshot of the nearest spectators.

Pollard is one of the most admirable sights of a cricket field. His hair is red, his face is ruddy, his flesh is pink and you see much flesh on his arms because Dick rolls his sleeves up higher than anybody else in the game. He is, and looks, the perfect and most honest tradesman imaginable. He gives a huge day's work. He never falters in his job and there are, with him, no middle of the pitch tantrums. If he has misfortune—and he has more than his fair amount of this—he turns side-on to the batsman, faces cover, puts his hands on his hips, whistles and then bursts out laughing. His pace is medium-fast. The keeper stands back to him and every now and then he bowls a faster ball, but he can move the ball in the air and off the pitch and, always, his length is splendid. So is his direction, mainly at the leg-stump. Off field, he plays the piano splendidly.

Hassett and Morris played soundly to offset these two English giants. Bedser bowled for an hour and a half unchanged, and the Australians finally had the satisfaction of seeing both take a sweater with the air of finality, for a period at least.

Hassett fell that night. Possibly remembering how Young had tied the Australians down at Nottingham and of how he, Hassett, had there experienced a successful onslaught on Young, the Australian evidently determined that he would soon settle the Young issue. He tried to drive him over the heads of the in-field, mistimed, and was caught at cover. It was well worth trying. This made Australia 82—3. Miller saw it through with

B.F.D.   I the dependable Morris, and Australia, at stumps, was 126—3, Morris 48 and Miller 23.

I have rarely seen runs look more difficult than in the first hour of the next day. It was a lovely, sunny day, this Saturday, and the gates were closed at nine o'clock—a fact which should not be mentioned without a thought again to all those travelling and enthusiastic thousands who came innumerable miles only to see the gates barred against them. This, happening in all Tests, was the saddest occurrence of the season. So big was the crowd this day (the playing arena again being dictated by the crowd) that Pollard, indeed, seemed to start his run just on the fringe of them.

The new ball was soon due and it brought intense distress of mind to Keith Miller. Three times in one over he flicked at Bedser in a manner which suggested defeat off the pitch. Whilst this was going on, there were the usual shouts and roars of "Sit down" from the early birds, who were finding that if there were any worms' eye-views about, the late birds were catching them.

Miller was first to go. Like Bradman, he was beaten off the pitch by Pollard and was leg before. The only difference between the two Pollard feats was that there were some more Lancashire thousands to roar its approval to high heaven as Miller walked back. This brought Barnes to the middle and applause accompanied him all the way.

Barnes had had a bad night. He had been in much distress, though, in typical style, he had refused to stay in hospital. He chose a moment when the rest of his team-mates were not looking to go to the nets behind the pavilion at Old Trafford, but it was obvious he was in no state to bat. I saw his ribs and they were all colours. He collapsed at the nets and certainly should not have come to bat, but probably Bradman accepted his offer when he saw the difficulty his other batsmen were in against the new ball.

On the way out, Barnes shook hands with Pollard—a nice gesture—and both smiled. It had taken Morris 21 minutes to make his first run this day, and it was not until a quarter past twelve that he made the single for his 50. This fast run was too much for Barnes. He collapsed after holding his end up for 30 minutes for one run and was assisted off the field, Bradman coming on to help. It was courageous of Barnes to make the effort. He was in no way to achieve big deeds.

This complete loss of Barnes made Australia's position worse

than it was—and that was bad enough—but Morris was soon out
and though Loxton, in his first Test, batted very brightly and
was not dismayed by the position, and Lindwall and Tallon made
some handy runs, the Australian rout was complete at 2.35 p.m.
It was nothing more or less than sheer collapse on a perfect
batting pitch, and it was almost entirely due to Bedser and
Pollard. England had taken a colossal risk in entering this Test
with only three recognised bowlers. Bedser and Pollard had to
carry the burden. Young was the third stock bowler, but Edrich
and Yardley were, naturally, only change bowlers. This cheap
dismissal of Australia, therefore, was in the light of an unexpected
miracle.

During the latter part of the Australian innings there happened one of the most interesting things of the whole season.
When Lindwall came to bat, Edrich deliberately bowled bouncers
at him. He gave him four in the first over and off one he was
hit on the hand. At the end of that over, Lindwall looked to the
Australian dressing-room, smiled and gave a Churchillian
thumbs-up salute. But these bouncers gave the Australian a big
shock. Though he was adept in bowling them he had, apparently,
no batting practice against them and looked none too sure of
things. Whilst this was going on, I made a mental note of what
Edrich was preparing for himself in the second innings.

Emmett was soon to find that a Test life can be very hard if
luck is not with one. Some very capable cricketers have never got
a second chance in a Test because luck was dead against them in
their first try, and Emmett could well be in this category. Dr.
Roy Park, father-in-law of Ian Johnson, is one who comes to
mind. Chosen after much publicity for Australia against England
in December, 1930, he was tumultuously cheered all the way to
the wickets in Melbourne, was clean-bowled first ball by Howell,
didn't have a second innings and was never chosen again. In
Lindwall's first over, he had to shape against one on the off-
stump but it swung away late. Emmett nicked it, and Tallon,
diving, brilliantly caught it one hand on his right. Such is fate!
It snubbed Emmett but flirted outrageously with Washbrook.

Edrich was next and we sat up to take notice. Lindwall took
it very quietly. He is very level-headed in his bowling. He
always works up pace gradually but there was a surprise when
Miller prepared to bowl the other end. Only the day before,
Miller thought it likely that he might not bowl fast again on
this tour, but it might well have been that the bouncers he saw

Edrich aim at Lindwall had decided Miller to push himself, despite strains and pains, in the defence of his Australian cobber.

This first Miller over was very fast, much faster than Lindwall's. He beat Washbrook completely, shaving the stumps, and there was a hint of desperation in Washbrook's technique as he swung Miller high to the on. Then he perfectly on-drove Lindwall for four, but in Miller's next over there was a bouncer that cleared Washbrook's head by four feet. There was no mistaking the feeling in the middle at this time. It recalled vividly to me the days of Jardine and Larwood.

There will always be feeling when bouncers are about, but a good quick exchange of them by both sides will often clear the air. Lindwall, thoroughly warm, began to let them fly next over and there was a sensation when Davies no-balled him. This was obviously for dragging, as Davies showed Lindwall a mark a foot behind the white line and drew it for him with his toe. Evidently Davies wanted Lindwall to comply with this mark—which recalled memories of Lindwall in Australia, what the English critics had written of his dragging, and also recalled the fact that he had not previously been no-balled in England for dragging.

This incident seemed to add more feeling to things because Lindwall took the matter up with Davies again after the next ball. At the end of the over, Davies needlessly and somewhat bad-manneredly threw Lindwall's sweater not so much to as at him—a gesture which Lindwall rightly resented. Bradman had a word with Lindwall before he commenced his next over and the fast bowler shook his head in disagreement, but fortunately there now happened an incident which took everybody's mind off this obvious wrangle.

Washbrook could no longer restrain himself and again fell into the Lindwall trap. He played his now celebrated hook and the ball flew straight to Hassett on the fine-leg boundary. Hassett had not to move a foot in positioning himself for the catch but he dropped it at the third fumbling attempt. I can't remember seeing Hassett drop a catch before. The cricketer has never lived who hasn't dropped one at some time or other, but this was a most vital one as Washbrook was then 21. It is always difficult on a crowded Test ground to sight the ball against the dark mass of people, but it is interesting to reflect that had Washbrook then been caught he would probably have been outed from the next Test because of misdemeanours. This hook stroke had got

Washbrook and England into a lot of trouble, and Washbrook's main fault as a Test opener was in not ignoring this bait.

At the end of this over, Davies handed Lindwall his sweater —a peace offer. Loxton gave Lindwall a rest and hereabouts Washbrook batted well, concentrating upon keeping the ball down on the leg-side. I noticed here again what initial trouble Edrich gets himself into by his fault in taking the bat out and around in his back-swing, not straight back as the text-book teaches.

Confidence returned to Washbrook with a rush. He played some lovely strokes on both sides, and the cheering as he reached 50 was terrific. This took him only 70 minutes and the total was 80. A funny game, this cricket! On this ground the two previous days, booksellers were finding it hard to dispose of a little booklet on Washbrook's career. When he reached 50, they were selling like Test tickets. Had Hassett held that catch, Washbrook would have been in direst disgrace, but at this time he was almost equalling Pollard as the county's hero.

When Lindwall came back, Washbrook almost moved his head into a very fast bouncer. I found myself, at this stage, becoming very intolerant of these bouncers. They were grossly overdone, and the game always falls from high estate when they are around in quantity. Edrich found his form after tea and nicely on-drove Miller for four, at which Miller flushed and bounced four in succession at Edrich. The second hit Edrich on the elbow and there were loud hoots when Miller followed with two more. I was right in thinking that there would be some especial bouncers for Edrich after his treatment of Lindwall. Bradman, after this over, spoke words of sympathy and apology to Edrich and had a word with Miller before he bowled his next over—in which there were no bouncers at all.

Edrich now began to bat more in keeping with his form of the preceding series in Australia. The ball began to go off his bat with timing and judgment, and I laughed once when some young codger, as they frequently do on all English Test grounds, began to run in front of the sight-screen as Toshack was beginning his run-up. The angry shouts of "Sit down" dropped the young chap in his tracks. Old Trafford was not going to have the splurge of English fours stopped at this juncture.

Edrich ran to his 50 with speed with a four to long-on and a lovely hit for six over long-off by Toshack. He had restored himself fully in all English eyes. We were just noting that this was England's biggest partnership of the series and wondering what would happen when Edrich began to operate on Johnson's slows, when Edrich was unfortunately run out. It looked like a faulty Washbrook call that was further embarrassed by hesitancy (always fatal!) in the middle of the pitch. Whatever it was, Arthur Morris capped it by a quick throw that knocked back the stumps. It was tragic to see Edrich go in such a manner and at a time when it looked that he would make good those other Test failures.

Compton was no sooner in than he was out, beautifully caught by Miller in the slips off Toshack. There is an Australian saying, attributed to Ponsford, that after the Lord Mayor's carriage comes the rubbish cart—to clear away the mess of celebration. And it was a true saying in Compton's case. An unconquered century in the first innings was followed by *nil* in the second.

England lost no more wickets that Saturday evening. Washbrook was not out at 85 and Crapp the same at 19, and with 174—3 England was 316 runs ahead—a delightful position for Yardley to face the week-end. I have written that England lost no more wickets that afternoon but Washbrook had two more lives. He went through the same hooking ritual off Lindwall at 78; the ball went to Hassett in the same position and again did Hassett drop it. I couldn't believe my eyes. Hassett, biting his lips and blinking his eyes furiously at this disgrace, borrowed a helmet off a nearby bobby and prepared himself for the next catch—which gave the crowd a great laugh. Ian Johnson missed Washbrook two runs later in the slips off Loxton and that ended the day's thrills.

This was, in many ways, a lovely day's cricket and it was a pity that such grand stuff was coloured by the feeling over the bouncers. There was a period after lunch when the Australians, as they did during the Compton-Bedser partnership of the first innings, by no means looked a good side let alone a great side. But all teams have their off days. In the pavilion, after play, Washbrook sent Hassett a drink along with his compliments. And umpire Davies sent Lindwall one also!

English cricket spent a happy week-end in Manchester and it was good to sense it. The Mother Country had had many ups and downs but there were many times during the post-war, in Australia and now in this series in England, when England had its chances. It looked as if Manchester was to be the turning-point but, alas, the weather! A group of English players and officials seemed to be constantly grouped about the weather apparatus in the lobby of the Midland Hotel on the Sunday and the line was going sharply down. On Monday, we awoke to familiar Manchester sounds—the clippety-clop of horses' hooves along the cobbled streets and the sound of rain.

This, for England, was wretched luck. It was, too, for the game of cricket because, undoubtedly, we would have seen some grand deeds on that Monday as England pushed the scoring rate along. Some 21,000 people went to Old Trafford and sat, huddled, in the rain. Super-enthusiasts and optimists they were, because not for one minute on Monday did play look at all possible. The forecast said a depression, centred near the Faroes, was moving south-east and the weather would be mainly cloudy. It was— all day. It is an interesting point that the 21,000 people had no money refunded nor received tickets for the final day. This seemed unjust, but all English grounds make a point of stating that no money will be refunded in case of no play. The saddest figure I saw that dripping, dejected day was a blind man, tap-tap-tapping his way with a stick out of the ground and through the puddles of water. He'd come to hear the game!

The glass had gone up slightly next morning, and again did the thousands crowd down to Old Trafford. At eleven o'clock, Yardley, Edrich and Washbrook had a look at the pitch and Yardley immediately declared. It was amusing to see Yardley and Bradman make their inspection. Yardley was in flannels; Bradman, overcoated and muffled to the ears, looked as if he were contemplating a trip to the South Pole. The condition of the pitch, to captains, is nearly always dictated by the state of the game and it was obvious the captains would disagree. They did and then entered the umpires. Chester and Davies spent a long time in the middle, helping the ground staff to soak up water. They said they would look again at noon, then at two, and finally decided on a 2.15 start.

As preparations were made (and what more warming sight is there on a cricket field than preparations for play after hours of wait?) we looked up the records. It was here, in 1921, that Herby Collins played one of the most remarkable innings in Test history, stone-walling for four and a half hours for 40 in a successful attempt to draw the game for Australia when rain interrupted play (they keep that slug always set, incidentally, in all Manchester newspaper offices). Collins did not want runs.

He played only for time. Once, when the ball went down towards the boundary, he didn't run but said to his partner in a mid-pitch chat whilst the ball was being fielded, "Why should I run and destroy my patience and stamina. I want time, not runs. Go back to your end."

Bradman used the light roller and a succession of maiden overs opened the play. The first over showed what the result was to be. The ground was too wet, there was no sun, the pitch would play slowly with turn but not exaggerated turn, and it was apparent that England had not the slightest chance of forcing a win—particularly when two showers came to make the ball greasy for the bowlers. Counting the wicket-keeper, Yardley had eight men close in around the batsman, but this was to try and impress something upon the batsmen that didn't exist in the pitch.

England could not take a wicket until ten to three, well outside the time-limit for victory. Young relieved Pollard and Ian Johnson swept him fine for four, the ball being well fielded by a dignified policeman. Next ball Johnson edged to Crapp and that was the end of Johnson who, after loitering as if he couldn't believe the worst had happened, sadly wended his way pavilionwards.

Bradman played eleven balls from Young without scoring. Morris played two uppish strokes from Bedser that went for four apiece, but the strange feature of this batting was that Morris kept to one end and Bradman the other. Yardley might have done much better by quickly calling on the pace of Edrich, but, though there was much clapping for maiden overs, I thought Bradman wasn't at all worried about runs or the bowlers. He was making Young look more difficult than he was, and Compton also. I think Bradman fooled Yardley to keep his pace off, and it was not until he had been batting for an hour that Yardley tried Edrich against Bradman. Edrich, however, tried to bowl off-breaks. Bradman viciously hooked two and that was the end of Edrich.

Several showers interrupted play, and it was significant that Edrich and Compton were the first to move off the field, Bradman and Morris the last. This, too, showed that Australia was in no trouble though Bradman indulged in hefty pitch-smacking after every ball. Morris did not budge from his top end for a whole hour and three-quarters, and when he did hit a single and call, Bradman seemed so surprised that he wanted to send him back. Bradman played only eight balls at that end. Johnson played none, so that Morris played all the rest. It took Bradman 28 minutes to score his first run. The game, after several more interruptions, fizzled out at 13 minutes to six with Australia losing only Johnson's wicket.

Hard things were said of Manchester's weather after this game. In London newspapers there was a demand to know why Manchester, with its very bad record, should be given a Test. The last Test finished at Manchester was 43 years ago—in 1905 —and in 1890 and 1938 the Tests were abandoned without a ball being bowled. The cotton industry was established in Manchester because the looms always work better in damp weather. The thread does not break and the damp air gives the cotton some special texture. This makes Manchester famous for its cotton but notorious for its cricketing weather.

As far as it had gone, however, this Manchester Test showed that there were cracks in the Australian side which could be exploited. It showed, too, that confidence was fast returning to the English batsmen.

CHAPTER ELEVEN

BRADMAN AT LEEDS

HEADINGLEY, Leeds, provided England with its last chance in the Test rubber. England had to win at Leeds to retain chances of halving the rubber; a draw would give the series to Australia. Headingley has not been a good ground for England. The last home victory there was in 1905 and, since the twenties, Macartney and Bradman have given England's bowlers perhaps the greatest drubbings in Test history. It was here that Carr dropped one of the most publicised chances in cricket when he floored Macartney first ball in the slips in 1926. Macartney made a hundred before lunch, and it was here in 1930 that Bradman made his world's record Test score (to 1938) of 334. Bradman made 304 in 1934, so that these, together with his 103 in 1938, showed Leeds as his most favoured Test ground. And showed Leeds also as England's worst Test ground ever.

Macartney and Bradman are the types to make sensational scores on any type of ground, but it is well to have a mental picture of Leeds. It is not pretentious in its accommodation and the playing area is small and exceedingly fast. There are places where it falls away quickly from the pitch, and as I walked on it after one of the Test days of this match I found it exceedingly bumpy. Mailey declares when a fieldsman is in one particular part of the outfield, only the batsman's head is visible, but this is somewhat exaggerated. There were times during this Test, however, when I was looking at the smallest Test field in the world. Particularly was this so on the Monday when the crowd of 39,000 converged on the field and the white boundary line was lost far from view. Sydney enthusiasts will have an idea of the playing area of this day when I declare that it was no bigger than the Mosman ground, which is notoriously small.

Barnes was not considered fit for this Test. A day previously he had had a net at Lord's but felt giddy after it. Pollard had certainly dealt a heavy blow for England when he laid Barnes low at Old Trafford and it was strange, seeing that he had played in the Nottingham and Lord's Tests as a number six batsman, that Brown was not chosen in the Australian side as an opener.

This, one thought, was where Brown was wanted and indeed would have been invaluable, but he was made twelfth and Australia had to improvise an opener in Hassett.

Hutton, of course, was a natural choice again for England. It was never clear what the English selectors set out to achieve by dropping him for Old Trafford, but as this fourth Test was being played in Yorkshire it was only politic of the selectors to assume that they had achieved their publicly unknown objective, and further, Hutton's form in the Gentlemen-Players game at Lord's, which he dominated in both captaincy and batting, gave the selectors the chance to reinstate him. Which they did, we can assume, with great rapidity and no discussion.

In the game at Leeds in 1938, Australia won inside three days, Hassett gaining victory with a death-or-glory innings as rain loomed overhead. This game had been dominated by spinners. Australia had O'Reilly and Fleetwood-Smith, and England had Verity, Wright and Bowes. It might seem strange that I put Bowes in the spinning class, but he could cut the ball either way and was a persistent menace on English pitches. In view, then, of Leeds' 1938 history it was passing strange that the selectors of both sides should not have included an orthodox leg-break bowler, and England went further than this on the morning of the game by omitting Young, who, as a left-hander, spun from the leg. This was to make a vital difference on the final day when England, generally, would have given one or two of its remaining colonies for a leg-spinner.

In the train up from London the preceding day were both English and Australian cricketers, and I noticed this time that the Englishmen were not present as if they had an apology in their pockets. They met the Australians on level terms and this, stemming from what happened at Manchester, augured well for the fourth Test. Unless Manchester was a flash in the pan (or a splash on the pitch, to retain the Manchester metaphor), English cricket had at long last found itself.

At Manchester came the realisation—over-long in its coming —that Bradman's team was not quite the unbeatable one many had at first imagined it to be. Some ominous cracks opened in the Australian batting, bowling and fielding, and all Australians who played in that game or watched it were agreed that England had this particular Test in its pocket on Saturday night.

Of course there had been other times when England seemed to have the position in pocket only for it to disappear mysteriously down some unfathomable hole. There was Lord's the first day; there was Nottingham on the fourth day when England had placed herself for a draw, but at Manchester, more than in any Test of this series or the preceding one in Australia, did England seem to be at Australia's cricketing throat in the old accustomed manner.

England could not afford to go back at Leeds. It had to advance from its retrenched position, and so we looked forward to the best Test of the series. It was so in 1938, and in that highly exciting game I remember that our "baby," Sydney Barnes, was so pent up at the vital period that he could watch no longer. He left the ground and wandered down a side street until it was all over.

The Headingley ground was all push, bustle and crowd on this bright July morning. Queues, of tortuous length, wound up and down the side streets, and as one entered the ground it was obvious that thousands upon thousands outside had no earthly chance of admission. This is always a sad thought as a Test begins. Many outside at Leeds had travelled miles since early morn to see the game, and the ones I felt very sorry for were the boys, who, doubtlessly, had been looking forward to this plum for weeks and weeks. I often wondered how many Test players are lost to the game when the small boys can't gain entrance, because inspiration and emulation are the beginning of many Test careers.

Unsung heroes of the pre-Test were Mrs. Alice Boulton and Miss Louie Cope, two hearty souls who, between them, washed 5,000 glasses and 10,000 cups and saucers to be ready for the big day. The married men of the Press-box saluted them silently as we read this before the captains tossed, and then came the first of innumerable announcements over the amplifiers. It was a policeman's voice. He bade us good morning. He wanted us to watch our pockets as well as the game. Pickpockets were on the job, he said, and it was our money they were after. Arthur Mailey observed that many caterers were after that ever since the tour had started!

Yardley began the day well by winning the toss, and the reception given Len Hutton by this densely-packed crowd was worth the trip to Leeds alone. Intensely loyal are the Yorkshire people, and the roar of delight as Hutton scored a single in Lindwall's first over was thrilling. Miller bowled from the other end but he had no speed and he bowled three full tosses. The outfield was exceedingly fast, running downhill in places and very bumpy in others, and I noticed there were no sight-boards —a change to 1938 when there was one at the opposite end to the pavilion.

Both Lindwall and Miller felt their legs in between overs, and Johnston, who had a back chill the day before, was stretching himself in an ominous manner. A long tour is a tremendous strain on fast bowlers, and I began to contemplate just what trouble this Australian side would be in if Lindwall and Miller were both to break down. Early, too, I noticed that without the adventuresome Barnes the Australian fielding had lost much aggressiveness. There was no silly-leg. Instead, Hassett was sedately back some ten yards.

Miller bowled only two overs. There was nothing of great moment in the first ten minutes, the runs being matched by the number of announcements over the air. At one stage Master Somebody was asked to report to the nearest policeman, who would bring him to his father, who was waiting at the secretary's office. A great cheer greeted the dignified bobby as he led a minute lad around the edge of the field. And Arthur, of the ground staff, had already gone adrift, as they say in the Navy. By the end of this game, the loud-speaker made Arthur seem almost like a relative.

A momentous happening occurred at ten to one when up came England's 50—the first 50 partnership of the series for England's opening batsmen. Hutton and Washbrook did not seem to worry much about the applause for this signal achievement. They appeared to be concentrating upon the hundred partnership, and indeed it seemed as if they had both piously promised before leaving the English dressing-room that there would be no cuts and no pulls for the first two hours at least. The runs came mostly in singles.

Hutton had a streaky one through the slips from Toshack, and at 25 Hassett dropped from him a smart catch behind square-leg from Loxton. Loxton was thus having plenty of ups and downs in getting his first Test wicket. This made Hassett's third dropped catch in succession, and I saw through the glasses that he had a very wry smile on his face. But these things happen to everybody who plays the game, and there's no accounting for it.

Hutton played a glorious square drive that left point flat-footed, and I liked the manner in which Washbrook once got a rising ball down to ground and to the boundary, beating Harvey, who was lurking on the boundary for the usual Washbrook pull. At lunch England was 88—o, Hutton 46 and Washbrook 41. It was a grand start for England, not so much in runs, although these were coming at a good bat nearing lunch, but it was satisfying in that the openers were still together. Bradman took some posers to lunch with him.

Tallon, injured, was standing down and Saggers was in his first Test. We noted this most when Lindwall, after lunch, appealed very confidently for l.b.w. against Washbrook. He appealed alone. Saggers barely raises his voice in an appeal, which is not encouraging to a bowler.

Hutton opened out on Toshack after lunch. He drove him beautifully past point to reach his 50 in 125 minutes; he clipped him next ball, again past point, for another four, and when Washbrook neatly back-cut Lindwall to the boundary England had reached its first opening century, something that had been needed all the series. A superb on-drive gave Washbrook his 50, and as the two Englishmen looked full of confidence and runs, I noticed that Bradman, with stooped shoulders, was looking at the ground in most contemplative mood.

The Australian bowling was atrociously bad. There were full tosses in every over, and again did one think that an Australian leg-break bowler, in form, would have been invaluable in the middle at this period. There were two small stops for rain, but nothing could stop the Englishmen and the 150 came at twenty to four. Brilliant sunshine then flooded the ground and, after a mid-wicket talk with Hassett, Bradman brought on Ian Johnson who, strangely, had bowled only three overs to this stage.

Bradman copied Yardley's "wheel" field of Nottingham. He had no slip for Johnson and it was obvious he wanted to tie down the rate of scoring—unusual for a winning side like Australia, and just after midway on the very first day.

While Johnson bowled two successive maidens, Washbrook was making merry at the other end. At one stage Hutton was 73 and Washbrook 61. Soon Washbrook was 85 to Hutton's 75, and then Bradman took the new ball at 165. Hutton greeted Lindwall with a lovely on-drive for four, and here again I noticed that the ball had only to cleave the field to become four.

Lindwall got Hutton next ball. He was clean bowled playing forward, as had happened so often before to him and to other Englishmen. The way to play any fast bowler, surely, depends upon length and not upon any preconceived notions. If it is well up and the ball can be covered on the full or half volley, the way to play is forward; if not well up, then surely the correct thing to do is play back so that one can get the pace and swing off the pitch. Those, at least, are the Australian ideas.

Hutton had performed his job nobly for England and reinstated himself, if such were needed, with everybody. Yorkshire's joy would have been complete had he rounded off the job with a hundred, but he had laid the path for the rest who followed. This opening partnership had made 168, Hutton 81 and Washbrook 85.

Edrich, who had the dual task of consolidating England's position and proving that his recaptured form at Manchester had come to stay, saw Washbrook go to his hundred at five o'clock. It had taken him 230 minutes and knew 16 boundaries; it was his second Test century against Australia, the other being 112 in Melbourne, January of 1947. It was remarkable in that it was chanceless and that he had batted all through in a sweater. One wondered, too, whether Washbrook would have been persevered with had Hassett caught him out at Manchester when 21. Probably not. His Test scores then would have been 6, 1, 8, 37, 11 and 21. Who says there's no luck in cricket? The game is full of it, more, I think, than any other game.

Washbrook was out that night, but it was probably to fatigue as much as to Johnston, and the burly Bedser came in as the "night watchman," conserving Compton from the final few minutes. England, at stumps, was 268—2, and, with 41, Edrich was again justifying himself.

The longer this first day went, the more the value was borne in on us of a good opening partnership. England went on and on while Australia never recovered but, indeed, went progressively downhill. It was Australia's poorest day in attack in post-war history. I have never before seen such an abundance of full tosses in a Test day, but most things are relative and it is probably true that our bowlers performed just as well as they were allowed.

Bradman seemed weighed down by his bowling problems, and one sensed it would not be long before there would be a general bemoaning of the absence of a leg-break bowler. The pitch was not a good one for the pace men. Lindwall stuck manfully to his job; Miller never seemed to gain his hostility, and Loxton, though he tried hard, is cast more in the batting than the bowling mould.

The day's honours were with Hutton, Washbrook and Edrich for batting full of sound, common sense. They kept closely to a policy all day and that was, mainly, not to take any risks but to stay there and let time bring its own reward. England was well on top after this first day. The toss had been won; it had been capitalised; Edrich was on the way to a good score; Compton had still to come, and wear and weather would favour England.

England's policy was clearly defined for the second day. It was to gain a good start again and then push the scoring rate along. The objective was 600 runs by the close of play.

There was even a bigger crowd crammed into the ground than the preceding day. The light was very dull, and sighting from the pavilion end was made more difficult by the line of trees on the embankment at the top of the ground. Edrich and Bedser cleaved at the air with probing bats. They were finding the ball hard to sight and, judging by the antics of the slip fieldsmen, were going close to edging catches.

The start was more in keeping with the funeral of a notable national figure than a cricket game. Heavy clouds loomed over the ground; the cricket was slow, solemn and decorous. Two miserly singles came in 15 minutes. Just across from where we were writing (on seats, incidentally, as hard as the Russians at that moment in their Berlin policy and as confined as the air corridor there) I could see the English players and their ever-attendant army of former players and officials, and they were looking at the sky more than the play. England had to win this match to save the rubber. A draw was useless. No delay was wanted by the weather and runs had to come at a good rate.

Bradman stepped the field as if he had no immediate worries, nor, indeed, had he any, because slow scoring by England suited him admirably. He posted his men far and wide, and scoring runs seemed about as difficult as coping with inflation and Blackmarketeers. Bedser's bat looked broad and, just as one was wondering whether he wouldn't be better suited by sacrificing his wicket for runs, Bradman took the second new ball and Bedser's wicket became even more important to England.

If Bedser could see this new ball through, he would pave the way for Compton and the rest. The sun peeped through at noon and in this thirty minutes England had scored four runs. It was not good enough, but I could sense what trouble the batsmen were having in sighting the ball. At eighteen minutes past twelve Edrich played his first free stroke of the day and he went to 50 in 193 minutes. It was a struggling affair but he was still there, and he and Bedser had seen through the new ball.

It was Bedser who opened out first. He received, it seemed, the portent he wanted when Hassett had just a touch off a stroke to fine-leg. England had made 22 runs in the first hour when Bedser opened his shoulders and he chose Toshack as the victim. Off four successive balls he took 14—a straight hit which bounced into the crowd, two fours to the on and a two. This was too much for Bradman. He sacked Toshack immediately and dismissed him, seemingly without a reference, to the outfield; but Bedser, looking meekly at Johnson's slow wares for an over, made up his mind about him also, and so came another 14 in an over. This was made up of a huge six over long-on into the massed, black crowd, and two hefty smites to the on for four apiece. I wouldn't vouch for it, but in the outfield I thought I saw Toshack with a look of righteous rectitude on his face. Or probably it was a smirk.

There was an agonised "oh" from Loxton as Bedser almost gave him a caught and bowled, but, collecting himself, Bedser, whose run of 14's had taken him to 47, went calmly on to 50, and his 50, in respect of temperament, control of the situation and stroke-play, was as good a 50 as we had seen in the series. The "night watchman," sent in to protect Compton overnight, had come to stay. Sitting behind me was Maurice Tate, who had once "night-watched" against South Africa to the extent of a century. Bedser's 50 had taken 117 minutes, which was good time when one considers he had the anchor well down for an hour that morning.

Edrich, too, had run into stroke-play and, at lunch, Australia had received its severest whacking in post-war series with England 360—2, Edrich 76 and Bedser 52. The crowd was most jubilant. The ground after lunch was again bathed in sunshine with the gates, as usual, locked. It was a fair day for all but the Australian bowlers, but they had had a little of this coming to them for a long time.

The silent Saggers again allowed Lindwall to appeal on his own after lunch. This was Lindwall's fourth unsupported appeal, and one pondered on the difference between the two Australian wicket-keepers—one as vociferous as the other was silent. At this stage, Lindwall, whose heart is immense, had bowled 31 overs for 57 runs, an effort worthy of a stock and not a shock bowler.

Hereabouts, too, came the hundred partnership between Edrich and Bedser, the second in succession for Bedser because he had participated in the one with Compton at Manchester. England scored 22 in 30 minutes after lunch, and Johnson came to bowl round the wicket. Edrich, at 90, hit him straight into the stand, a powerful stroke, and at three he placed a long-hop from Morris (whose presence at the crease showed Bradman's bowling dilemma) where it belonged on the leg-side and thus reached his century. There had been many brickbats for the English selectors up to this time; they deserved a bountiful bouquet for their courage in sticking to Edrich.

Bedser now took a particular interest in Morris's slow, seductive lobs and hit him with a beautiful, soaring stroke high over square-leg into the crowd. I noticed a gentleman in shirt sleeves nonchalantly take the catch as if he had been taking them all his life. I looked hard at Hassett through Ray Robinson's binoculars. I think he was blushing.

The surprise element of Morris's bowling was working in reverse and so Bradman called afar off to Toshack, who seemed, at that particular moment, as if he were more interested in a passing plane than the game. But he came to the business end of the pitch and delivered a maiden. Over on the English balcony I saw Robins look at his watch and do some mental calculations. England would have to sacrifice some wickets to get runs quickly, but at that moment, just after the 150 partnership, Bedser was out—caught and bowled by Johnson.

What worried Bedser most, I think, was not that particular ball. I think it had suddenly occurred to him that he was on the verge of a Test century. He couldn't seem to associate himself with the idea and, whilst weighing up the situation, played quietly at a ball which he might otherwise have hit far, far away. Of this I am sure. Bedser was very embarrassed as he walked back down the long Leeds lane of spectators that springs up on the field as soon as something happens in the middle. He had batted 177 minutes for his 79 with eight fours and two sixes. He left the position comfortably in the hands of the accredited and supposedly more gifted men to follow.

As so happens when a big partnership is dissolved, the second member of the company did not stay much longer. In trying to force Johnson to the on, Edrich holed out to Morris and that made England 426—4. Crapp was over-eager and was bowled by Toshack, and a quick change had come over the game. England wanted runs quickly but this was unprofitable.

Though Johnson and Toshack had wrought this change, Bradman somewhat surprisingly took the new ball, which Compton appreciated, but when the sheen had gone, Compton lingered on 23 for 25 minutes. He got no further. Saggers picked him up nicely off Lindwall on the leg-side, and so Saggers, whose keeping had been of a high order, had chosen a pretty good one to begin his Test career.

Loxton took Cranston's wicket, which feat induced Loxton to turn himself almost inside out in ecstasies. He is a tearaway bowler, halting at the moment just before delivery, but he certainly has spirit. Had chances been taken, he would have had his first Test wicket long before this, so his exuberance can be understood.

England's tail crashed badly. Instead of getting quick and cheap runs, the side collapsed for 496. Eight wickets had fallen at one period for only 73 runs. This was execrable after such a bright outlook, but it really seemed that the Englishmen had encountered something which they had not known in post-war Tests with Australia and did not know how to handle it. They had wickets to spare and wanted runs quickly but didn't quite know how to go about it.

Due credit must be given Bradman, in his captaincy, and his bowlers, particularly Lindwall. This grand fast bowler held the side together splendidly and answered every call. Johnston, Toshack, Johnson and Loxton also did much hard work, and Saggers gave a neat display behind the stumps, making an able substitute for Tallon.

Australia had lost Morris's wicket overnight for 63. Morris, carelessly for him, played into the pitch of a ball from Bedser and was well caught mid-wicket by Cranston on the run on the on-side. Bradman received a remarkable reception, the like of which I have not seen approached on any ground. Thousands of people lined up many deep three-quarters of the way to the pitch. With three policemen as a bodyguard, Bradman came to bat down this long lane, his green cap faintly showing every now and then among his adulators. He was enthusiastically clapped, patted and pummelled as he walked along.

Bradman emerged from the lane to a thunderous applause which continued for the rest of the way to the middle. The

Australian acknowledged it with a merry raising of his cap, but this seemed insufficient so he gaily waved his bat to the crowd. This, surely, will always rank as the greatest tribute paid any cricketer, and, be it noted, this was not, like Hutton, Bradman being welcomed on his home ground. He was an Australian in England but, more than any cricketer of modern days, Bradman belonged more to the game of cricket than to any country. There were strong rumours at this time that he would some day receive a knighthood. If it should be a higher honour, the title suggests itself. As it was Montgomery of El Alamein, so would it be Bradman of Leeds, for on this field he has won his greatest honours; nowhere else has he been so idolatrously acclaimed.

Fittingly, Bradman got off the mark with his first ball and, racing along the boundary, Compton made an Arsenal drive with his foot as he saved the boundary. While Hassett established himself as the usual rock, Bradman made short work of the English attack. Edrich tried to bowl bouncers, so Bradman took three fours off him in that over, and at stumps Australia was 63—1, Bradman 31 and Hassett 13.

It was a day that left the position open, though England still had wear and tear on its side—advantages which would have been inconsiderable had the first-innings total, as it surely should have done, reached 600. An hour after play had finished, as we were getting away our final despatches, I saw a delectable scene. Just finished work at a booth, a woman walked across the ground and, in her high heels, plumb across the centre of the sacred strip of pitch. A workmate called her back. She answered and returned —across the pitch! She came on her way, finally—and again across the pitch! What a lovely reflection, I thought, on all the grim seriousness of Test cricket. She will never know the sacrilege she committed.

The third day of the Leeds Test will always be remembered in Yorkshire. It was as perfect a day's cricket as man would ever wish to see, blurred only by the inability of the English bowlers to dismiss the Australian tail in the final two hours. It was hot in the morning, on the sultry side. It might have been a coincidence that as O'Reilly and I entered the ground there came the police warning again over the amplifiers that "very suspicious characters were in the ground to-day and, please, do watch your pockets." Everybody, literally, sat pocket to pocket in this dense throng.

There had been a Leeds shower at seven that morning and,

returning from the practice pitch, which is on the ground, Bradman and Hassett seemed to have puckered brows. Again Bradman received a tumultuous welcome and, as if to show that he knew how to join in the spirit of things, Bedser gave Bradman a no-ball which the champion tucked away square for two. As if to show the other side of his nature, Mr. Bedser then gave Mr. Bradman a spiteful ball which kicked and hit the Australian a nasty abdominal blow. Bradman was careful for the rest of the over.

Pollard got Hassett with his second ball from the pavilion end. It propped quickly and Hassett couldn't get his bat out of the way. It was a nasty one to get so early and Hassett nicked it to Crapp, who accepted it. In came Miller to see Edrich polishing the ball on his socks for Pollard. Out walked Bradman to greet Miller and have a serious talk with him. The Australian captain looked worried, and then Miller knocked off Edrich's imparted sheen with a drive for three. That brought Bradman against Pollard and he was out, clean bowled, first ball.

This was a palpable instance of killing the two birds (and what rare birds!) with the one ball. The ball that got Hassett also got Bradman. Bradman remembered that Hassett's ball propped and he expected the same. He drew away, momentarily, the better to deal with the ball as it rose, but it skidded through with ordinary height and increased pace and, miraculously, found Bradman's bat not at home. Over went Bradman's off-stumps and the tumult that greeted this amazing beginning of the day by Pollard and England was wondrous to witness. This hour was to be—it had already begun—one of the richest in all Test history, and I looked down on almost indescribable scenes of bedlam as Bradman walked slowly and thoughtfully back. These scenes were in themselves a tribute to Bradman's greatness. He was the overnight danger to England's thrust.

What a setting for one's first Test innings! And what a setting, moreover, when that one is only 19 years of age, but I don't think Neil Harvey, capless, so diminutive that every mother's heart on the ground warmed to him, gave the situation more than a second's thought as he emerged, quizzically, from the end of the human tunnel and looked about as if wondering what all the fuss was about. Every now and then Australian cricket throws up one like Harvey. There was Trumper, there was Archie Jackson (164 against England in a vital Test when the same age as Harvey), there was McCabe, there was Bradman himself, and here, now, walked in Harvey. Where some others have to fight their way up, learning by experience and taking step by step, these few others walk boldly and composedly into crises as if they have been dealing with them for decades.

Down at Kennington Oval one day, young Harvey wanted to know in the dressing-room why the two Australian batsmen in the middle did not use other tactics against a particular Surrey bowler. The two batsmen, I must state, were Bradman and Hassett! It was, admittedly, somewhat precocious for the baby of the side to voice his thoughts and of two such proven players, but Harvey, I am sure, did not mean wrong by it. Bradman always had his own mind on the game, and what is sometimes interpreted in youth as cheek is merely self-confidence and individuality.

Harvey, before this Test, had had his ups and downs. He began the tour badly. He couldn't fathom the English pitches, and the bat he bore with him to the Leeds middle told its own eloquent tale of snicks and mishits. It was peppered along both edges, but the lad had won his way to the top, he had thrown out bold challenges for inclusion in all three previous Tests, and those who knew him had for him not pity but confidence as they saw him walk out in this crisis. As Harvey passed Miller, walking to the other end, he said, "What's going on out here? Let's get into them, eh?" Rather perky chit-chat, to be sure, for a youngster approaching his first Test crease—and in a crisis, too.

Australia was 68—3. Harvey, who was in his crawling rompers when some against him were even then first-class cricketers, took block with the air of a veteran, and Miller, I noticed, began to sniff the air with appreciation. Miller is a fighter. He is never one to accept runs when they are there for the taking. I have seen averages studiously built up from time to time by others, but in similar circumstances I have seen Miller deliberately miss the ball and be bowled. I acknowledge myself the supreme believer in Miller as a cricketer. He has given me joy in the game unapproached by others.

I wrote this, then, of Harvey's beginning: "Harvey was soon off the mark against England with a forcing stroke behind point—a stroke to note because you will hear a lot of this lad in the years to come."

Miller was superb. He drove and cut and pulled, and Australia's score raced past the century. Laker came on and Miller hit his first ball, a long hop, straight into the square-leg

crowd for six. This was a beautiful, virile stroke. Harvey, too,
played superbly with cuts and drives with every now and then
picking one fine to leg. It was batting of the highest possible
order, challenging and stirring stuff which was throwing England's gesture back in the face of Yardley and his men. I don't
think I have known a more enjoyable hour of cricket than that
of this day.

Pollard, gallant, honest soul, was trying his best to break
this partnership, but it seemed, so well were they batting, that
he would be the first to break—that is if one could visualise
Pollard breaking down in anything. Bedser, too, was toiling
away, his huge body whipping the ball into the pitch, but Yardley
had to make quick changes (the half-century of this partnership
came in only 43 minutes) and on came Laker for Harvey's especial
benefit. Laker's off-spin turns from Harvey's legs, as he is left-
handed, and once Laker spun one high over Harvey's bat and
stumps.

Miller made the decision from the other end. Something
would have to be done about Laker. So Miller cleverly got the
youngster away from the strike and then hit Laker past mid-off
like a bullet. No cricket field has seen a more killing stroke.
Miller's off-drive is one of the beautiful things in life. Miller
tried to get into Laker again next ball, but the bowler had cun-
ningly dropped it short and Miller jammed down on it hard and
in a hurry. At that the crowd laughed. Miller threw back his
hair, turned and laughed with them, but he had the last laugh
very next ball when he hit Laker straight and skimmingly,
almost for six. This went so fast that the small Yorkshire boys
who usually run in to field the ball scattered in all directions.

This appealed to me as one of the loveliest overs in cricket,
full of character, challenge and thrills. Laker had threatened
Harvey, so, like an older brother protecting his young one from
a bully, Miller took charge of proceedings. Then Harvey decided
that what Miller could do, he could at least try and he succeeded.
Twice off successive balls he crashed Laker for four, the second
being almost a six. What cheek for a nineteen-year-old! Then
Harvey took another four off Laker to make his score 44 to
Miller's 42.

It was delectable cricket; lovely stuff of light and shade. In
an hour and a half, Australia had put on almost a hundred runs
at a time of great threat, and at a few minutes to one Pollard,
his head perspiring but unbowed, finally took his sweater. His

grand piece of sustained bowling had yielded two wickets for 40 runs off ten overs. (But they dropped him for the next Test!)

The pitch was against the bowlers. Hassett was unlucky in getting one of the three balls that propped. Bradman got one, the one that hit him, and Harvey had the other, the one that got up over his stumps.

About this time Miller became a public menace. He hit Laker as high as any bowler, surely, has ever been hit. Out on the long-off boundary, Hutton, eyes on the ball, edged back and back, but the ball cleared his head by yards and fell into the crowd. This time somebody was hit. Hutton delved among the crowd to find the ball and ambulance officers entered also to lead away a blonde girl in a green dress, who was limping badly. I recalled, at this stage, the Leicester youth Miller had put into the infirmary over the week-end with a blow on his knob.

Yardley, the partnership-breaker, thought it high time he tried to do something with those cheeky Australians, but there was a great scatter beyond long-on when Miller bounced him into the crowd. Next ball, Miller scattered the crowd on the other side of the ground when he sent a raking stroke through the covers. Yardley had had enough of this. He waved his field to the on-side and distributed them about. Miller accepted the challenge. Yardley bowled his next ball wide outside the leg-stump and Miller, heaving mightily, tried to hit him out of the ground, possibly out of the county. He overbalanced, and in falling somehow or other just tipped the ball, which tipped Evans on his cranium, and, diving from short fine-leg, like a Rugby international diving for the line with the score 13-all and the final whistle blowing, Edrich caught the ball on the tips of his fingers and Miller was out. What a sensational piece of work this was! Judging by their demented behaviour, it looked as if some of the spectators should go outside and pay their admittance money again. They were certainly enjoying themselves.

If one sat down with pencil and paper he could not have planned a more sensational dismissal. The crowd was on its feet roaring and the noise changed only in character and not in volume, continuing on in its intensity as Miller entered the lane. This was one of the rarest gems in the Test collection of all time. Every now and then we see such an innings as Miller's, which sets the blood tingling, but the feature of this particular morning's play, after Pollard's most sensational over, was that we saw two such innings at the same time. That rarely happens in Test cricket. Generally, the heroics in a partnership come from one man at a time. Here they came from Miller and Harvey.

I retain a vivid mental picture of Miller as he walked back that sunny Leeds day. When he is embarrassed by the applause, his eyes sweep the sky as if searching for Nazi planes. He tossed back his hair with a jerk of his head; he plucked at his shirt over his chest with his left hand and, with the right, he waggled his bat aloft to the crowd in appreciation of their appreciation. And then a tall, dark, handsome figure in his white flannels, he disappeared from view down the slapping, clapping lane with his police escort. This was an innings, this was a moment to live in the cricket memory.

Was Harvey upset by the loss of his brilliant and guiding partner? Not at all. I do not think anything on a cricket field could upset Harvey. He's just not made that way. He drove Cranston square for four, he hooked him square for four, and when Yardley and Cranston in consultation took the man from fine and put him square, Harvey then disdainfully, it seemed, flicked Cranston fine for three. Loxton was in bother to Bedser but at lunch, after this dazzling morning of brilliant reverses and recoveries, Australia was 204—4, with Harvey 70.

Things were somewhat quiet, by comparison, for a long spell after lunch. Loxton was in trouble and did not look like a big innings at all. It was felt that the new ball would fix him, but with it came a remarkable change in Loxton's batting. He swung Pollard high to the on for four, almost a six, and then hit three fours off another Pollard over. Harvey, too, relished the new ball. He took the English bowling by the scruff of the neck and twisted it in all directions. The total for this partnership raced past the hundred and the total past 250, and just on half-past three came Harvey's first Test century against England. And goodness only knows of how many it is the forerunner! Loxton was so delighted that he chased down the pitch and, in his boisterous manner, vigorously pumped the hand of his young Victorian friend. Harvey, for his part, grinned, waved his bat on high and then flicked a spot off the pitch. The reception for this could not have been excelled on his home ground of Melbourne. It was a chanceless display. I can remember only that ball from Laker giving him a fright in any way. His century included 14 fours and had taken 177 minutes.

The spotlight, hereabouts, shifted from Harvey to Loxton. Loxton had played his first Test innings at Manchester and played some vigorous drives when the position for Australia was not healthy. Loxton is square-jawed and serious-faced until he breaks out into the widest of grins, and his boyish vitality was most marked in the field during England's first innings at Leeds. He hurdled small boys in the outfield as he chased the ball; he took no pains to conceal his unfeigned joy when he took his first Test wicket, and, in every action to this innings, Loxton showed that he was on the field to enjoy his Test cricket—not merely to participate in it or be overcome by it. I have a very deep appreciation of the cricketing soul who refuses to be depressed by the Test atmosphere and nobody, in my experience, has brought more actual and visual enjoyment to the game than Loxton.

Loxton is athletically built, not quite six feet in height. He moves with ease and power and has a broad pair of shoulders. He showed his disregard for his first Test fifty by not creeping on it with traditional singles but by opening his shoulders and hitting Cranston high into the pavilion for the biggest six of the match. This was such a glorious hit that all the fieldsmen spontaneously applauded.

Harvey was out to his worst stroke. Indeed, he will never play one worse in all his career. He played a rank, cross-bat sweep to a well-pitched ball and was clean bowled. Just across on the balcony I saw Bradman throw back his head, clutch it as if in agony, and then walk into the dressing-room. At such a time and at such a score, Bradman would never have played such a stroke. It showed that Harvey was perfectly satisfied with making just the century. Bradman's gesture showed that he thought Harvey should have gone on and on, but I saw something in the lad to admire in the manner of his dismissal. He had done a grand job under difficult circumstances and was, no doubt, soon forgiven this indiscretion. Such was his general demeanour that one would have thought he was playing in his twentieth Test against England, not his first.

Loxton then began his onslaught in vicious fashion. He hit Laker for two sixes to the on and then two successive sixes over mid-off, where Miller had hit his in the morning. This, indeed, was a hazardous place for spectators that day, but a very hurried scatter left safe openings for all of Loxton's sixes. That made five sixes off Laker to that period. At Lord's, in the match against the M.C.C., the Australians hit ten sixes off Laker, so this, at Leeds, was no new experience for him. He is the ideal bowler for six-hitting as he turns into the bat and is hit with the swing.

On came Yardley again to see what he could do, and bless me if he didn't break a partnership again! He clean-bowled Loxton. The batsman made a wild, cross-bat swish somewhat after Harvey's style. I never remember seeing a man in the nineties in a Test playing such a stroke before and, judging by the look on Loxton's face, as he returned, he will never forgive himself. His 93, an incredibly and highly thrilling Test innings, came in only 135 minutes with five sixes and eight fours.

It was four o'clock when Johnston came in. Johnson and Saggers had not lasted long, so that meant England had only to dismiss Johnston and Toshack to be well over a hundred ahead with valuable batting time that same afternoon in case the weather broke overnight.

That period from four o'clock onwards was when England, so splendidly placed, failed to win this Leeds Test. In retrospect, one can usually find a time in the game when an opportunity offers and the taking or losing of it means the result of the game. Such a time was from four to five at Leeds that Saturday, and it was a bad jolt, a sorry anti-climax to the Englishmen, when 6.30 came and Lindwall and Toshack were still in possession.

Lindwall, of course, is a gifted batsman, but even such a one can do little when left with two abject tail-enders. Johnston and Toshack possess much too good a sense of humour to take their batting seriously, but Johnston hung on until twenty to six, and Toshack for the final fifty minutes. Lindwall played grandly, as he always does when he makes runs. He makes them in brilliant fashion, but it was a terrible reflection on the English attack that the others could not have been quickly hustled back. Douglas Wright, at this stage, would have been invaluable. Tail-enders don't like spin that comes quickly from the pitch, but on this pitch which saw the 1938 Test finished inside three days because of the spinners, the English selectors had not chosen Wright and, on the morning of the game, had dropped Young, who spins from the leg.

Toshack, whose injured knee had at last given out, limped badly. Johnston remained on, in much confusion, until the limping Toshack was seen, to run for Toshack, and this gave us the laugh of the day. Johnston has a run all his own. He runs somewhat like a grasshopper would if it didn't hop, and Smiling Bill enjoyed himself immensely as he ran some 15 feet out, almost in the next paddock. He told me later that he had never run for anybody before and found it difficult enough to run for himself. He had the umpires twisting their heads and taking their lines across from the crease as he bounded along, like an outsider in a race, very wide out.

And so this hectic day of mingled roars, claps, thrills, skill and humour ended with England being repulsed badly. A grand day for Australia, but look at it from the English viewpoint! Two heroes, including the Don, dismissed in one over in the morning; two rabbits nibbling on for two hours and a half in the evening! England was barely a hundred ahead at the end of the day. Whilst it could be said that England failed badly to push home the advantage gained in the first few minutes of the day, just homage should be paid Harvey, Miller, Loxton and Lindwall—and, in less degree, Johnston and Toshack.

CHAPTER TWELVE

A TEST OUT OF HAND

THERE was no rain on Sunday and Monday was very summery, somewhat like a February day in Sydney or Adelaide. Each year the towns in the North of England take turns in having a week's holiday. It is known as Wakes Week and this Monday was the beginning of the week locally. As one entered the ground, it seemed that all employed in the heavy woollens industry were outside the ground, trying to gain admittance. At eleven the gates were closed. This was inevitable but sad as thousands outside were queued up and down the streets.

The closing of the gates had been delayed, too, because there were too many inside. Long before play began there were shouts from the left of the ground like lions being fed at meal-time. They were growling at the late-comers to sit down. As the players came out, the boundary line had disappeared completely as people sat inside the ground. The playing area was smaller than ever.

The Australian innings closed in the third over of the day. Crapp caught Lindwall beautifully in the slips in his left hand as he fell to the ground. Australia finished only 38 runs behind. Hutton and Washbrook took a good look at the Australian bowling and then began to attack it with neat strokes and quick, efficient running between the wickets. Lindwall once bounced one high over Washbrook, and bowler and batsmen both intently studied the pitch while those looking on all asked whether it was beginning to show wear at last.

Nearing one, Bradman spoke to the umpires and they walked to the left of the ground, where the roars had continued all the morning, and tried to move the people back. For ten minutes before Bradman spoke to the umpires, I noticed more and more people encroaching on the field so that the boundary, which had begun play well behind the lines, was still farther back. Chester and Baldwin spent eight minutes of the game trying to move the people back. It was hopeless. They edged back, but as soon as the umpires moved away, a forward surge took place again. It seemed that the game was getting out of hand. The boundaries were ridiculously short.

157

As the umpires were doing their best to improve matters, there was a ludicrous happening as a child ran on the field, right to the centre, and sought autographs. This encroachment on the field is a very bad feature of English cricket as the boundary changes so much. It could not happen in Australia, where on all the first-class grounds the boundary is defined by a picket fence—and this never changes over the years. Bradman had to hit his Australian boundaries as far as Trumper, but some of the hits that passed for boundaries in this 1948 series deserved no more than two runs at the outside.

England's fifty came in just over even time; at lunch, England was 72 for none, Hutton 40 and Washbrook 28. England was thus 110 runs ahead.

Thirty policemen around the ring after lunch tried to get the crowd to move back but it was impossible. Too many had been allowed into the ground. They squashed back for the bobby, and forward as he moved on, and all during lunch, on this crowded, sweltering day, the amplifier blared for little Willie or wee Mary or Mr. Somebody or other to come to the secretary's office. And, as usual, the gentleman on the ground staff was constantly being sought. He seemed to be about as difficult to find as a spot on the pitch.

Hutton and Washbrook played splendid cricket after lunch. Bradman tried to quell them with defensive fields, but Washbrook hit a six, straight, off Johnson, and Hutton did the same at 98 to raise England's hundred, the second time for the match. The person sitting far off in the tree at the top of the ground could tell this was a six, so far into the crowd did it land, but umpire Chester busily bustled off to the side, ferreted in among the crowd to find the white line, bustled back and then imperiously raised his hands above his head. A thorough umpire is Chester.

That made Hutton's half-century in 125 minutes, and Bradman, scenting some long stick for Johnson, had him off and Lindwall back. Washbrook square-cut him like a flash to pass his 50. Lindwall did not seem to appreciate this and finished the over with two bumpers. The crowd shouted "Eh, eh!" in admonitory tones. Washbrook had tasted blood. He swung at one of Johnston's and hit it high in the air. Bradman, running back and trying to judge at the same time, almost got the ball on his cranium.

Some youth got himself lost at this stage and so we had another announcement, and then, thrice during the one over, small boys walking along the field at the back of the bowler's arm, stopped the play. One began to think that the spectators were doing everything in this game but the batting and bowling. The truth was, of course, that yet another English ground was incapable of holding the inordinately large crowds which wished to see Test cricket.

Washbrook was having one of those delightful batting days when everything goes swimmingly, but nevertheless he was batting beautifully. He played his hook once too often again, however, and out on the boundary Harvey sprinted like an Olympian, stooped on the run to catch the ball at his toes, tossed himself up a little catch, caught it again and, while on the run, drop-kicked the ball the rest of the way in to wicket-keeper Saggers. This was the catch of the season—or, indeed, would have been had Harvey not turned on several magnificent aerial performances down at the Oval in London earlier in the tour.

It is strange how often, when one man goes in a big partner-ship, the other soon follows. Hutton was out without another run being added, Bradman taking a good running catch. England was then 167 runs ahead with eight wickets in hand, but then Edrich and Compton entered the doldrums. Edrich managed 13 runs in thirty minutes but Compton, in the same time, could make only two. This was bad for England, but Bradman was calling the tune with defensive fields and his men were bowling to it—Lindwall several times having no slip.

Compton did not like the way things were going. He hit his pads in a disgusted manner at the end of one Johnson over and then looked most impatient when, next over, he again failed to get Johnson away. He made up his mind before the next ball was bowled, ran down the pitch and swung it to leg for his first four. This had taken him 45 minutes to achieve. England's hero could not cope with the situation and was obviously very upset about it, slapping his leg with the bat and tossing his head about. Yorkshire is a bad scoring county for him, but when the new ball came Compton nicely back-cut Lindwall for four, Edrich brilliantly drove Miller for four (Miller replying next ball with his customary bouncer), and soon afterwards came the fifty partnership in an hour, Edrich making 24 in that time and Compton 21.

At this stage, Lindwall found trouble with the foot-holes at the delivery crease. They were very worn and, after having a good look at the ground, Lindwall changed to round the wicket.

He bowled two balls and then umpire Baldwin inspected the pitch. He had a talk with Lindwall, evidently about running on the pitch after delivery. Bradman joined in the talk and Lindwall changed to over the wicket again. It evidently nettled him because he almost took Compton's chin off with a bouncer. This was very interesting. As Australia had to bat last, it would have served England's purposes admirably if Lindwall had damaged the pitch, but the worn foot-holes were causing him great concern. Apropos of this, Duckworth once told me that McDonald was never worried by worn foot-holes. He could bowl from any place on the crease, whereas Larwood, according to Duckworth, always brought his feet down in the same place.

Edrich lingered on 25 for a long time, but then Compton played one of the loveliest strokes ever seen—a full-blooded pull off a bouncer from Lindwall. It crashed its way to the boundary. Compton hooked Johnston very finely also, and at tea England was 209—2, Compton 42 and Edrich 33. England was then 247 runs ahead. It was apparent that England would have to go for the "Doctor" in a big way after tea.

Edrich began the job quickly. In Johnson's second over he hit 4, 4, 4 and 6, the latter soaring half-way up the mound, but bless me if umpire Chester didn't wish to go aroving again, and off he went to the edge of the field, delved again, emerged, returned and waved six three minutes after everybody had entered it in their books. I almost expected the amplifier to blare for Mr. Chester as a missing person and would he please return immediately to the middle of the ground.

Lindwall soon trapped Edrich leg before; Crapp had a short life but a gay one; Harvey hurdled a small boy on the field as he gathered the ball; Yardley deliberately put one high through the slips off Lindwall with nobody there; Compton batted in his best form and Yardley, trying a big hit off Johnston, was caught in aerial fashion by Harvey. Cranston lasted two balls and England became 268—6—a collapse as sudden as in the first innings.

Bedser's first innings success had not led to promotion, and Evans had luck first ball as he snicked one high through the cordon. As Compton hit Lindwall for a lovely boundary straight the amplifier broke in on the beauty of it by wanting Arthur of the ground staff. One wanted nerves of steel with this persistent amplifier, and soon afterwards Compton slashed one towards cover without moving his feet and was caught. With 45 minutes

22. *Neil Harvey, pulls one with vigour in his Leeds century. Note the perfect position of his feet*

21. *Out goes Bradman. Pollard gets through his defences in the first innings at Leeds*

23.   *The master in action. Bradman scores a boundary off Pollard at Leeds*

left for play, England was 331 runs ahead, but Evans, dealing mainly in fours, improved the final spell for England with dashing batting. At stumps England was 362—8, Evans 47 and Laker 14.

The air was full of speculation the next day. It was fine. If Yardley declared, Australia had to score at the rate of 400 runs in six hours—an unprecedented rate on the fifth and last day of a match. It was wondered whether Bradman would accept the challenge and push for victory. It was known that a draw would suit as well the purposes of the Australians as this would give them the rubber, whereas a defeat to Australia gave England the chance to halve the rubber.

We saw the first show of tactics immediately. Yardley batted on for two overs in which three runs were scored. By continuing his innings, Yardley thus had the option of which roller to use before play began and, possibly remembering that Bradman had done this the preceding series in Australia, he ordered the heaviest roller. The object of this was clear. If the pitch is breaking, the heavy roller helps it on its way, and love and war are not the only things in which all is fair and above board. In articles following this tour, Bradman went to great pains to deny any malice aforethought with a preference late in the match, just before a declaration, for the heavy roller. But I, for one, was left unconvinced. He did not mention that he also used his prerogative, on this Sydney occasion, of keeping the grass on the pitch uncut also. As Yardley observed in his articles following on Bradman's (these Test captains nowadays scribble almost as much as a professional journalist), Bradman is a shrewd and a hard captain who gave nothing away, not even, wrote Yardley, in a festival game.

Yardley barely took time to make his appearance on the balcony, accept the congratulations of his fellows on the birth the night before of a son (both well!), before he waved his arms to the middle and England had declared. Australia had to score 404 runs to win in 344 minutes. Bradman used no roller at all. Some players told me the night before that the pitch was beginning to sport a patch but the point was whether England had the bowlers to make use of it. Not many balls played up the day before, and England lost wickets mainly in a chase for runs.

In between innings, the police made an announcement that lost children and their parents should go immediately to the office and wait there without having messages put over the air, so that gave everybody a chance to watch the cricket and write about it. I wondered whether Yardley's tactics with the heavy roller would, in turn, lead Bradman to be tough and play solely for a draw.

In Bedser's second over, Morris again played that on-side stroke that dismissed him in the first innings, but this time the ball fell just wide of Cranston. After fifteen minutes, Australia was 10 but this signified nothing. Care is always necessary at the start of an innings, and thus we had to wait for the tactics of the game to unfold.

Yardley did not wait long to exploit spin. After three overs by Bedser, he called on Laker, England's sole spinning agent. Hassett hit a four and a single, Morris hit a four but one lifted quickly and beat Morris altogether. Morris hit the next for four. It was a poor over but the next was better, and after that Hutton had a long and serious talk with Laker. No immediate results were seen.

All the English bowlers were over-pitching the ball, but at the end of 45 minutes Australia was only 32, each batsman 13. It did not look that the batsmen had orders to push it along. There were cries from the crowd of "Have a go" and "Windy." A single by Morris was cheered ironically and then Evans missed a difficult leg-side stumping off Hassett. The next ball lifted. The pitch was there all right, but were the bowlers? Bedser got another up, this time to Morris. He looked much more dangerous than the spinner, Laker.

With so many runs to play with and the clock being well ahead of Australians, Yardley gave Compton a bowl-up, but this, at first, provided some easy runs. Morris took two fours and Australia's 50 came in 64 minutes. But in Compton's next over Evans had another miss and a costly one it was, too. Morris had moved out to Compton, missed, and was stranded down the pitch, but Evans couldn't get the ball down into his gloves. This was a rare chance. Morris was then 32 and the total 55.

Laker spun one up sharply and away to Morris, to whom he is most trouble, coming from his legs, and I noticed Hassett look to his fellows in the pavilion, grin hugely and measure off a foot on his bat. In cricketing language, this was saying that the pitch was now a real spinner's one, turning a foot. The pitch was there but I wasn't satisfied that I had yet seen a bowler to take advantage of it.

Compton got Hassett and well deserved it. He spun one very

sharply, caught the edge of Hassett's bat and, following through fast, Compton took a thrilling left-handed catch inches off the ground. Australia was 57—1 in 75 minutes, Hassett 17. In came Bradman to his last Test innings at Leeds, and the demonstration was even more amazing than his first innings. He was escorted again by the police and clapped and cheered terrifically all the way to the middle. The stage was set for him and his last innings on his most noble ground. Australia was well behind the clock.

Bradman pushed Compton for a single immediately. He followed with a pull in the grand Bradman manner; he off-drove Laker for a resounding four and was 12 in six minutes. Then Yardley brought on Hutton. I could imagine Yardley's desire to get all the spin he could on this pitch, but I think it might have been wiser to have had a few overs from Bedser and Pollard first. Hutton rarely bowls. He throws up leg-breaks but they are not good ones, usually lacking in length. Morris took three fours in a rather terrible over and became 51.

Compton bowled a good over from the other end but Hutton continued his poor stuff, Bradman collecting two fours in succession. He almost hit the next to Yardley, the ball falling just short, and with this spurt off Hutton's bowling Australia was now 96 in 90 minutes. A big leeway had been made good.

Then came a most incredible over from Compton. This is worthy of close description because I think it ranks as Bradman's most uncomfortable over in his whole Test career. Bradman failed, first of all, to detect a bosie. He snicked it very luckily past Crapp at first slip for four, an accident of a stroke. Up came another slip and Bradman glanced Compton for four. Next ball he failed to pick Compton's bosie again, played for an off-break, snicked it as it went the other way and was missed by Crapp, yes, Crapp, in the slips. The last ball of the over beat Bradman again completely and rapped him on the pads. Phew! What an over of excitement this was!

Unperturbed, Morris continued to enjoy Hutton at the other end. We were seeing some strange mixtures of cricket but never such poor Test leg-breaks as from Hutton. That Yardley should have used him at all was a confession of how much he needed a leg-spinner on such a pitch. Four overs from Hutton cost 30 runs. At lunch, Australia was 121—1, Morris 63 and Bradman 35—but both had been missed. Had chances been taken in this pre-lunch session, England, of a surety, would have had this game won before tea. Hassett, Morris and Bradman out would have left the Australians gasping because this pitch was a very different proposition to the plumb one of the first innings when Miller, Harvey, Loxton and Lindwall were so successful.

Compton was again on after lunch, naturally, but he had seen his best. He is not a regular bowler and here, in Compton and Hutton, we had two very St. Swithin's Day bowlers trying to do the job of a Test match-winning bowler. This, in itself, was sufficient condemnation of the team England sent into the field. It was not balanced; it was chosen in the face of Leeds' history.

After lunch, Morris took seven fours in two overs of indescribably bad bowling. He entered the nineties 14 minutes after lunch and got his century with another four. It had taken him just over two hours. After lunch he had scored 37 runs while Bradman made three, but Morris was getting the choice offerings.

Bradman was missed again just after he had gone to his 50 in 60 minutes. Yardley dropped him at point off Cranston but it was not an easy one. Bradman tried to drive, mistimed and spooned the ball up behind point. Yardley dived, got the ball into his hands but could not hold it. The 200 came at ten past three, Laker giving Morris two awful full tosses in succession. The English bowling was very bad indeed. Here was a pitch made for bowlers and the Australians were pegging fours in all directions.

Then came an incident above the ordinary. Bradman hooked Cranston viciously for a boundary and finished the stroke by clutching his side. He was in great pain. It looked like a return of the injury which caused him to retire in Melbourne the preceding February when 57 against the Indians in a Test—his last Test innings in Australia. He hooked another four but winced visibly and had Pollard rub him vigorously.

They all had a breather then while Crapp brought out drinks. This was the first time I had noticed drinks this series. It was certainly not the summer for a thirst. The 250 came at four, Morris 133 and Bradman 92. A few minutes later came the 200 partnership, and at ten past four Bradman reached his century in the very fast time of 147 minutes. It was not one of his best centuries. It had that nightmarish Compton over but it was, nevertheless, quite a good one. It was his second of the series, his 19th in all against England and his 112th in first-class games.

Then Evans had another miss and Bradman was again the fortunate one. Laker drew him two yards down the pitch but

Evans couldn't finish the job. Bradman was 108, and then in the next over, off Compton, Laker dropped Morris in front of square-leg. He got the catch into both hands but could not hold it. Morris was then 136. The English out-cricket had been such all day that the side did not deserve to win. At tea, Australia wanted only 112 to win in 105 minutes.

Australia coasted to easy victory at 15 minutes past six—15 minutes to spare. Morris did not stay to see it through, and Miller tried to win the game in a few hits, so that Australia still had seven wickets in hand when victory came with Bradman, fittingly in his final Leeds appearance, unconquered at 173. It would have been fitting, also, had Bradman made the winning run in this game but, most unselfishly, he worked the strike so that Harvey could make the winning run because of the lad's great deeds in the first innings.

Harvey nonchalantly hit the winning run with a four, turned about as he cut short his follow-through with the bat, whipped out a stump as a souvenir, and as Bradman ran gaily down and patted him on the back Harvey searched about to find a bail or two on the ground. Bradman fled the ground as the thousands converged on him. It was a memorable scene. Bradman's 173 not out goes to join his 334, 304, and 103 at Leeds. Truly has it been his greatest ground.

It was, of course, a great Australian victory and Bradman deserved every credit for the manner in which he pushed along for victory. The Australian honours were well shared. Morris played in his own enchanting style in the second innings and Lindwall was fit to rank with any in playing his part. The Australian win was due to teamwork, Bradman's incentive and captaincy, but due allowance must also be made for England's ignoble cricket on this final day. It was wretched stuff. No side can afford to miss Bradman, Morris and Hassett and still expect victory. Fate is not like that. The Leeds Test gave us some lovely memories, but England's bad cricket on this final day watered down the taste. But what are we to think of selectors who refused to choose a leg-break bowler for this place, above all? Even if the Australians followed suit, they did have Johnston to spin them from leg. A Wright or a Hollies and England would have won this game on the last day. Had the chances been taken England would still have won.

CHAPTER THIRTEEN

ON YORKSHIRE'S GROUNDS

WHEN we were very young we played cricket on a rough-
and-ready parkland across which rolled the pleasant noise
of the Pacific boomers as they broke on the nearby Bondi Beach.
The name of our cricket field changed each week with each
"Test." First it would be Old Trafford, then Headingley at Leeds,
then Lord's, then Bramall Lane (our infant minds must have been
subconsciously alert, you'll agree, to give Yorkshire two Tests),
and then, finally, the Oval.

The Sydney ground, then, was the only Australian ground
we knew, but there was more romance in aping the English
grounds. This was about the time Macartney had made his
immortal 100 before lunch. Our field was strewn with Macartneys,
Sutcliffes, Hobbs, Jack Gregorys, Wilfred Rhodes, and so on.
Indeed, we even aped the mannerisms of each as we read about
them and so, after all those years, it is most interesting for one
to come and see, first as an Australian player, and then as a
Pressman, the grounds we knew only in imagination.

Each English ground has its own particular atmosphere, but
nowhere in England does an Australian enjoy playing as much
as in Yorkshire. There is about Yorkshire crowds something
which is lacking in the crowds in the South, and not approached
even by the fabled crowds of nearby Lancashire or Nottinghamshire. Yorkshire crowds are like our own Australian ones. They
are part and parcel of the game, and all Test players will tell you
that a chirping, appreciative crowd in the background makes
much more for atmosphere and is more inspiring than a polite
crowd which claps the good stuff and, by silence, ignores ignoble
stuff which is deserving of censure. There have been Test players,
they will tell you, who have been put off their stride by the
barrackers, or the chirrupers; but these are only being found out
early in their careers. If a little free and easy advice would upset
them, how much more so, when it came along, would a Test
crisis?

Leeds, Bradford and Sheffield all have atmosphere rampant.
I discovered that very early in our game at Bramall Lane in 1938

—in fact, I discovered it the very first ball of the day from Bowes. Bowes appealed for l.b.w., so did the wicket-keeper, Wood, so did point and, indeed (this must be true because of the roar from the field), did fine-leg. So, too, did some 30,000 spectators. I did not take this amiss. It was Yorkshire's way of telling me that the game had started, the battle was joined and nobody wanted any stuff or nonsense. It is not for "nowt" they call the spectators the "Grinders" at Sheffield, but let me assure you that Australians love this atmosphere. It is what we are reared in at home, and no Australian will ever begrudge the man-in-the-street, who puts in his few bob at the turnstiles, what he considers is a rightful part in the game.

What we notice most in England is that far too few people are allowed to pay their shillings at the turnstiles. Your grounds are hopelessly inadequate when it comes to housing all those thousands who wish to see a Test match between England and Australia. One of the saddest sights I have ever seen in the game was that outside Headingley in 1948, when thousands and thousands, patiently queued up and down innumerable side streets, were locked out from a lovely day's cricket. These thousands won't come a second time to be disappointed—and who can say how many Test players were lost to England on Monday when hundreds of small boys could not find entrance to see how their heroes treat this great game of cricket?

That must be a thought which agitates your cricket legislators. Your grounds have not only been inadequate since the war. All through the 'thirties there was the same experience. I saw it at Leeds in 1938, at Bramall Lane and even more so at Scarborough.

The Melbourne cricket ground houses 90,000 people—and it does so in extreme comfort which gives everybody a seat, and a seat, moreover (and this was not the case in the Leeds Press-box, at least, where the seats were as hard as the Russians in Berlin), where one could expand and stretch one's legs over six hours of play. The Melbourne spectator, too, has a roof over his head in that huge double-deck concrete stand which accommodates 60,000. Sydney can house 60,000 and so can Adelaide.

But, as an Australian, I do not want to be over-critical of things as we see them in England. We realise the many difficulties which confront the game in England and we know, too (though sometimes we listen incredulously), that cricket and football cannot be played on the same grounds here. It is only because football and cricket share the expenses of the grounds in Australia that we can enlarge. A month after our middle is a churning mass of Rugby mud our grade cricketers are stealing to and fro.

They tell us in England that the climatic and grass conditions simply will not allow of a ground being used all the year round. It would dig the pitches up too much (I could suggest a few here that ought to be dug up, incidentally), and if that is so, then I cannot see how your grounds can ever be enlarged to accommodate the huge crowds which, it could be argued, congregate only every four years. I cannot see, either, how things can be made more comfortable for those who watch; or how a band, which is one of the most pleasant things I know of at a cricket match, could be used to entertain people during those weary waits for play; or, finally, how your crowds can be given those huge scoring-boards of ours which tell you, at a glance, the position of the game and the names of those fielding the ball so that, at once, you feel as if you belong in the very game itself.

Some tell us that we are trying to upset customs and traditions here that have withstood the years. No, it is not that. We think more people should be catered for in the game of cricket in England and the game made more comfortable in all ways. The average person will withstand discomfort in a football game of 90 minutes; he is entitled to expect something better over $7\frac{1}{2}$ hours. And those who come early should not have their view obstructed by late-comers.

I have not mentioned the spirit of Yorkshire for "nowt." This county leads English cricket in many ways. I mentioned early the rough nature of our own "Leeds" at Bondi. That's where we learnt to watch the ball. On our concrete pitches we later learnt to play the game correctly. Let Yorkshire be the first to string such pitches in the country. There has been only talk about them so far in England.

CHAPTER FOURTEEN

FIASCO IN THE FIFTH

THE fifth Test match at Kennington Oval could well be remembered as the poorest Test ever between England and Australia—or, better still, it could well be forgotten altogether. It was over in twenty minutes over the three days with Australia winning by an innings and 149 runs from a total of 389. If we recall that play was delayed for half an hour on the first day, it could be said that the game finished inside the three days.

The Oval Test is rarely a satisfactory affair. Usually, as the result of the rubber hinges upon its result, it is played to a finish, and huge scores there by Ponsford and Bradman, for Australia, and Hutton, for England, have given these Oval Tests the flavour of attrition, but this game of 1948 differed in that it was limited to five days. Australia had already won the rubber.

The English selectors continued their team-changing habits. Crapp was originally dropped from the Leeds team but he was recalled when Washbrook, struck several times on the thumb in his benefit game against Australia at Manchester, was unfit. Pollard, though he had taken Bradman's wicket at Manchester and Leeds, was dropped, and so, too, was Laker. The additions were Hollies, whose feats at Birmingham made him an obvious choice, Dewes, of Cambridge, and Watkins of Glamorgan, the first Welshman to play against Australia in a Test.

These changes brought England's tally of players in the five Tests up to 22. The selectors had chopped and changed so much, in other words, that they fielded two complete teams against Australia. This, naturally, could not make for efficient team-work, and that is one advantage a touring side has over the home team. With all the country's players on hand, there is the temptation to change the team at home, particularly if it is a losing side, whereas a touring side is restricted in its choice. Ring came into the Australian side for the first time; Ian Johnson was dropped to twelfth man and Barnes, being fit again, took the injured Toshack's place. This meant that Australia had played fifteen men in the series, but three of these were entirely due to injuries to Toshack, Barnes and Tallon, so that Australia preserved an almost identical team throughout the series.

There had been much bad weather in England just before this game. The Australians were rained off in their second day against Durham at Sunderland, and made their path back to London along a railway line that had been so severely damaged that bridges were washed away and the Flying Scot, indeed, was lost in transit for some hours. This weather seriously interfered with the preparation of the Oval pitch, which was water-logged 24 hours before play began.

It was apparent, therefore, even before the game began that we would not see one of the usually tedious Oval Tests in which the bat completely dominates the ball. As we watched Yardley (in flannels) and Bradman (in mufti) walk to the middle, I thought that the side winning the toss here would have a big advantage. Yardley won it. In Australia one knows soon after the toss which side has won the toss and what is happening. It is put on the scoring-board but, unless one of the captains gives a sign, it is often necessary in England to wait until the players come on the field before knowing which side is batting.

When I saw Bradman lead out the Australians I took it for granted that he had won the toss and had sent the Englishmen in. It was not so. It transpired that Yardley had won the toss and decided to bat first.

Did Yardley err in this? It is very easy to be wise after the event. I feel certain Bradman would not have batted had he won the toss, but in making up my mind that had I been the English skipper and had won the toss Australia would certainly have been sent in to bat, I did so without seeing the pitch. Bradman and Yardley inspected it before the toss and everything that happened in that innings supported Yardley's opinion that the pitch would play in good style. From the psychological angle, however, I still would have had a hankering to ask Australia to bat first. Because of our lack of practice on rain-affected pitches, our chaps feel somewhat apprehensive if the pitch is in doubt, but nothing that happened in the two English innings suggested that had Yardley sent Australia in first and had Bradman's men been dismissed for a tolerable score, England would then have amassed a big one.

The truth was that the English batting was the poorest in modern memory. It might have had its counterpart in Armstrong's tour in 1921 but I did not see that series. My knowledge of the Tests dates only from 1928 but it is true that in score —and, probably, in technique—nothing as weak as England's first innings has ever been seen before in the game by this country. England was all out for 52. This was one run lower than England's previous lowest at Lord's in 1888. At Edgbaston, in Birmingham, in 1902, Australia made 36.

Dewes took strike. Yardley was criticised for sending him in first to open the innings, but a captain has no alternative but to use his team as the selectors give it to him. Dewes was included in the side as an opening batsman; therefore he had, of necessity, to open the innings. One must enter a Test match ready to take all that is coming and, undoubtedly, Dewes himself did not want any attempt to shelter him lower down the list.

Dewes took one in the first over by Lindwall. He took strike to open the game and after Miller, his nightmare opponent, had bowled one ball and then sprinkled sawdust on the approach for the next, Dewes was clean bowled. Miller seems always to be doing this to Dewes. That is why I have referred to him as Dewes' nightmare opponent, because if Dewes has feverish dreams about cricket (and what Test cricketer doesn't?) Miller must always figure in them. Miller skittled him when he was in England with the Services' team and Miller skittled Dewes again at Cambridge. This was where Dewes wore towels to protect his body against Miller. He remembered him from the Services' games.

Dewes played a weak stroke. He played across the line of flight, and when an opening batsman does that only trouble can follow. That was 1—1. Hutton and Edrich proceeded warily. Bradman made quick changes, trying to exploit the pitch early if there was anything in it to be exploited. Johnston dropped one short and Edrich played his hook. He did not get it in the meaty part of the bat, however, and it went slowly enough to allow Hassett to make a sideways dive just behind square-leg, some ten yards away, and catch the ball two-handed. It was a splendid catch. What are we to think of the stroke ? Well, in playing a hook stroke, plenty of things can go wrong. It only needs the slightest slip and there is trouble. This short ball deserved hooking, but the old adage in Test cricket is not to hook for the first hour at least. It is a stroke in which, once committed, the batsman cannot go back. He puts his leg across the pitch and he gets into position to play this cross-bat stroke. He must go through with it, and of all strokes, I think, this is the riskiest. This was another case of the hook costing England dearly.

Compton was next and did not look too comfortable. Lindwall bounced one at him and Compton, putting his bat to it, edged it up high. It seemed that this would be a simple catch for one of the slips but it cleared the bunker there and went on down to Hassett, who ran around from third man. In his surprise, Compton dropped his bat and while Hutton was calling and running, Compton, with one eye on Hassett, was fumbling on the ground for his bat. Hassett had the ball in hand while Compton was still fumbling, but, very nobly I thought, he held the ball while Compton regained his bat and his composure and scurried off to the other end. This was a pleasant gesture on a Test field and Hassett was warmly applauded.

But the let-off profited Compton nothing. A few minutes later Lindwall dropped another ball short and Compton played the hook. He got the ball cleanly but close in, and around square, Morris, quickly on the move, took a most spectacular catch. This was one of the catches of the season. A batsman, possibly, is unlucky to be out to such a catch but here was the hook again! It could not have assuaged Compton's disappointment, either, when Bradman told him that he had remembered that particular stroke from the Oval of ten years before and had placed Morris specially in position for it!

Crapp batted twenty minutes without scoring and then followed away one from Miller which made England 23—4. Off six overs, Miller had taken two wickets for three runs, and so England went to lunch with Hutton, who had never been in the slightest difficulty, 17 and Yardley 4, the hopes of the side.

Lindwall sent back Yardley's stumps soon after lunch with a yorker and Watkins came to bat in his first Test—indeed, this was the first game of any calibre Watkins had played in away from his Glamorgan county and so he must have felt very strange about everything. He hooked viciously at a bouncer and missed, took another bouncer on the point of his shoulder and was out leg before for nil to Johnston, playing across a ball. Bedser came and went with a new bat, not a mark on it before or after his innings, Evans and Young had their stumps uprooted by Lindwall, and with the last man, Hollies, for company, Hutton hit the only four of the innings when he hit Lindwall high and straight. This was not far off a six but Hutton, who looked like going right through the innings and, indeed, was never ill at ease at any stage, leg-glanced Lindwall fine and Tallon, diving, scooped the ball up in his extended left hand. This was one of the grandest leg-side catches by a keeper I ever wish to see.

Lindwall took six wickets for 20 off 16.1-overs. His figures after lunch were 8.1 overs, four maidens, five wickets for eight. He bowled as well in this innings as at any stage of his career. Probably it was the best he has ever bowled, and often as I watched him I thought that I was watching a man the equal of Larwood in pace. One of his greatest assets is the ability to change his pace without any notice of it in his action. Truly, a great bowler.

The bottom of this game had thus fallen out of it soon after it had started. There was a feeling of intense gloom as England took the field, and it increased during the sunny afternoon as Morris and Barnes piled on the agony. The fifty of the partnership came in quick time with neither batsman worried by the pitch or the bowlers; the 100 came at 5.30 with Barnes 52 and Morris 47, and it was not until 117 that Hollies, who immediately impressed as the most hostile English bowler, had Barnes play at one that went away and snick it to Evans.

Bradman was next and received a royal reception, a splendid tribute from the huge crowd which must have felt sick indeed at the sickly failure of its home men. Hundreds in this crowd had queued all night. They had slept on wet pavements so that they could see this final Test and the final appearance of Bradman, and his reception could not have been bettered. He came a lithe, athletic figure down the steps, and he fingered his cap to the applause as he made his way to the middle, his trunk slightly bent forward off his legs.

The reception he received must have been embarrassing for him. It lasted all the way to the middle, and there Yardley had assembled his team and called for three cheers for Bradman. This the English team gave heartily and Yardley shook Bradman by the hand. Bradman took guard, looked about and settled himself. Hollies bowled him a good one which Bradman played off the back foot. The next was pitched slightly farther up. It drew Bradman forward, he missed and the ball crashed into his stumps. And what a roar there was from the crowd!

This was one of the strangest experiences I have ever known on a cricketing ground. One moment the crowd was acknowledging Bradman lavishly in his farewell appearance in Test cricket against England; that noise had barely died on the afternoon air when it was rent again with the crowd shrieking at Bradman's dismissal. As the game gives, so the game takes away! Bradman looked back at his stumps, seemed not able to believe what he saw there, turned slowly and very, very slowly retraced his steps to the pavilion and a sympathetic reception. The game that had given him so much had denied him at the very last Test appearance.

On the Australian balcony, during all this, was Barnes. He had gone into the dressing-room, whipped up his camera before taking his pads off and from the balcony filmed the last Test innings of his captain. There is no more enthusiastic photographer than Barnes. Adjusting his camera, he entered the dressing-room and unbuckled his pads with his skipper and told him he had got all his innings!

At stumps that night Australia was 153—2, Morris 77 and Hassett 10. Next day Morris moved to his century with never a doubt. It had taken him 208 minutes with six fours. This was his second in succession and his third in the series. As he had made three in the series before in Australia, this made him now six Test centuries against England. Many famous players have played a lifetime of Test cricket against England without achieving anything like this, and at the time I remembered thinking that perhaps Morris is the best left-handed batsman Australia has ever produced. He stands upright, looking down as the bowler approaches, and his bat and legs are always in the correct position for either attack or defence. Perhaps his best scoring stroke is through the covers and he achieves the maximum force with a minimum of back-swing.

Hassett anchored himself 100 minutes this next day for 27 to total 37 when Young had him leg before. Miller was soon out, stumped off Hollies as he stretched forward. Harvey began with the confidence and impetuosity of youth. His feet twinkled against Young and he hit him straight for four; then he pulled him cheekily for another four but Hollies could not get Harvey against him. When he did he tricked him with a catch to Young and that made Hollies 95—4. The splendid bowling of this Warwickshire player was a bright spot in England's day, and he continued to worry all the Australians with the exception of Morris.

Morris was out in the only possible way. He was run out. He answered a short call by Tallon and was beaten by inches. It was unfortunate that he missed his first double century against England by four runs, but he had established the highest score of the series and he had topped Bradman's aggregate in Australia of 680, which was the highest post-war Test aggregate. In every way, this innings by Morris was the innings of a master.

Hollies was the English bowling star. He took 131—5 off 56 overs. An average of under three an over is very inexpensive bowling by a slow man, but as good as his figures was the manner in which Hollies achieved them. He was rarely, if ever, short in a length. He kept the ball always well up to the batsmen, inviting strokes, and it is this initiative by a slow bowler which gains him many wickets. Hollies, too, had spin and direction. He nagged at the off-stump, breaking away, and every now and then whipped his bosie back from the off, and Bradman, in the pavilion, could have testified to the deceptiveness of that particular ball.

This huge Oval crowd cheered every run when Hutton and Dewes opened again, but Dewes was not to last long. He played several strange-looking strokes for a Test arena and then was clean bowled without attempting a stroke against Lindwall. Obviously, Dewes was not yet fitted for the Test heights. He seemed to have a fault in leaning forward on his front foot before the ball was bowled and this, no doubt, explained why his footwork was all astray.

Hutton, again batting beautifully, and Edrich hung on that night with England 54—1—still 283 runs behind. With so many unreliable batsmen, it was felt next morning that all depended upon Hutton, Edrich and Compton, but there was an early setback when Edrich, playing across the flight again, was cleanbowled by Lindwall. The 100 came up at ten to one, and though Compton, early, was very unlike his true self, he later found some form and at lunch England was 121—2, Hutton 42 and Compton 37. It had not been a morning of attack by any means. The batsmen had scored 67 in 100 minutes, but it was consoling for England that they were still together. Hutton had scored only 23 in the 100 minutes. A feature of the morning's play was that Ring bowled 13 overs straight and bowled them well. This was his best sustained piece of bowling on the tour—indeed, it was the best chance he had received.

Compton was out to a freak slip catch by Lindwall after lunch. It was one of those catches when the ball just stays in the hand. This sent England's stocks down again and then Hutton, after several beautiful shots through the covers, was again caught by Tallon, but this time off Miller.

The end was just a matter of time. Crapp knew nothing of a ball from Miller which found his stumps; Watkins blazed to the leg off Ring and Hassett had not to move on the boundary for the catch (this was Ring's first wicket against England); Evans had his stumps knocked back, and a light appeal by Yardley saved the finish for the next morning.

Twenty minutes saw the end next day. Had Lindwall taken the final three wickets he would have established an all-time high for an Australian bowler's bag against England. Grimmett holds this with 29. O'Reilly is next with 28, but it was lanky Bill Johnston who tumbled over the last three wickets. Lindwall did not take one, and so Johnston equalled Lindwall's bag of 27, the highest ever achieved by a speed bowler and established in the 'twenties by Ted McDonald.

It was a sad finish to a sad game. Little can be said of what was, undoubtedly, the poorest Test in living memory. The English team never looked at ease with the bat though Hollies' grand bowling did redeem the side in the field. Indeed, had it not been for Arthur Morris, England would have dismissed Australia for a remarkably low score, but the pitiful batting by England had taken all interest out of the game.

On that black Saturday, Walter Robins, the leading member of the English selection committee, went off to Dover to play against Kent. I played against Robins in a club game on the Sunday and he told me he had never felt so ill as when he heard the progressive English scores. Brian Valentine, the Kent skipper, sent Holmes, another selector, a telegram to the Oval which read, "Robins has shot himself."

Probably one or two of the selectors must have felt like doing that. Several selections in this English team looked bad ones, but one wondered whether they were the fault of the selectors so much as the fault of the system under which English cricket is played. Watkins, for instance, had never played an important game away from his Glamorgan side and thus could not be expected to fit into a Test combination. The previous season he had not bowled at all in county cricket. To the time of the Oval Test, he had taken 35 wickets, but this was poor recommendation for the position of opening Test bowler against Australia.

There were farewells to Bradman at the close of the game but I liked particularly the gesture by Miller as he left the field. There was the usual scramble for stumps as souvenirs, and these were uprooted and claimed long before Morris took the catch at mid-on which finished the game. Miller won a bail in the scramble and tossed it high to the outer as a present for one of the small boys. A little lad in front of the Press-box could hardly

24. *Bradman at work in his century against England at Leeds. Note the combination of concentration and balance in this powerful stroke*

25. *At full stretch and out! Miller stumped by Evans in the final Test at the Oval*

26. *The leg trap. Compton catches Bradman off Whitcombe at Lord's. He is in the position where Hutton caught Bradman three times*

believe his eyes when he saw it tumbling to him. The pleased
look on his face as he clasped the bail in his two hands was one
of the sights of the game.

In his address to the people below the pavilion, Bradman said
that it was a sad occasion for him. "No matter what you may
read to the contrary," he said, "this is definitely my last Test
match ever. I am sorry my personal contribution has been so
small. There are two reasons for that. One was the generosity
of the reception I received and, secondly, the very fine ball bowled
to me. It has been a great pleasure for me to come on this tour
and I would like you all to know how much I have appreciated
it. Our most important matches are over. We have played
against a very lovable opposing skipper. He has been kind to us
in every way and it is a great pleasure for us to have him captain
England against us. The captain of the losing side has a very
difficult job. Yardley had the misfortune to run against one of
the strongest Australian teams ever. It will not be my pleasure
to play ever again on this Oval but I hope it will not be the last
time I come to England."

Said Norman Yardley: "In saying good-bye to Don we are
saying good-bye to the greatest cricketer of all time. He is not
only a great cricketer but a great sportsman, on and off the field.
I hope this is not the last time we see Don Bradman in this
country."

And, giving three cheers and singing "For he's a jolly good
fellow," the Oval people wandered off sadly home and to the
city. The game did, in no manner, befit the occasion.

CHAPTER FIFTEEN

NO SHOCKS OR LOSSES

THE county games between and after the Test matches have not the same appeal as those prior to the first Test. When the series begins, the Tests occupy first place, and as the touring Test side is usually a settled business by the time of the first Test, the county games that follow are generally used to give as much cricket as possible to those members of the touring team who do not make the Test side.

This tour of 1948 was somewhat different because, in his desire to have an unbeaten record, Bradman was not disposed to take a risk with *any* county side. Thus either Lindwall or Miller was in every game, sometimes both together, and Bill Johnston was another who found himself with plenty of work to do. This often deprived McCool and Ring of extended bowling trials, nor did Bradman believe in changing his batting order to give some of the less talented ones a chance to show their ability. An instance of this was at Birmingham. The Australians needed only 40 runs to win outright in the second innings, but Bradman sent in Brown and Morris and came in himself first wicket down, while in the dressing-room the "Untouchables" sang their now-familiar "Ground Staff."

Northants provided weak opposition after the first Test, but Australia again struck some spirited stuff from Yorkshire, this time at Bramall Lane, Sheffield, in the return game on the eve of the second Test. This game heard barracking and hooting, as spirited as at Nottingham, because of Miller's bouncers, and it finished in Bradman running off the field amid loud booing. The Sheffield crowd thought very poorly of his captaincy in leaving Yorkshire only an hour to bat with a leeway of 328 runs.

It was at Bramall Lane that Yorkshire almost toppled Australia in 1938. Rain beat Yorkshire to a victory then and Bradman, playing himself with a special trip to London on the Sunday to sign 3,600 autograph bats, took no risks with his side this time. He played a very strong team. The scenes outside the ground before play began were remarkable. As at Leeds later, thousands queued around the nearby streets only to have the gates closed on them. This led to a noisy scene when those with tickets clamoured for, and eventually gained, admission. They call the Sheffield people " Grinders" because of the town's affinity with the cutlery industry, and the spectators believe in the principle that once inside the ground they are part of the game. As a result, the game at Sheffield is always a very chirpy one, and the roar this opening day when 40,000 people saw Barnes clean-bowled third ball was something to remember.

Yardley was Yorkshire's skipper. I had often thought, in Australia and at Nottingham in the first Test, that Yardley would not hesitate a moment in replying with bouncers if he had someone who could do the job, and we had an indication of this when Aspinall tried to bounce them at Bradman. But Aspinall was no faster than any other bowler in England and Bradman just thrived on his short stuff, which gave him plenty of time to get into position. Bradman made a sparkling 50 in 76 minutes with Brown only 19 in the same time, but the sensation of the game came in the second innings when Bradman at 86 was caught in the Bedser-O'Reilly position at short fine-leg. Again the fieldsman was Hutton, and again Bradman fell in precisely the same manner as he had twice fallen in the Nottingham Test.

Bradman's 54 was top score in Australia's first innings but the innings of the match belonged to Harvey. He was absolutely brilliant and, with boundaries in all directions, he probably gained the respect of this most discerning crowd more quickly than any other cricketer in recent years. Harvey made a tremendous impression. With this innings he had clearly shown Bradman and his co-selectors that in him Australia had the left-handed reply in the Tests to the slowing-down policy which Yardley had used with such good effect at Nottingham.

Hamence had to struggle hard for his 48 here, but he was receiving few chances and thus could hardly be expected to show confidence. Had the Yorkshiremen held their chances here, Australia would have been out for less than 200. At least eight chances went to ground, and even then Australia could manage only 249 so that after the first day Yorkshire was well in the game.

This was the innings in which Coxon took 66—4 off 26 overs and thus gained Test selection. His bowling was steady but not impressive in the Test sense. He is medium-fast only and, as I have written in my Test chapters, dug the pitch up badly.

Another mannerism he possessed was in changing the ball over from his left hand to right in the middle of his run. Just before delivery he puts his right elbow out at right angles, a habit which gives the umpire a few anxious moments and which the wary avoid by standing back a few yards.

Though eight Yorkshiremen passed double figures, the county could total only 206. Hutton topped with 39 and, as usual, he was the main recipient of the bouncers. Halliday received some nasty blows from Miller, and in a following over Miller bowled two well his own side of half-way which whistled over Hutton's bent head. This was too much for the "Grinders." They went into loud and voluble action and resented it all very much. There were shouts, as at Nottingham, of "What about Larwood?" and one reflected, again, what unpleasantness bouncers bring into a game and particularly when the other side is incapable of retaliating. In stressing the difference between the Australian bouncers and those of the Jardine-Larwood era, it must be always understood that the Australians have never packed the leg-field and, since those days, the umpires have been fully empowered to stop these tactics if they think them improper. As I have written in other places, the umpires, however, have never spoken to the Australian fast bowlers about their tactics.

In this game, Brown made his fifth century, equalling Bradman, but it was a very studious affair of four hours with no risks. Brown was a perfect study of concentration and defence. He knew his selection for this tour was criticised and he was out to justify himself with a huge packet of runs but, as at Yorkshire and elsewhere on this tour, he made many critics for himself with his posed and deliberate defence. Many wished that he would enter into the spirit of a final trip and enjoy it. Though Bradman made 84 in the second innings, Harvey's deeds were again the sensation of the innings. His form by now was truly splendid. He had picked up the pace and height of English pitches to perfection, and full-blooded strokes flowed from his bat in all directions.

In this land of rations, McCool and Ring were assuming proportions of aldermanic state because of lack of work. It was wrong of Bradman not to give either of them one single over in the first Yorkshire innings, and especially as the two Test bowlers Johnston (41 overs) and Toshack (40), were greatly overworked but this was one of the many instances we had on the tour of Bradman's disinclination to take the slightest risk of defeat.

From this aspect and the experiences of the last day, this was a disappointing match and in most ways unworthy of the £6,911 which the thousands of spectators paid in admission money. There was no reason why Bradman should have continued batting after lunch. Because of a very early finish to catch the train back to London for the Test, only two hours remained for play after lunch and Australia were then 297 runs ahead. At no time on that final day did the Australians give the impression that they would try and force a win, and the "Grinders" were not slow to give vent to their feelings when Yorkshire was left with an hour and a leeway of 328. The game developed into a farce in the final two hours when Yardley retaliated by bowling everybody and then giving his tail-enders promotion in the batting order. It was no wonder, perhaps, that this game at Bramall Lane should have ended on the note of hoots. The Yorkshire people are the last in the world to put up with any nonsense at cricket. It was a poor finish to what could easily have been the county game of the season.

The Australians did not hesitate, however, in disposing of Surrey in the return game at Kennington Oval after the second test, and here Bradman enjoyed a great triumph in his batting. In a speech at the Surrey dinner to his team, Bradman had hinted with a smile (referring to when he broke his ankle in the Test of 1938 and when Hutton took the world's record Test score from him) that the Oval owed him something, but when Bradman made 128 in this second Surrey game, which followed upon 146 in the first, the Surrey men might have thought of reminding him that it was against England, not Surrey, that he had his grudge at the Oval. This 128 was a lovely innings, with 15 fours in his hundred, made in 140 minutes. Hassett topped with a neat 139 and, like Bradman, he also made a gift of his wicket after the century.

The "Ground Staff" were singing their particular ditty with great gusto at this stage. They were feeling very much out of things, but the slow men were given long spells in this game. McCool bowled 48 overs, 117—6, and Ring 45, 102—4, so that this time they did not have much breath left for singing. Parker, who once played a season with the Gordon (Sydney) club, had a good game here with 81 and 76, and Fishlock again did well with 61 and 31. Errol Holmes, avenging his feelings on Toshack with three successive fours, had a bright 54, but it was now becoming the habit for Harvey to steal the thunder from everybody.

In the first game at the Oval and again in this, Harvey took several of the most sensational aerobatic catches ever seen on the ground. They sent everybody into ecstasies and he seemed to pluck one from the middle of a flock of pigeons. This was the day of the Wimbledon tennis final, in which the Australian, John Bromwich, played "Go-Slow" Falkenburg, and the Australians were keen to finish the game against Surrey so that they could see the tennis. "I'll get it over quickly for you, if you let me," said Harvey with youthful confidence to Bradman and the skipper gave him the chance. The 122 runs were made in just over the hour, Harvey making 73, and the Australians got to the tennis in plenty of time, thanks to Harvey.

This could have been a red-letter day in the monetary sense for the cricketers. Bradman received a telegram at the Oval from the connections of Bowral Boy, giving him the "good oil." With Bowral Boy's name came the names of two other horses—and all three won! Though some of the Australians liked their plunge, they were in such a hurry to get to the tennis that they let the good things go unsupported.

The train to Bristol that night was a sad affair with Bromwich losing the Wimbledon final after having it thrice in his pocket. Saddest of all was Ray Lindwall, a fellow club member of Bromwich's at home. Lindwall was utterly inconsolable. It is odd at times how upsets in other sports mean much more than a personal downfall to a champion himself.

I found Bristol most interesting. Not even London, I thought, had more character about it than this hilly city of churches and types, and not many English cities and towns are hilly. There was one Bristol lass, a bus conductress, who had more than her share of character. At the head of our Australian Press crowd, I timidly asked one morning whether her bus went to the cricket ground. She did not repeat herself for at least five minutes in an address to the world at large on the general stupidity of passengers who did not use their eyes. She had evidently been asked that question so often this morning that she decided the next questioner would, so to speak, stop something. And it had to be me! O'Reilly, in particular, was highly amused at my discomfiture, but we won her over and she actually apologised before we left the bus. Being an Australian can be very handy at times.

The preceding season, Gloucestershire had run Middlesex very close for the championship but, against the Australians,

Gloucester, the county of the Graces and Wally Hammond, looked poor stuff. It was strange how many counties lacked confidence against the Australians. On the first day, before a record crowd, Australia made 560—5, Morris making 290. This Bristol pitch had rather a reputation for favouring the bowlers so attempts were made in the off season to build it up, experts coming down from Bingley, in Yorkshire, to advise on the subject. They built it up well enough for the Australians as the huge scoring proceeded on the second day until Hassett closed at 774—7, this beating the previous best at Southend of 721. Harvey was still knocking at a Test door that could, advantageously and with justice, have been opened long before this. He had 95, Loxton handed in an extremely vigorous 159 unconquered, McCool had 76, one of his few batting successes of the tour, and Miller 51.

This Bristol ground is a very pleasant one. It is high, looking far out to the hills beyond, and there is gay but sad colour in the uniformed orphans who cram the walls along the side of the ground and their huge home. The crowd is tremendously keen and in three days there was the record attendance of 43,000. Tom Goddard is the local hero. Tom seems to be as much a Gloucester institution as Dr. W. G. Grace and there is always a hum when he takes up the ball. At 48 years of age, Goddard is still erectly tall and wiry. He is slow to slow-medium and is one of the fathers of that innumerable English breed of off-tweakers who deliver round the stumps. Tom runs seven paces, swinging out from behind the umpire in the last few yards. He wheels his arm in practice as he places the field and wipes his fingers on the ground to get grip of the ball. Every ball he bowls is greeted with some comment by the loquacious ones who sit behind his arm in the pavilion: "Good, Tom"—"Well bowled, Tom"— "Nice ball, Tom." You feel that Tom is very much one of the family.

The crowd laughed and the knowing ones said "Ah, Tom," as the veteran beat Barnes, but the next one Barnes square-cut with the speed of sound. I declare I have never seen any one to equal Barnes on the square-cut. He stands alone with possibly Dudley Nourse, of South Africa, next in line of succession. A back-cut a few moments later by Morris off Cook stood in my mind as the most artistic stroke of the whole year, but one barely had time this day to notice one particular stroke before it was crowded out by another.

The Gloucestershire bowling was amazingly weak. It looked so that day as Morris flayed it in all directions and we found it to be so again the next day when, in the Duke of Beaufort's team, we played the entire Gloucestershire team in a benefit game for Goddard and beat them by eight wickets in a single-innings game. I found that the years had made "Old Tom" pretty hard in the head. Wally Hammond was on our side (with O'Reilly, Wyatt, Captain Grace, a grand-nephew of Dr. Grace, who was a magnificent fieldsman, Reg Sinfield, Mailey, McGilvray and several others). Rain cut down play, and Goddard, when I had reached a quick half-century with some sixes, suggested I might make way for Hammond. I fully agreed. I said I had been trying to hit sixes or get out for the past ten minutes, but Tom seemed disinclined to keep the ball up. "You toss them up, Tom," I said, "and it will be either sixes or out." "No," said Tom, "you can easily walk down the pitch, miss one and be stumped." The years had made Tom a hard man. I compromised by walking out as Lyon caught a bump-ball.

Crapp and Emmett heard on this day, one of the most enjoyable we spent in England (tasting venison for the first time, meeting the Duke's charming wife, and feeling close to England and war with an inspiring memorial service), that they had been chosen for the third Test. The next day Crapp crept on his century from 91. It was a close call, as he made no attempt to push matters along as the tail crumbled. This was the third century against the Australians, the others being Hardstaff (for Notts) and Compton (in the first Test). Crapp looked very solid but neither he nor Emmett looked a worthy man to replace Len Hutton in the English team.

The county men made a poor fist of playing Ian Johnson, particularly, and Ring. The first took 100—11 and Ring 130—7. Goddard had 186—0. "Tom is not used to batsmen using their feet to him," said Maurice Tate as Morris and Harvey indulged in a spate of fours. "The county batsmen diddle and diddle to him and that gets him many wickets."

One day in a Bristol street we met a small lad who told me, most politely, that he came from an infirmary (as a school is called in some English quarters). He was dressed in a long, flowing black robe like a monk with a little white necklet of a barrister. He wore black socks with yellow tops, like football socks, and he wore buckled shoes. He was the most colourful schoolboy I have seen, but then Bristol was full of colour from the bus conductress to the inspiring Severn gorge, from the nails (on which money, in the old days, was paid down to clinch a business deal; but the nails are not what they sound but are, indeed, more like a drinking fountain as they stand in the street) down to the grim war relic which now stands, jaggedly, in the grounds of St. Mary Redcliffe ("The fairest, goodliest and most famous Parish Church in all England."—Queen Elizabeth). This relic is part of a tramway line which was flung by a bomb over tall houses to land and embed itself in the lawn of the church. But possibly we met nobody more colourful in Bristol than our good hosts, the Harveys, and that bubbling character, the night porter, as round and as jovial as Falstaff himself, who said to his companion as they struggled with a big case one night, "Thee coosen't canteen oop bit, coost?" That means, in English, "You couldn't cant it up a bit, could you?" For good measure, before we left Bristol, we had a private inspection of the huge Brabazon, the giant plane, then nearing completion.

The champion county, Middlesex, fared no better than the runners-up against the Australians. Bradman fell again to the leg-trap, Compton catching him off Whitcombe, the Oxford bowler, this time for six, and Morris and Loxton made a century apiece. This meant Morris had made 504, with his Test 51 and 54 not out, in just over the week. He was at the very peak of his form and was destined to follow his score against Middlesex with 6 and 182 at Leeds in the fourth Test. Compton had 62 here and laconic, rolling Jim Sims, who went to Australia in 1936-37 and always enters a cricket field as if he's just come from a long sea voyage, had 65—6 off 24 overs, one of the best pieces of bowling the Australians met in the whole tour. But as Middlesex scored only 203 and 135 (Dewes 51), Australia was not hard pushed to win by ten wickets. This was the innings that forced Dewes into favour for the final Test but he didn't quite look that class in this Lord's game.

It was a somewhat elderly insurance manager named Gothard, grey-haired and bespectacled, who clean bowled Bradman for 62 at Derby. The county was leading in the championship when the game was played against the Australians, and what added interest to Gothard's feat was that all the rest of the season he had taken only five wickets at 38 apiece. Probably Gothard's best piece of work, considering his avocation in life, was to remove the fieldsman from short-leg when Miller came to bat. Bradman was out in playing his favourite pull stroke but the ball kept low on him.

Both Barnes and Bradman showed up Brown's rate of scoring. Brown by this had lost his Test place and he seemed eager to regain it with big scores, irrespective of the time factor. He took three hours and five minutes to make 50 and, by this time, hadn't a friend left on the ground. "Simmo," who sold the souvenir booklets, said sales had dropped to a minimum. "We'll not buy book if photo of yon so-and-so is in it," said the spectators sourly to Simmons, and he didn't go on the rounds again until Brown smartened and made his second 50 in 37 minutes. Brown is a lovely stroke-player when in the mood but his concentration on defence for long periods set us all to write letters home in the knowledge that things wouldn't be happening for some time.

George Pope looked on here and didn't play because of some foot trouble though he played in the match before and the match after the Australian one. It seemed as if George was being artful. From the Derbyshire point of view, Gladwin's bowling was good. He is a medium-pacer who runs the ball away as well as in, and I liked also the look of Jackson, a medium-pacer who spends his time between the cricket field and a colliery. Rhodes, a leg-breaker, looked also a bowler of class, and as Denis Smith made 88, the highest Derbyshire score ever against the Australians, the county reaped reward other than the financial ones from the big gates. They had a good keeper, too, in Dawkes.

Rain, unfortunately, ruined the Glamorgan game after Glamorgan had made 197 and Australia had replied with 215—3. This was a pity because the game in Wales, the only one in that country, drew record crowds who swarmed past the dull placards outside the ground of "No play guaranteed"—"No money refunded"—"No pass-out tickets issued"—No this and no that. This was one of the many grounds during the tour which gave me the impression that spectators were not sought but were suffered, being provided with the minimum of consideration and comfort.

Clift looked a batsman of promise at Swansea and Watkins set about the bouncers with gusto. This Welsh team, ultimately to become champions for the first time in cricketing history, looked the part in the field, and it was generally conceded that in attack and in holding the catches, rather than in possessing any outstanding batsmen, had this Welsh team won its way to the top. When we played in Swansea ten years ago, J. C. Clay,

English selector, said he thought he was too old to play in such a game and stood down. He must have had some gland treatment because he played in this game and bowled very well until Harvey attacked him. If we exclude the Irishman, Boucher, who took 18 wickets at an average of 8, Clay headed the English bowling with 41 wickets at 14, and the ones he took were at a vital time in the championship. This was a remarkable feat for an off-tweaker (as usual, round the wickets) who was in his 51st year and had played in Glamorgan's second county game in 1921.

It was at Bournemouth that Glamorgan clinched the championship with an innings victory over Hampshire and, fittingly, a Welsh umpire, Dai Davies, gave the last Hants batsman out. Some there told me the decision *might* have been tinged with the flavour of that decision by the country umpire, who answered a l.b.w. appeal with "He's out and we've won, hooray," but Dai and the Glamorgan team were in no mood then to put up with any nonsense as victory was assured and was greeted in traditional Welsh fashion with song and celebration. There was stump-seizing on the Test match model and, wrote Brian Chapman, people tut-tutted when the loud-speaker requested: "Will the groundsman please collect the stumps and the ball." This victory, wrote Chapman, might have been more fitting at Cardiff or Swansea, where leeks could have been tied to the stumps and spectators shinned up the scoring-board,[1] but at all events, the Welsh sang "Sospan Fach" all the way home.

The Welsh were very disappointed when Bradman did not play or come to Swansea. It was pointed out that he couldn't play in all matches and that he had to consider himself and his team, but the Welsh would have none of that. "We are different. We are a country and he should have played here, or, at least, visited us," they claimed. But one can always side-track the Welsh by talking Rugby. On the walls of the pavilion are photos of Welsh teams who won here and there. "Has no Welsh team ever been beaten?" I facetiously asked a Glamorganite, "or don't you photograph your losing teams?" But they are good sports, the Welsh. They are full of spirit and love to meet overseas sportsmen.

Out from Swansea is Port Eynon, where one drinks ale with the villagers in their 350-year-old inn, the whole constructed of

[1]This is the traditional Welsh happening at a Rugby international when spectators shin up the goal-posts and tie leeks to the top for luck. 'Sospan Fach' had its origin when Llanelly beat the Australian Rugby team.

timber from wrecked ships and having, in its inside, the enveloping atmosphere of an old sailing ship with its heavily-timbered roof, its ship clocks, green and red lights and all the odds and ends of ship life. They say, of the old Port Eynon folk, that they used to tie lamps to the tails of their grazing cows in order to bring about a shipwreck. If you tell the modern generation this, they will point to the framed prayer on the wall of the nearby village: "Lord, on this night of tempest and storm, remember and protect the poor sailors on the sea and guide their ships to a safe haven—but, Lord, if, in Thy infinite wisdom, it doth please Thee to wreck a ship, wreck her in the Parish of Rhossilli and not among the sinners in the Parish of Port Eynon farther down the Coast.—Amen." At least, say the Port Eynon folk, their predecessors were honest about their wrecks!

At Swansea happened the most amazing batting feat I had ever seen. Keith Miller hit a six with one hand. It happened like this. Watkins, medium and left-hander, bowled a ball wide on the leg. Miller put his left foot up the pitch and then, with his left hand, played what would have been a left-handed back-hand shot at tennis. The ball flew fine and into the crowd. This was positively an unbelievable stroke. Someone told me that Miller had once played a similar stroke in Australia but he cannot remember it though he thinks he did do it to somebody or other. That is typical of Miller, not being able to remember such a happening.

Miller gave the Glamorgan people thrills galore. He opened fire on the Glamorgan skipper, Wilf Wooller, and hit him off successive balls for six over the sight-board and then six over long-off. Miller had 42 of his 50 runs in boundaries and was out at 84 when going for another six, this time off Clay. By the lunge he made, it seemed that Keith wanted to hit Clay back into England.

With Hassett in charge, O'Reilly and I were invited to accompany the team in its coach to Birmingham. This would not have happened with Bradman. It is a wise ruling that the Press should not travel with the team nor, in ordinary circumstances, does the Press want to travel with the cricketers, but those who have pulled their weight in other Test series and tours of England sometimes have hard thoughts as they see a huge and roomy coach go by on a direct route while they are trudging off, carting luggage, on a train journey with several changes. One expects and receives an occasional gesture from Hassett, and Keith

Johnston, as manager, made us welcome and had us to afternoon tea at historic Hereford. It was quite like old times as we joined in the team songs. It was a touch of kindness that we greatly appreciated—and, as far as I could see, contaminated no one.

Strange as it may seem, a touring cricketer does not see much of England's beauty. The games are played where the crowds are biggest, and so the cricketing round is usually from one drab industrial town to another, so that a coach trip up the Welsh hills and into this lovely town of Hereford was doubly enjoyable. The speed-cops pulled the coach up once but promptly tore the ticket up when they recognised the team. They took autographs instead. They knew how to entertain in Hereford in the old days. Parties (for men only) given by the Duke of Norfolk would begin at 3 p.m. and continue on to midnight. After dinner, port wine was introduced (three bottles to each person) and, in time, one member after another of the party would disappear under the table, where a boy had been stationed to loosen their neckcloths and place in a comfortable position each citizen in turn. I shall never forget, on that run up through Wales.

Birmingham's game against Warwickshire was a triumph for Eric Hollies, a blonde slow bowler whose every movement in the field is greeted with the most amazing roars of appreciation by the young brigade. These teen-agers had given the county committee much trouble in the games before the Australians. There were times when they had almost taken charge of the game and much damage had been done to the ground's property. The result was that war was declared against the youths for the Australian game. They were told they had to behave themselves —or else! As usual, thousands queued before the game began, but no youths were to be allowed into the ground unless accompanied by a parent. It was amazing the number of "adoptions" there were that morning in the streets outside the Edgbaston ground but, generally, the youths behaved themselves well during the Australian game—though grim authority could not stop them paying noisy tribute to Hollies every time he moved or even appeared on the field. When he bowled Bradman, I thought the ground would explode. Not even Bradman has known such youthful adulation.

Hollies is a good bowler. That must be said at once. The Edgbaston pitch did not look a good one but Hollies was later to show at the Oval that he would have bowled well against the Australians on any pitch. Again, as he rolled over eight of the

Australians, were there sighs that a man like him had not been present at Leeds. That Leeds Test will be fought over and over again for years to come. Hollies has perfect control. He has nice flight, gives the ball plenty of air yet, withal, is not too slow through the air. He bowls an excellent bosie and I was interested to see him bowl around the stumps to Arthur Morris. Most slow bowlers dislike bowling to left-handers, but Hollies bowled exceedingly well to Morris.

The Australians told me that Hollies does not spin the ball very much but, indeed, bowls many top-spinners. It was one of these which clean bowled Bradman when he was 31 at Birmingham and the huge crowd became delirious at this pronounced success by "Our Eric," as Hollies is known throughout the county. Bradman played what seemed a somewhat careless stroke and played outside the ball. Hassett batted best for the Australians here with a neat 68, but it was the failure of Warwickshire's batting that twice let the county down. The county men could not cope with Lindwall, Johnston, Johnson and Loxton in the first innings, nor Colin McCool or Johnston in the second. This was rather a happier game for McCool. At first slip, he took, perhaps, the outstanding slip-catch of the tour and his bowling was really good in the second innings.

Another word about Hollies. He is 37 years of age and his father was the last lob-bowler in Birmingham League cricket. The Hollies come from Old Hill, in the Black part of England, so-called. The mind of young Hollies, after his first game against the talkative Yorkshiremen, must have been worth probing. From the quiet complacency of Old Hill, he wondered what he had struck. "I heard words," he said, "I had never heard in Old Hill." In 1946 he took all ten Notts wickets—seven bowled and three leg before, which is surely a novel way of taking all ten wickets. He dislikes Test cricket. He was chosen for M.C.C. in 1935 but ricked his neck and did not play in a Test until 1946. He didn't think much of it as he had to play second string to Doug. Wright. When he was chosen in 1948 for the Oval Test, Hollies wanted to withdraw, but the county committee persuaded him to play.

Two New Zealanders in Donnelly and Pritchard and an Indian in Kardar played for Warwickshire. Donnelly could not strike the form of the previous season, when his century for Gents against the Players was the talk of the country, nor could Pritchard, a wag of a fellow, strike form against the Australians.

Pritchard had a grand year in county games. His 172 wickets (at 18.75) was next best to the Australian, Jack Walsh (174 at 19.56) in the county championship, but Pritchard took 35—0 off 16 overs against the Australians. He is not fast as Miller and Lindwall are fast, but he cuts the ball nicely and has good control. Kardar almost dismissed Bradman with his first ball, and then Bradman, with his old tigerishness, decided to "do" for Kardar. He hit him for three successive fours and Kardar wilted, changing his field. It was a very quick Bradman victory but, at least, it gave Kardar a taste of what Mankad and Co. had known from Bradman in Australia a few months before.

Though Ikin and Roberts had splendid individual successes, Lancashire again failed to put up a true Lancastrian performance in the return game at Old Trafford, a game which the county gave to Washbrook for his benefit. Hilton did not play and so there could be no further Bradman duel with him, but Roberts, we thought, bowled well enough to gain a Test place in the final game at the Oval. But evidently Roberts had left his run too late because Young was preferred.

This pitch was a green-top and caused the Australians many anxious moments on the first day but, strangely, Roberts was not tried until sixth change and immediately met with success. At one stage he had bowled 24 overs for 24—4, and that included Bradman's wicket with two lives to Bradman not showing in his figures. How odd to have Bradman's wicket virtually three times in an innings! Roberts is a true left-handed type. He comes from round the stumps but flights the ball better than most English left-handers. He is a superb fieldsman to his bowling, and once caught Ronnie Hamence and had the ball pocketed before the batsman was quite aware he was out. Ikin, too, bowled splendidly. He bowled 39 overs for 80—1 and Roberts finished with 42—14—73—6. It should have won him a Test place, but the English selectors do not jump to things as quickly as their Australian counterparts.

Bradman said good-bye to Old Trafford with a century but it was not one of his best. I deal with it, mostly, in another place so will not discuss it here other than to say that in making it he batted on so long that, as at Yorkshire, he left his bowlers little time in which to achieve victory. Ikin played gloriously for 99. He fell to the new ball which Bradman took with only six minutes left for play. Washbrook had his thumb split here and could not play in the fifth Test, but he had the advantage of a bumper benefit. Cyril seemed to spend as much time off the field as on in making thanking speeches over the amplifier.

For the remaining games, the Australians never once stood in fear of defeat. Kent, for such a county, put up a hopelessly inefficient display of batting and was out twice within a day for 51 and 124, Pawson and Evans putting some delayed sparkle and spirit into the proceedings. Somerset suffered much the same fate, falling for 115 and 71, but the Gentlemen, with Simpson making a splendid 60 in the first innings, and Edrich a grand 128 in the second, did much better at Lord's with 245 and 284 against Australia's 610—5 (Hassett 200 not out, Bradman 150, Brown 120 and Miller 69).

In another place I deal with Bradman's last match and innings at Lord's but, hereabouts, two older members of the eleven, Brown and Hassett, were dominating the scoring. Hassett had a grand eight days. He put his nose to the pitch at Lord's in his farewell appearance and followed his double century here with 103 the next innings at Taunton and 151 at Hastings. That soared Hassett up the aggregate list. Brown's century at Canterbury (where, incidentally, we once met the very colourful Dean of Canterbury in an early-morning stroll) had made him many critics. It was a most laborious affair. He saw Morris, Bradman and Harvey come and go with the sparkle and dash of tail-end innings, but Brown refused to relax for a moment—or to attack. He wanted a century and he got it to the tune of ironic clapping. He began at 11.30; it was 4.45 when he reached his objective. I thought at the time, considering that it was his last trip, that William Alfred would have left a better impression in Canterbury had he gone down the town instead and had a few beers with the locals, but nobody could quibble about Brown's final century in the next game against the Gentlemen at Lord's. It was a superlative effort and, in brilliancy, Brown far outshone Bradman while the two were batting together. Brown has always looked the class batsman that he is when playing at Lord's, and this superb century, so different in conception and execution to the one at Canterbury, made one reflect what a grand opening batsman this series of Tests had done without. What a gain he would have been to England!

Harvey had a glorious century, also, against Somerset in the final county game of the season and everybody was sorry, here, to see Ron Hamence miss his first century in England by one run. Hamence is a very bright tourist. There was criticism of his selection in this side, but had the war not intervened he undoubt-edly would have made a trip before to the Home Country. Hamence received very few chances on this tour and, even when played in the side, invariably had to come in after the better-known names, but he played some fine innings, nevertheless. He twice missed a century—at Taunton and again at Cambridge, where he made 92.

There was practically no competitive flavour about the two Festival games, the one at Hastings and the other at Scarborough. Bradman was "toey" in both these games. He kept his team right up to the mark to avoid defeat, but this never looked likely in either game and there was, too, the insistence by the Australians that the game at Scarborough should reflect its nature and not be a post-Test Test. The Australians insisted that only a certain number of Test men should play in this game and they had their way. And so the curtain was rung down on the first-class deeds of the only unbeaten Australian team ever to tour England.

CHAPTER SIXTEEN

RECORDS, RUNS AND BRADMAN

ON the sunny afternoon of 10th September, 1948, Don Bradman was dismissed for the last time on English soil in a first-class match. Indulging in a hectic splurge of boundaries and running his score to 153, thus topping Barnes' 151 for the highest score in the match, Bradman singled out Bedser for his wicket and hit a ball high into the covers. By fate, it was Len Hutton, who, ten years before at the Kennington Oval, had taken the record score for the Test series from Bradman, who stood underneath the catch, but whilst the ball was yet soaring, Bradman turned, took off his cap and ran full pelt for the pavilion.

By the time that Hutton's two safe hands had closed on the ball, Bradman was half-way to the pavilion. He did not turn to see whether the catch had been taken. He continued running, gloves, cap and bat fluttering from his hands, and almost before this huge Yorkshire crowd at the Scarborough Festival had had time to warm its hands in appreciation to him, Bradman was lost to view for ever as a first-class batsman on an English ground. It was the end of his 120th innings in England. He had scored the last run of his mammoth total in four tours of 9,837 runs; the statisticians were already discovering that he had averaged 96 runs per innings.

This was a most significant moment in cricketing history. Devotees of a game in a country in which many of its most illustrious players had continued long after 40 years of age, could not credit that one so brilliant and so chockful of runs could possibly think of retirement when still lord and master of the cricketing domain. But the grim, purposeful Bradman had stated, before leaving Australia in March, that this would definitely be his last tour of England, no matter what happened. Not for him a repetition of the closing career of another illustrious Australian, Dame Nellie Melba, whose indefinite "definite farewell appearance" became the joking butt of the country.

"Never," said Sir Norman Birkett, at a London dinner in

April, after Bradman, in a speech, had reiterated his intention to make this his final tour, "never have I heard more tragic words fall from the lips of any man—but there is given to all men a chance to repent and, maybe, Bradman will yet repent words and an intention that seem intolerable to us."

But those of us who knew Bradman, knew full well at Scarborough that September day that we were watching him leave an English field as a batsman for the last time. It was, as I have written, a most significant moment in cricketing history. We had seen the thousands gather in front of the blitz-scarred Kennington Oval pavilion and applaud him most generously when he appeared and spoke to them at the end of his last Test match against England. Exactly a week later, he came, after hundreds had whistled and cheered and called for him, on to the pavilion balcony at Lord's and waved to the crowd below. This was at the finish of the game against the Gentlemen of England and everybody knew then that Lord's was seeing Bradman for the last time. A few minutes before he had fled from the field at the head of his Australian team as the match finished in yet another hollow victory. Bradman invariably fled from an English ground where, unlike the Australian grounds, there are no pickets to keep out the invading throng, and the invaders, as one, always made straight for Bradman at the game's finish.

He was burning, in this summer of 1948, his English pavilions behind him. On all famous grounds, as he made his farewell appearance, he was clapped to the centre as he walked slowly— always, all his cricketing lifetime, had he walked slowly to the middle as a batsman—but, at the finish of the game, a quick sprint took him soon from view. At Leeds, the most famous of all his happy hunting grounds, there was that lovely but practically unnoticed gesture of the English man-in-the-street to Bradman as a very old and very squat Yorkshireman stood clapping, gnarled pipe in mouth and the most intent look and smile of appreciation on his face, as Bradman sprinted past him to the dressing-room. "Ah," said the aged Yorkshireman, forgiving in a trice all the humiliation which Bradman had showered on his bowling heroes, "you ——!" In Australia you may call a man such a name and it is a compliment when you say it with a smile. At Leeds, this day, this simple old Yorkshireman epitomised what the English cricketing public thought of Bradman over the years. The smile; the clap; the all-embracing look of intense pleasure which the retreating form had given him and, finally, the complimentary epitaph which spoke so well the thought that Bradman had been just too good—too good for every country and everybody if we except the turbulent period of bodyline when the most vicious form of attack known to the game was devised to curb the greatest batting automaton the game of cricket had produced.

Scarborough was the end of all this. Scarborough was the end of what Sir Pelham Warner has aptly termed in another place in this book "the Bradman era." English cricket was free, at long last, of the Bradman plague, the Bradman scourge, the Bradman blight, call it what you will. On this lovely September afternoon, the cricket world far removed from that outside world of trouble and limitless and abortive peace talks, Bradman yielded up his batting ghost for the last time to English cricket, and his remark on returning to the pavilion, made in all good humour, was typical of the man.

On his entry, a sleepy Hassett stretched on a form.

"Ahhuum," yawned Hassett, "what happened? Did you chuck it away?"

"Well," said Bradman, with a wide smile, "I worked it out that to average a hundred for every innings I have had in England, I would have had to make about 500 not out—and this game, as you know, *is* limited to three days."

A few days later, at Balmoral, in Scotland, the Australian cricketers were entertained by their Majesties, the King and Queen.

"Tell me, Mr. Ferguson," said the King, with a twinkle, to "Fergie," the official Australian scorer, "do you use an adding machine when the Don comes to bat?"

"Fergie" laughed and was stumped for an appropriate answer but he knew that, over the years, the King's suggestion would have been a good one. "Fergie" is a wizard scorer. He has a system all his own. He not only notes the bare details but he keeps diagrams which show, at a glance, where the batsman's runs have flowed and off which particular bowler; and, for good measure, he sketches on his sheet during the game a view he might have of steeples or trees or nearby houses. His scoring sheets, therefore, are things of rare attraction but, over the 20 years he scored during the Cricket King's Reign, "Fergie" had no time for extraneous sketches. The Don kept him too busy for that and often, too, "Fergie" had seen scoring-boards go haywire in trying to keep up with Bradman's phenomenal flow of runs. It might be here that the scoring-board had not sufficient numerals in the hundreds to register after the second or third one; it might be there that the total got out of hand whilst a demented scoring attendant on the board tried to do justice by Bradman's and the side's totals at the same time. For never in the history of the game, Grace, Trumper, Hobbs and all the others notwithstanding, had the game known a batsman to approach Bradman's profligacy in the scoring of runs.

Here, in barest figures, are the details of Bradman's phenomenal career:—

RECORD IN DETAILS

	Matches	Innings	No. out	Runs	Highest Score	Average
1927-8	5	10	1	416	134*	46.22
1928-9	13	24	6	1690	340*	93.88
1929-30	11	16	2	1586	452*	113.28
1930 (in Eng.) ..	27	36	6	2960	334	98.66
1930-1	12	18	0	1422	258	79.00
1931-2	10	13	1	1403	229*	116.91
1932-3	11	21	2	1171	238	61.63
1933-4	7	11	2	1192	253	132.44
1934 (in Eng.) ..	22	27	3	2020	304	84.16
1935-6	8	9	0	1173	369	130.33
1936-7	12	19	1	1552	270	86.33
1937-8	12	18	2	1437	246	89.65
1938 (in Eng.) ..	20	26	5	2429	278	115.66
1938-39	7	7	1	919	225	153.16
1939-40	9	15	3	1475	267	122.91
1940-1	2	4	0	18	12	4.50
1945-6	2	3	1	232	112	116.00
1946-7	9	14	1	1032	234	79.38
1947-8	8	11	2	1181	201	131.22
1948 (in Eng.) ..	23	31	4	2428	187	89.92

TEST MATCH FIGURES

	Matches	Innings	No. out	Runs	Highest Score	Average
v. England	37	63	7	5028	334	89.78
v. South Africa ..	5	5	1	806	299*	201.50
v. West Indies ..	5	6	0	447	223	74.50
v. India	5	6	2	715	201	178.75

* Not out

Those figures reveal much but not everything. They do not

tell, for instance, that Bradman took to himself almost every record worth the taking in first-class cricket; they do not tell, as Sir Pelham Warner points out, that Bradman made a century, on an average, once in every three visits to the wickets (not counting the times—and they were many—when he made two or three hundred); but more, perhaps, than any other great batsman in the game, figures do Bradman justice. They show his complete mastery during the time he played the game; they show, with the exception of those four innings in 1940-41, when war crowded everything else off the stage, his uncanny consistency.

People will tell you that figures do not do justice to the superlative art that was Trumper's. Macartney was another whose skill was not revealed by figures, and the same, in my time, applied to McCabe. But as long as cricket lives, figures *will* tell the revealing story of Bradman. They will not tell, perhaps, of the murderous upsurge which happened whenever a ball was pitched short and Bradman fell into his very individual pull shot, but they will tell for all time how Bradman made runs and how he went on and on making runs.

In his pen picture of Bradman, in another chapter, Major Vincent, of *The Times*, tells how many people found themselves with a desire to go and have a beer after watching Bradman bat for some time. That was true but it applied more to Bradman in the post-bodyline period than before the days when Jardine and Larwood, the decision having been made that his batting technique was above them, decided to probe him on the physical side. Bodyline *did* leave its imprint on Bradman—as it did on all other Australian class batsmen who struck its full fire. Seldom, if ever, afterwards did Bradman's batting have the same jaunty air, if one may so term it, which distinguished his batting in 1929, 1930 (in England) and 1930-31 and 1931-32 in Australia. The bodyline sear was still there in 1934 in England when he experienced the only known run of outs in his whole first-class career.

Nothing I have experienced or read since has influenced me to alter, in the slightest, the bodyline story which I told in *Cricket Crisis*, and that historic happening in cricket was unimpeachably because of Bradman's influence and dominance in cricket. Bodyline was specially prepared, nurtured for and expended on him and, in consequence, his technique underwent a change quicker than might have been the case with the passage of time. Bodyline plucked something vibrant from his art.

It so happened, too, that soon after the bodyline period, Bradman became the Australian captain. This has to be considered in the general picture of Bradman's change of technique because it can be accepted that Bradman the batsman often became subservient to Bradman the captain. This was so, particularly, in the Australian season of 1936-37 when he had an uphill captaincy fight after Australia had lost the first two matches of the rubber. I batted almost the whole of one Test day with him in Melbourne when he refused to take the slightest risk because of the state of the game, and he did that again, often, in the series of 1938 (in England), 1946-47 (Australia) and, finally, this last season of 1948 in England.

Yardley quietened him for over after over in the first Test at Nottingham with leg-theory. The 1930 Bradman would have thrived on such stuff; nor would the 1930 Bradman have adopted the 1948 technique of pushing his pads at the ball in negative answer to Bedser's threat of the fine-leg trap.

This, of a certainty, is not a criticism of Bradman. It is but another way of asserting that (a) nobody would have gone for a glass of beer while Bradman was batting in 1930 and (b) how successfully he changed his run-getting technique to suit requirements and the passage of years.

There were, I think, three periods of the Bradman era. One was pre-bodyline; the other was from then to the beginning of the world war, and the final was from 1945 to the end of 1948. In his first post-war game against England (for South Australia in Adelaide) Bradman found that his mind was moving quicker than his legs. He accommodated his technique to that, but in all periods of his era, though his technique changed considerably, Bradman retained to the last the most remarkable appetite for runs that the game of cricket has surely ever known.

As at Scarborough in his last innings, Bradman threw his wicket away on a number of occasions in England in 1948, but never until he had reached his objective, and Bradman, in all his career, never began an innings in any game without an objective. As I read his mind, he had two objectives before this 1948 tour started. One was to lead an unbeaten team through England (which had never happened before) and the other was to be cock of the batting walk until the very last. And he achieved both. No side beat this twentieth Australian Eleven, and Bradman, with 2,428 runs, was well ahead of the next batsman, Morris (1,922), though Morris and Barnes beat him in the Test averages.

I retain one vivid picture of Bradman's insatiable appetite for
runs. It was late in the tour at Manchester and on the final day,
when Bradman's decision to bat on denied the game any reasonable chance of a decision. All competitive interest had long since
flown the game. Bradman had left his mark on it and Old
Trafford by making a century, but in the 120's he scuttled as
hard to run a three as a tyro would in running a three to make
his first century in any type of a game. That was typical of
Bradman. He never tired of making runs, even in his fortieth
year. There was one previous occasion in this game when Bradman might have had a quick two, but the inimitable Sydney
Barnes had his own ideas about the sharing of the strike. As
Bradman turned for the two, Barnes had his broad back turned
at the other end. It was a clear case of disagreement and, from
the outside, it was apparent that Bradman rebuked Barnes down
the length of the pitch.

Barnes, not easily rebuked, motioned to Bradman and made
as if to walk out while the Lancashire men enjoyed the general
situation. It transpired that Barnes said to Bradman: "Here,
you come and have it all. I'll have none."

Bradman planned everything and, in his long career, I saw
his complacency only twice rattled. Once was during the bodyline days and the other whenever a "sticky" pitch happened
along. Sir Pelham Warner writes of when Bradman scored a
masterly 71 on a bad Sydney pitch in 1932. To be true, that was
a lovely innings, but there was no fast English bowler playing
that day, and for each of the few times Bradman succeeded on a
bad pitch one could name half a dozen times when he failed. It
was reputed of Dr. Grace ("Strange to say, champion and all as
W.G. was, he was not in any way a wonder on a sticky pitch"—
Jack Worrell) that he had his limitations when the pitch was not
good, and Bradman, though possessed of all the fundamentals
to succeed, certainly had his. Bradman's limitations on a bad
pitch were, I think, largely psychological. His whole demeanour
changed on a sticky pitch and the psychologist had something
to work on at Old Trafford on the final day of the third Test
when Bradman, after every ball, walked down the pitch and
energetically patted it, whereas, at the other end, Morris barely
worried about it. This pitch was not bad. Something has happened to English pitches so that nowadays one rarely gets a bad
one, and the turf certainly did not lift at Old Trafford this day.
It was a sodden pitch, but Bradman's exaggerated patting of it

was as if to suggest that it was a nasty business. Not a single ball flew.

That was one side to Bradman's batting nature and, to the student and historian, an interesting one, but, on good pitches, none will deny that this most amazing cricketer was the *greatest* personality the game has ever known. Much has been said and written of the "jealousy" of those who played with and against Bradman, but those best qualified to speak are those who played with him, and I have never met a single first-class cricketer of Bradman's age who was not ever ready, indeed eager, to declare that the game of cricket had never known his like before. He had his critics, and will always have, I suppose, for his somewhat indifferent, cold and unfriendly attitude towards most of those with whom he played, but not one, I repeat, has ever denied the greatness which rightly belongs to Bradman. On good pitches, he stood in a class of his own as a scoring machine; and, more-over, the game has never known one to approach, yes, even approach, his miraculous consistency. When you boiled Bradman down, when you analysed his eyesight, his footwork, his judg-ment, his range of strokes, there was still something left in which he was also superior to all others, and that was consistency.

What was the secret of Bradman's consistency? That is a subject which will be always fresh as long as cricket is played, but I am inclined to think that the answer is to be found not so much in anything physical as in the mind. With the exception of those two perturbing instances I have mentioned, Bradman's mind was always cool, calm and analytical and, in its sphere, was as great a taskmaster of the body as man could possess. His mind gave his body no rest. His mind called the tune and his body, gifted as it was in peerless footwork, eyesight, judgment and a perfect dynamo of ceaseless energy, danced to it. The only times the dance became agitated were against bodyline and on sticky pitches.

One does well to try and analyse Bradman's mind because, in all cricket, I met no other like it. He was the only cricketer I knew who never tired of the game, who never became bored by it, who never became stale—or, if his body did, his mind would not allow it to be so.

Trumper, it was said, looked about for some deserving fellow after he had made a century and, unobtrusively, allowed him his wicket. It was said, further, that some English professional down on his luck often found himself back in the good books with

Trumper's wicket against his name. A batsman like McCabe, after a run of good scores, would find himself bored and allow himself to become careless, but Bradman never allowed himself to relax or relent until his objective had been achieved. After a good day, the average cricketer, feeling at peace with the world, would seek out his comrades for a yarn and a little jollification in the evening, but Bradman either denied himself or did not want such mundane pleasures. He was not to be found.

Bradman's ways were not those of the ordinary cricketer. In the 1930 days of youthful rectitude, he made a very strong public statement against strong drink. Somewhat unkindly, impassioned zealots blazoned that statement out from notice-boards wherever Bradman went in England in 1948. He had changed somewhat in that direction but he had not changed in his general mixing. Down the Suez Canal, in October of 1948, a hot and dusty R.A.F. lad bawled across the canal to the ship on which Bradman and his men were travelling: "Hey, there, where are those Ashes? We'll get them from you next time, Don." A day later came a lovely wireless message from Aden, arid, barren, rocky, sizzling Aden of all places, and in its message of greetings to Bradman and his men it concluded with a challenge to play the cricket-weary Aussies at cricket. It was from the R.A.F. there, the R.A.F. in one of the grimmest outposts in the whole world, and the day the *Orontes* arrived at Aden an R.A.F. launch bobbed up and down, officers in cummerbunds and white mess jackets, waiting to take the cricketers off and entertain them.

Almost as one, but without Bradman, the Australians tumbled into the launch. Late at night they returned to the ship, singing "Waltzing Matilda" and good cobbers for life with the men of the R.A.F. They had had a champion time. A few minutes after entering the Mess, the C.O. dropped all formality by doffing his black tie and cummerbund. "They were such good fellows," said one of the team, "that, bless me, if we had stayed another day in Aden, we jolly well *would* have played them a game of cricket."

It was a warm thought that the game of cricket should have its ties in such outlandish places and, thinking of the desolate lives the R.A.F. must endure there, of what the British Empire owes to such men and how they worshipped and venerated him, it might be thought that Bradman, for once, would have yielded and gone to give, and have, pleasure. But here again was an instance of that mind which would not allow him to depart from a set course.

Do these interludes reveal anything of Bradman and his attitude towards cricket? I think they do because they show his mind and how he would never allow it to relax. Probably he reasoned that if he relaxed, if he became, mixed and lived like one of the ordinary cricketers, his concentration would be spoilt. You gathered that same concentration in conversation with him. There was the long pause, the slow, studied and concise reply.

In another chapter, Charles Bray criticises Bradman for his dealings with the Press, and it is true that his connections there were not always happy ones. He not only resented criticism but made the bad mistake of regarding it as personal. Of course, over the years, he had been worried often by the Press—what prominent figure hasn't?—but, like others, Bradman owed much in life to the publicity he, and cricket, had received from news-papers. Then, too, he had worked for some time on a newspaper, so that he should have had tolerance for working pressmen.

The gossip-writer of the Manchester *Evening News*, an esteemed member of his profession throughout Lancashire, wrote this of an experience with Bradman: " After five embarrassing minutes in his company I am compelled to the opinion that while Mr. Bradman may be the greatest cricketer in the world he is hardly one of the most tactful. While the foyer of the Midland Hotel swarmed with cricketers old and young, and small boys with autograph books waited patiently, the great Bradman, like Achilles of old, remained in his hotel room.

" For half an hour, receptionists and page-boys tried to locate him. I was then given a message that Mr. Bradman would be down in a few minutes, but he declined to be interviewed on the subject of where Barnes stood in relation to the bat in the match against the M.C.C.

" When he arrived I introduced myself and made it quite clear at once that I was only interested in him as a distinguished visitor. His replies to my two perfectly simple questions—was he well and how did he like being back at Old Trafford and Manchester—were completely offhand and, after rebuffing me, he stalked out and drove away, ignoring also the worshipping small boys."

Pressmen, as Bray has indicated, have not found Bradman an easy subject to interview. They, for their part, accustomed as they are in their profession to dealing with much more serious and telling things in life than cricket and cricketers, generally

resented him as much as he visibly resented them. He did not
have the facility to deal with pressmen. As I say, he resented
criticism and regarded it as personal. He could have learnt much
from the lovely blend of humour and understanding which the
Australian Prime Minister, the Right Hon. J. B. Chifley, and the
Leader of the Opposition, the Right Hon. R. G. Menzies, show at
their 'Xmas Press parties in Canberra when they forgive all with
their "Now come and have a drink with me, you chaps. I know
sometimes you have to write stuff about me that you may not
want to write. I know you've got a job to do, the same as me."

As the *Orontes* steamed into Adelaide Outer Harbour, pressmen seeking Bradman found this notice scribbled on his cabin
door: "Abandon hope all ye who enter here." It was Arthur
Mailey's way of waggishly stating the obvious.

These little facets of Bradman's character have to be written
and understood so that we can interpret the mind which he
brought to the game of cricket—a mind the game of cricket has
surely not known before. D. R. Jardine was one of the few who
did not give Bradman bouquets for his captaincy in England in
1948 but that might have been a harkback, on Jardine's part, to
bodyline days. "To suggest," wrote Jardine, in his cold, austere
manner, "that the captaincy of 1948 was brilliant or inspired
would be flattery, but it was adequate and more than adequate."

Bradman, in 1948, was a very sound captain. He had the
advantage of leading a side that was overpowering in all directions
and that against very weak opposition, but just praise must be
given him for moulding that side and for being equal to
emergencies. He had one fault, I thought, as a captain and that
was in having his favourites, particularly when it came to bowling
out the tail-enders. Those not in the beam of his smile often
received scant opportunities, so that this English tour was not
a happy one for some. Midway through the tour, those who did
not make the Test side, rightly thinking they might have been
given more chances in other games, devised a song which they
sang with rare gusto in the dressing-room:

> *Ground staff bowlers is our name,*
> *Ground staff bowling is our game.*
> *At the nets, we bowl all day ;*
> *In a match, we're never asked to play.*
> *We're the heroes of the dressing-room ;*
> *Ground staff bowlers is our name.*

So weak was English cricket in 1948 that Bradman could well have given the "Ground Staff" more opportunities without risk of defeat, but he had set his heart on an unbeaten record and never once took a risk with it. The Australian Board of Control, not regarding kindly what are called Festival Games in England, stipulated that there should be only a certain number of English Test players included against the Australians. Bradman "policed" the opposing Scarborough selection pretty closely and then entered the field with his very own Test side. He was particularly "toey" in these two Festival games, being anxious that the unbeaten record should not topple at the end, and he remembered, also, that it was in one of these games that Armstrong's great side of 1921 came to grief.

As a captain, he had good control of his side. There was the occasion at Manchester in the third Test when he apologised to Edrich ("Sorry, Bill, but these chaps get out of control when they get excited") after Miller had given Edrich four roaring bouncers in succession, but that was the time when Miller and Lindwall were stung into hectic bouncer offensive after Edrich, earlier in the day, had bowled bouncers at Lindwall. He had more conferences on the field than any other captain I knew. He took longer to place a field and was constantly in attendance on most of his bowlers during an over, but he always knew what he was striving for and always had something in mind. I can remember only two occasions on this tour when the game got away from him. Once was the Saturday at Manchester, in the third Test, and the other during the Leeds Test, in England's first innings, when, strangely, he had Johnson emulating Yardley's defensive "wheel" field on the very first day of play. But, perhaps, there was some retaliation in this. In the final analysis, Bradman was, in every sense, a brilliant captain.

In calibre, Bradman's batting on this tour was, generally, only a shadow of what it had once been. He had some very jittery periods, particularly at the beginning of an innings and, often, against slow bowlers. He had difficulty in detecting the bosie, more difficulty than at any time of his career, but this, probably and naturally, was because his eyesight had lost its keen edge.

One day at Lord's, I stood with "Buster" Nupen, the South African player, who had never seen Bradman bat and had flown specially to England to do so. This was Bradman's most jittery period. Laker turned him almost inside out but the little chap battled it through—and Nupen was satisfied at the end that he had seen something pretty good.

In absolute brilliance, Bradman might have been only a flicker of his 1930 self, but we must remember that those who knew him then were judging him in 1948 by his highest standards. The post-war generation were seeing him for the first time and they were satisfied, too, that he fulfilled every expectation. In this year of 1948 he had centuries on every ground of note— Lord's, the Oval, Old Trafford, Leeds, Trent Bridge, Worcester, Southend, Brighton and the rest. The post-war generation in Australia were sadly disillusioned by what they saw of Hammond in 1946-47 but Bradman, his hesitant periods apart, knew only fame and success wherever he went in England.

This 1948 tour of England was, in every way, a fitting end to the greatest career the game has known. Bradman not only again made runs unlimited but he stood out, with another Australian in the golfer von Nida, as England's sporting personality of the year. His speeches were bright and witty; he was feted and received by the highest in the land. Together with all other cricketers of our generation, I salute him as the greatest player of his age, the greatest attraction the game of cricket has known. He did not make the friends in the game which others did but, possibly he reasoned, he would not have been the player he was had he allowed his concentration to be upset in the slightest manner. He brilliantly and decisively achieved the objective he set himself when he found his feet in first-class cricket—and that was to be, by far, the greatest run-getter and the greatest holder of records the game has known. And, in doing that, he gave to the man-in-the-street the greatest possible value for his admission money and he brought to cricket the most pronounced publicity the game had ever known.

CHAPTER SEVENTEEN

WHAT THE CRITICS THINK

TOWARDS the end of this tour, when I decided to write this book on Bradman's final tour of England, I realised how difficult it was to give a complete picture of Bradman. Each critic sees him in a varying light, and so I asked my critic-friends to give me their pen-picture of the Great Man. They responded most generously.

Sir Pelham Warner (former English captain and, in 1948, the G.O.M. of English cricket): Prophets seldom win renown in their own country but in an introduction which Mr. Bradman asked me to write in his book in 1930, after his first tour of England, I ventured to say this: "What is his future? Is he destined to break his own records? Will he one day play an innings of 600 or 700 or put the aggregates of Grace and Hobbs, and their number of centuries, in the shade? He seems certain to plague, and at the same time delight, England's bowlers for many future seasons—indeed boys yet unborn are destined to suffer at his hands." Well, I was as near correct in my estimate of his extraordinary abilities as a batsman as any "prophet" can hope to be. His amazing figures are known to all followers of cricket, and from them one gathers that he made a century (in some instances it was of over 200 and 300) once in every three innings. Whatever comparisons may be drawn between him and other great batsmen of the past or present, there surely can never have been a *greater* batsman. It is often said that bowlers win matches. They do, but Bradman has *won* many matches by giving his bowlers lots of runs to play with and he has also *saved* matches for Australia and his two states, N.S.W. and South Australia.

In each of his four tours of England he has headed the Australian batting averages. It is sometimes said that he is not a great batsman on bowlers' wickets, but with this I do not agree. I saw him make 71 out of a total of 182 on a sticky wicket at Sydney in January, 1933, and a batsman who is equipped with every stroke, superb defence, extraordinary quickness of eye and foot and immense concentration—as he is—can surely adapt himself to any wicket. I do not think he is now the confident and dominating starter of an innings that he was on former tours in England, but let him get twenty or thirty runs and it was 2-1 on his making a century. Three times this season I made a bet—no money passing!—when he had made twenty or thereabouts that he would make a century. I won twice and on the third time he made 98! I think that, perhaps, the greatest innings he ever played was his 254 v. England, at Lord's, in 1930. Whatever the cricket historians of the future may say of him, they will surely have to call the period 1928-1948 the "Bradman Era."

He was in his earlier days a glorious fieldsman in the deep or at mid-off and if, naturally, at forty years of age, he is not so active as he was, he is still a good fieldsman on the off-side. As a captain he must be rated very high indeed. He knows everything there is to be known about cricket both from the tactical and strategical viewpoint, and his judgment of a cricketer is unfailing. The only strategical mistake of which he may be charged was his non-selection—he was captain of the side and no doubt had the last word—of Grinmett for the 1938 tour of this country. He thereby split the famous Grimmett-O'Reilly combination and Australia suffered as a consequence.

R. C. Robertson-Glasgow (London *Observer* and B.B.C.): Don Bradman has as many angles as a polygon; and, like that monster of geometry, Don was born to perplex students; and bowlers. Let's call him the greatest batsman of his time and sidetrack argument. But argument won't stand for sidetracking. And what do you mean by "his time"? Don and Jack Hobbs overlapped, just. I had the luck to play against both a time or two, and to watch both more than a time or two. And on "bad" pitches—sticky, dusty, broken, call them as you please—I'd put Jack ahead of all contemporaries. But, on "good" pitches—that is, to the bowler, 22 yards of dumb hell—Don was, perhaps is, the *nonpareil*. But I'd rather have watched Wally Hammond, twenty years back, off-driving; and I'd rather have seen Stan McCabe to the real fast stuff; he had more grace, and manner, more—what is the word?—*pride*. But you go the round of the great ones, and you come back—to Don and his figures. You can't answer *them*. They don't speak. They exist; and will exist; "a monument more enduring than bronze."

When I first saw Bradman, in England, he was an exquisitely heartless murderer of bowlers. He sliced them, into ever smaller pieces; danced on them, neatly and conclusively. There'll never be another innings like his 334 against England at Leeds in 1930;

27. *Bradman plays forward. Note the position of head, bat and feet*

28. *A tragic slip! Crapp misses Bradman off Compton at Leeds. Had this chance been taken England would surely have won the game*

never. Maurice Tate shaved Don's stumps with the first ball he bowled him, and George Duckworth, that tough and expert keeper of stumps, opened his mouth and let go four byes. From then on, Bradman batted as in dreams; or nightmares; and he never raised the ball from the grass.

In those days, you *saw* where he scored most of his runs; wide of mid-on, say; square-cuts, say, and so on. Nowadays you don't seem to *see* him run-getting; it just happens. He bats and, behold, a hundred pops up on the board against his name. But he doesn't murder any more; he *persuades*; persuades Fate to let him survive those early-middle-age gropings and soundings at the start of his innings, persuades the ball away from the best-placed fields, persuades himself back, almost, to a miracle-lad called Don Bradman, "self-taught, self-honoured, self-secure."

Oh, yes; Don's a genius; and geniuses are polygons, with many angles. And, this time, in English summer 1948, as a farewell, he showed us the new angle. Thanks, for that.

So much for Don the batsman. And, back to the start—is he the greatest ever? Nobody knows that. Certainly, the most successful. Good-bye, batsman Bradman. You've shown us something we'll never forget.

Reggie Spooner (brilliant English batsman before Bradman's days): Don Bradman is a wonderful batsman, a great captain and a most excellent speaker—surely a combination of qualities that is unique. It is, of course, impossible to compare him with batsmen of the past owing to ever-changing conditions, but it is difficult to believe that in my time anybody could have equalled his capacity as a run-getter, and although since the first World War the real sticky wickets have on most grounds disappeared there must be little doubt that he would have mastered them, if humanly possible. As a spectator of Don Bradman's play this year, I always admired his cleverness in adapting himself to what might be called the autumn of his grand career. We all pay tribute to his masterly skill and it is indeed sad that we in the British Isles are unlikely to have this great cricketer with us as a player again though he will be ever welcome when he can spare the time to visit us again.

Major Beau Vincent (*The Times* Cricket Correspondent): Back through the years with those many occasions when I have been privileged to watch Don Bradman bat and field—and never overlook, in glorifying his scoring power, the immense amount of runs this glorious fieldsman has saved—I have one particular recollection of him which remains constantly in my mind's memory. It was on his first visit to this country, and it was the evening before the first match of the tour at Worcester. He was sitting in front of the fireplace in the public writing-room—alone and thinking. And I feel that all through his illustrious cricket career he has always been thinking, concentrating upon what has to be done. Master of himself, just as he had unquestionably been the master of bowlers. There is a certitude in his batsmanship, mental as well as technical, which I cannot believe has belonged to any other cricketer since W.G. by his own force of character controlled every game in which he took part. I have heard it said this summer, "Oh! I don't want to watch Bradman. He's sure to make runs and be there all day. Let's have a glass of beer and wait until Hassett or Miller comes in." I have felt it myself. It may have been an indirect compliment to Bradman; but how false, for every stroke that he has played has been well worth the watching, preaching as it has the lesson of a perpetual concentration supporting genius.

Denzil Batchelor (Sydney *Morning Herald* correspondent and author): When I think of Bradman, my mind jumps back to summers of long ago, though I can almost feel the hot Sydney sunshine on my face, so close at hand do those vivid memories loom. I forget the shadow of the immortal who scratched and snicked and scraped and somehow survived at Nottingham this year; and who set the seal on victory at Leeds after an innings which included strokes that were not only heresies but were also hideous. I remember the rip-roaring bushranger of heroic stature who clubbed Fleetwood-Smith into eclipse in a double century at Sydney in 1931—the most consummately dominating feat I ever saw on any cricket ground. Yes, on a good wicket—but not on a bad one—he was in those days a magic bat, not subject to mortal laws at all. The footwork was audacious, the wrists well sprung, the eyes saw the opportunity—if not the ball—larger and quicker than any other player of our day.

I remember—perhaps as clearly as any snapshot memory holds—a sprint of 50 yards in chase of a hit to the boundary's rim from one of the West Indian batsmen. The flying Bradman took the ball inches from the fence in his finger-tips, and apparently straightening while still airborne, without putting foot to the ground, broke the far wicket with his throw-in.

And I remember above all, his captaincy against "Gubby"

Allen. Two down and three to play, he saved the rubber as by the divine right of Kingship. The third Test match at Melbourne was won almost in the style of a game of chess-by-correspondence: by sheer tactical superiority—bat and ball didn't come into it.

What was the secret of his success as the greatest run-getting robot? (which does less than justice to that imperious hook, that regal smashing into the deep field). It came, of course, from concentration and unbounded confidence. After the match was won was the time to talk about the game being more important than the result. Up till then—well, as 150 appeared on the board against his name, the superman must have felt the faint flush of satisfaction (glow is too strong a word) that ordinary batsmen feel when the cheers greet their fifty. After all, he was only half-way to a really good score. And when that was achieved there was no excuse for relaxing for a moment.

Jim Kilburn (*Yorkshire Post*): My cricketing heroes were created before Don Bradman was known. Therefore, I have never had to watch him in that prayerful discomfort born of more anxiety for a player's success than the player himself could know. I have never cared greatly whether or not Bradman was out— except in Test matches when I wanted him out, with all England's other enemies. I have seen Bradman clear, and would complete the allusion by saying I have seen him whole, except that I very much doubt if any one has ever seen Bradman whole because— as a cricketer, I mean—there is so much of him.

My belief is that he is beyond parallel. He may not have changed the form of cricket as W. G. Grace changed it, but he has carried the cricket of his time to its ultimate efficiency. To contain him it would have been necessary to institute a different conception. At his best he was absolute master of his medium, and when a threat was made to alter the medium the cricket world in general preferred the despotism of Don Bradman to the anarchy of Bodyline.

Bradman's genius must have been based on physical attributes outside the ordinary. Perhaps other cricketers between them had equally acute eyesight, equal speed of footwork, equal powers of enduring concentration, but no individual has shown quite such astonishing co-ordination of mind and muscle. His reactions were abnormal. No other batsman matched his capacity for avoiding error without falling into immobility. Times without number, Bradman has hit the ball easily from the wrong position; times without number he has appeared strokeless and defeated with the ball a yard away and yet contrived a full and faultless shot.

More than any one else Bradman took the initiative away from bowlers. In the glory of his youth and strength, he was the most relentless run-getter of all time. Some challenged, like Trumper; some charmed, like Ranjitsinhji; Bradman devastated —deliberately, coldly, ruthlessly. His power was his delight and his use of it the greatest single attraction in the cricket of his age. Wherever cricket lives, he will be discussed; dissected, perhaps decried, but never, never forgotten.

Charles Bray (London *Daily Herald* and former captain of Essex): To write in appreciation of Don Bradman as a cricketer is rather like praising perfection for this slim, sharp-featured, self-centred Australian has proved himself to be King of them all. I saw him on his first tour of this country. I watched him break bowlers' hearts on his second and third visits. I saw him lead Australia to their convincing victory in his own country in 1946-47, and I have now seen him during his triumphant "swansong"—a fitting climax to a great career.

It is not necessary to enumerate his deeds. They are written in letters of gold in the records. Yet in this, his final season of first-class cricket, the Don has made another niche for himself in cricket history. If the historians do their work properly, he will be classed as one of, if not the greatest, captains of all times, It is not difficult to fault a captain's technique on the field when one has the advantage of the detached view of a critic. It is easy, indeed, to look back on a day's play and say this or that should have been done by a captain striving to get the other side out. Yet I must confess that only on the rarest occasions have I been able to think, let alone write, that Bradman made a mistake in the handling of his bowlers or the setting of his field.

That is high praise, and while I shall always remember the Don for his many great innings I shall never forget his captaincy.

Before a ball was bowled in the 1948 series I publicly expressed my view that the Australian team was infinitely superior to any-thing England could produce. Not only had they the advantage of greater playing ability but they had the enormous asset of a brilliant captain. I would have liked to have seen the Don up against far stronger opposition. Unfortunately, we shall never see that now.

In a career of such outstanding success, it may seem churlish to suggest even that in one connection he failed. I mention it only to show that he is human and not as my old friend, Johnny Moyes, would have us believe in a book, absolute perfection. In his relations with the Press, Bradman has always been difficult. Very sensitive to criticism of any kind, he did not suffer pressmen gladly, yet the cricketing world was told of Bradman's deeds by those same pressmen. He seemed always to be aggressively on the defensive whenever a newspaper man talked to him. That has been my own experience and, I think, that of most others. It will be interesting to see whether he changes now that his playing days are over—or perhaps he will become one of us. Who knows?

Ray Robinson (Sydney *Sun* and author): One of the most remarkable things in Don Bradman's cricket after the war was the frequency with which he could change his mind in safety.

Many great batsmen have had the faculty of changing the stroke, but none in my time has done it as often as Bradman did on his last tour of Britain. Probably the reason was that in his fortieth year his sight was not so unerring as it was before the war. Mostly the change was from the beginnings of a forward stroke to a back stroke, usually defensive but sometimes for runs.

The most striking case was in the Australians' match against Yorkshire at Bramall Lane, Sheffield. The wicket was playing well and John Wardle, the slow left-hander from South Yorkshire, could get little out of it.

Bradman was in the act of playing one ball from Wardle near his off-stump when it jumped to chest height. The ball's prank was so sudden that no batsman need have been ashamed to have put up a catch. But, at the last moment, Bradman changed the course of his bat so that it passed away from the ball which hopped harmlessly to the wicket-keeper.

This ability to avert misfortune formed part of the working of the instinct for self-preservation which, I think, was one of the most important factors in Bradman's record-breaking career.

Brian Sellers (Yorkshire captain and former English selector): The first time I saw the Australians play cricket was at Leeds in 1926. I was then nineteen. I can remember it as well as if it were yesterday. I well remember that as I was about to sit down Tate bowled the first ball of the match to Warren Bardsley, who edged it to Herbert Sutcliffe at first slip and was caught. One down for nought was a shock for every one. I then saw a truly magnificent innings by Charlie Macartney, who scored a century before lunch.

Four years later, almost to the day, I saw Archie Jackson caught by Larwood off Tate for one. This time, Australia's first wicket fell at two, and as Jackson was walking out I wondered if I should see another innings similar to Macartney's and I certainly did. At the end of that day, July 11, 1930, Don Bradman was not out 303. What struck me most of all was the ease with which he got his runs. At no time did he appear in difficulties. His footwork and stroke-play were perfect.

It was four years later that I first had the pleasure of playing against the Don. It was for Yorkshire at Sheffield. He scored 140 after the first wicket had fallen for 16. Once again I noticed his footwork and stroke-play, but this time from the middle and I learnt plenty.

In my opinion, the Don is the greatest player the game has ever seen or is likely to see for many years to come. My father, who played with W. G. Grace, thought the same.

Many people have asked me why he is such a wonderful batsman, and I have replied that it is because he never tries to move his feet until the ball has left the bowler's hand and, moreover, his ability to concentrate on *every* ball that is bowled to him.

The time has now come for him to retire—a sad moment for any cricketer. He has given me and hundreds of thousands of others great pleasure during his wonderful career. Well played, Don!

John Arlott (B.B.C. and author): I believe that any opinion should be related to a standard—that in a vacuum it is valueless. The standard should be, of course, the sense of values of the man who expresses the opinion. I am, therefore, not being auto-biographical but merely providing a standard for the views I profess when I state that my enthusiasm for cricket is in continual strife with my sense of proportion. I believe that humanity and humour are greater than hundreds; that character transcends catches and that basic truth is bigger than bowling. A man may not be known as a man by the score-book. Averages can indicate no more than technical skill and temperament, but I do think that a man *may* be revealed by his cricket.

It has been impossible during the past twenty years in England to ignore Don Bradman. Some have been dazzled by him, others have feared him and another section, again, has given him unreserved admiration.

Here, I believe, is a phenomenon in that, wide-reaching as Bradman's activities have been, they have all been on one particular level of consciousness. If I were faced with a task, on a materialistic plane, I would sooner have Don Bradman to work with me than any other man I have ever met—provided he could, without hesitation, accept the terms offered. I feel he is capable of such single-minded concentration as to be able to achieve almost anything within his physical compass with utter competence and with an intensity rare in the human race.

Here is a man who works out what he wants to do and then does it. Upon what level of mind or soul he argues with himself about his aims I have no means of knowing. I do know, however, that he is capable of setting himself the semi-intangible target which is not to be found in the records books.

Bradman is a very clever man in the true sense of the word. He knows, and will always know, where he is going—on his chosen plane. He appears completely undisturbed by those doubts which often intrude from different spheres to disturb others.

Some cricketers have been content to settle for the records. Bradman, in his record-making, always retained the maximum of cricket beauty that was compatible with the "business" stroke. Others, again, have been content to be known for their play alone. Bradman has planted himself in the minds of men who follow cricket.

Not since W. G. Grace has cricket produced such a man who so combined technical skill, concentration, determination or who did so on a carefully planned course. I doubt that cricket will ever see another for cricket has a way of getting under a man's skin. I do not think cricket is under Bradman's skin but I believe that it is under his skull—in close control. Therefore he has missed something of cricket that less gifted and less memorable men have gained. How, I wonder, would Don Bradman define happiness?

Arthur Mailey (Sydney *Sunday Telegraph* and prince of slow bowlers): Don Bradman will be remembered as one of the most remarkable sportsmen who ever graced the sporting stage of any country.

Bradman is an enigma, a paradox; an idol of millions of people, yet, with a few, the most unpopular cricketer I have ever met.

People close to Bradman either like or dislike him; there is no half-way. To those who dislike him there is no compromise, no forgiveness, little tolerance. There are at least two major reasons: jealousy and this great cricketer's independence.

I have watched Bradman's career since he left Bowral, since he wore black braces on the Sydney Cricket Ground (he still swears he was never guilty of such sacrilege), have seen every innings he has played in Tests against any country, have seen him during periods of rich success and in his moments of embarrassment and frustration; have seen him pleased and annoyed; have seen him grin and sob almost in the one moment, but never have I seen him deviate very far from that line which was intended to lead him to power and success.

Unlike many people who attain power, Bradman has never, to my knowledge, resorted to political intrigue or compromise. His personal success on the cricket field has provided him with a passport which he never hesitates to use.

His intuition, tenacity, and calculating mind have given him an individualism which demands attention and, in most case's support.

Bradman has a very acute brain. But there are some aspects in his mental outlook which lack the benefit of finer thinking. He is dogmatic on subjects or opinions which even an expert or a master would treat with great care and discretion.

That he can express a more sensible opinion than most cricketers on any set of subjects, there is no doubt, and in this particular connection I would mention speechmaking. Bradman has surprised many listeners with his ability to make an after-dinner speech. His complete coverage of interesting points and somewhat unorthodox points of view have given him a reputation that a more efficient orator would be proud of.

During his career Bradman has fallen foul of many factions directly or indirectly connected with the game. The Board of Control fined him £50 for breaking the player-writer rule. Other players were disqualified for a similar breach, but Bradman was considered greater than the game, and certainly greater than the administration.

And, as a team-mate, I have always found Bradman dependable, a good sportsman. As an interviewer, I have found him reliable, fearless, and fair, but most unsatisfactory; unsatisfactory because he appears to be suspicious of the Press generally. Nobody handles his own publicity as well as Bradman himself. While he gives the impression of avoiding the spotlight, he is sensibly conscious and perhaps appreciative of its power.

When Bradman suggests an alteration to the laws of cricket he is listened to with the greatest respect.

Bradman is a law within himself. This has been proved over and over again, and it is his amazing success as a cricketer, plus his perfect timing and tremendous respect and faith in his own judgment, that have demanded attention where others have been ignored—in some cases ridiculed.

When I asked him if it were true that he had been offered a knighthood, he replied, "I know nothing about it."

"Would you accept it if it were offered?" I persisted.

"I cannot answer a question which to my knowledge has no foundation," said Don.

The dialogue was similar when I asked him if he intended to stand for Parliament.

A difference with the New South Wales Cricket Association probably caused Bradman to leave the State. There was a mild mutiny amongst certain players when he first led the Australian Eleven. Then he crossed pens several times with his old enemy, the Press.

In all these skirmishes he came out best, but there are still a number of his adversaries licking their wounds and waiting to have another "crack" at this "one-man" army.

Jealousy, according to the dictionary, is "apprehension of being supplanted in favour of another," and here we put a finger on the sore spot of Bradman's unpopularity with certain players.

The ambitious Master Bradman climbed right over the heads of his contemporaries, some of whom felt that priority entitled them to the plums of captaincy.

Many of these men had accepted the captaincy of Australia or their States in similar circumstances, but consoled themselves with the thought that, in their cases, it was a reward for efficiency.

Bradman was brought up the hard way, the lonely way. That's why he practised as a boy by hitting a ball up against a brick wall, and when he felt the cold draught of antagonism within the ranks he kept his counsel, remained unperturbed, and knew his greatest weapon was centuries and more centuries.

Apart from that, his tremendous successes on the field and his value as a box-office attraction made him a valuable asset to those who regard big gates as a proof of efficient administration. Bradman never made the mistake, common to many, of thinking that personal popularity is more potent than success.

Bradman's humour is not particularly subtle, although there is a cynicism about it which makes it more acceptable than the red-nose stage type of wit. Don is more alert than most people in repartee.

I believe that he is quite ready to "swap" wisecracks with Bernard Shaw or any other professional creator of smart sentences, not because he believes he can out-Shaw Shaw, but simply because he refuses to be silenced by greater personalities.

The Right Hon. R. G. Menzies (former Prime Minister of Australia, President of the Victorian Cricket Association, and a generally discerning cricket connoisseur): I write as a looker-on; as a lover of the game and its history and its beauty and the unforgettable pictures which it etches upon the visual memory. For twenty years I have been Don Bradman's beneficiary, for he is the greatest batsman, the most devastating stroke-maker, and the shrewdest and most concentrated tactician I ever hope to see. He is, of course, not without his critics; he has succeeded too gigantically to escape them. He has his faults, no doubt, but they are merely the defects inherent in those positive qualities which have given him his pre-eminence. In him we have witnessed the supreme cricketing combination; the quick eye ("sees the ball three yards sooner than any of the rest of us," Bill Ponsford once said to me), the instantaneous muscular response, the incisive and flashing intelligence. For, mark you, Don Bradman is a man of uucommon intelligence from whatever angle you consider him. I have been on the same bill with him for after-dinner speeches, and have marvelled at him. He has the born after-dinner speaker's faculties of wit, flexibility, and quick feeling for atmosphere. He has talked to me of politics with rare shrewdness and perception. His grasp of financial and economic matters, in which he had no early training, is impressive. He has a proper self-confidence and naturalness which carries him comfortably through a bewildering variety of social contacts. He believes in the virtue of concentrating all your mind upon the job in hand. He therefore plays to win. Once or twice I have thought that this ruthless quality might have been tempered with a little mercy; but reflection has almost always brought me back to the recognition that intense concentration IS a cardinal virtue, so rare that for its sake even much might be forgiven.

As a pavilion lover of the greatest of all games, I have balanced up the Bradman Account, and hereby acknowledge that so long as my memory lasts I shall owe him that which I can never repay.

CHAPTER EIGHTEEN

HOW GREAT WAS THIS TEAM?

THE 1948 Australians played 31 matches; they won 23 and drew eight. Of the 23 wins, 15 were by an innings. The Australians scored 15,120 runs against their opponents' 10,932, averaging 50.23 runs per wicket as against 19.66. There were 47 hundreds and 58 fifties scored for the Australians compared with seven hundreds and 41 fifties against them. There were 26 scores of nil by the Australians (Morris and Toshack, the latter being very pleased with himself, were the only Australians who did not qualify for the invidious honour of belonging to the Australian "duck" club) but there were as many as 82 scores of nil made against them.

The English century scorers were Compton (twice), Washbrook and Edrich in the Tests, and Edrich, Crapp and Hardstaff in the other games.

Such convincing figures led many critics to claim that this Australian team of 1948, the twentieth of its kind to visit England, was the best of all time. Bradman considered it the best team he had played with, and such an opinion must be given every respect. It shared with Vic Richardson's Australian team to South Africa in 1935-36 the honour of never being beaten abroad. But was it therefore the best of all time?

Figures are not reliable in answering such a question. The basis of evaluation must surely be standard, and there were reasons to believe that both in the quality and the spirit of its cricket, the English team of 1948 was the poorest that had played against Australia in the twentieth century. English teams which included McLaren, Hayward, J. T. Tyldesley, Quaife, Jessop, Jones, Lilley, Braund, Gunn, Barnes, Blythe, Fry, Ranjitsinhji, Jackson, Hirst, Lockwood, Rhodes, Warner, Foster, Fielder, Bosanquet, Hobbs, Crawford, Spooner, Smith and others, from 1900 to 1912, must be immediately above suspicion. On Australian wickets, in the 1911 season, English teams beat Australia in four out of five Tests, and the Australian teams of those days included Trumper, Armstrong, Syd Gregory, Bardsley, Macartney, Hill, Kelleway, Ransford, Carter, Hordern, Matthews, Cotter and Whitty.

The post-First World War saw Australia win 11 Tests and draw two before England won by an innings and 29 runs at Melbourne in February, 1925, but I feel convinced, from reading of the games, talking to those who played in them and on my own observations, that the English team of 1948 did not have five cricketers the equal of Jack Hobbs, Wilfred Rhodes, Frank Woolley, Parkin and Hendren. From 1926 to 1932 was a period of considerable English strength with Sutcliffe, Hammond, Tate, Larwood, Hobbs and Hendren the prominent players, and in 1936-37 and 1938 England very closely contested Australia's right to hold the Ashes.

The 1946-47 tour of Australia was an incredibly bad one for England but, on reflection, I think Hammond's team, indifferent as it was, played better cricket in Australia than this English one did on its home soil in 1948.

Robertson-Glasgow, a delightful personality whose writings always hit the century-mark, was very pessimistic about England's bowling at the end of 1947. He wanted to know who was going to get the Australians out. Those, he wrote, who don't care, were welcome to spread the newspaper over their heads and take thirty-nine winks, but on the evidence of 1947 the English bowling resources were:

   (i)   Fast bowlers—None at all.
  (ii)   Slow left-handers—None of true Test class.
 (iii)   Slow off-spinners—J. C. Clay, born 1898; T. W. Goddard, born 1900.
 (iv)   Leg-break and googly—One of true Test class.
  (v)   Medium and medium-fast right-handers—Dozens; nearly all willing; nearly all misdirected.

The one true bowler of Test class "Crusoe" referred to was Douglas Wright. It is interesting to recall that Bedser was dropped from the English Test team in 1947 against South Africa, something which never happened to Tate at the height of his career.

There was obvious apathy in English cricket in 1948 and I am not certain that the after-effects of the war were sufficient explanation. Due allowance must be made for the shortcomings in food, but I think it is in general cricketing conditions that Australia has gained ground over England.

There was much bad selection work by the English in this

series. To be true, the selectors were not helped greatly by the county standard. We often saw players in these matches who would barely measure up to our own second-grade club games in Sydney and, therefore, the English selectors found figures in county games were poor guides, but they made the blunder of choosing in Test matches several players who were not basically correct in their style and thus were foredoomed as Test failures. Then, too, English cricket has not changed with the times.

The economic life of England has changed so much that the amateur, as known in pre-World War One, is now non-existent. Life in England is now very real and earnest for everybody, with record production the aim of the nation, and, to Australian minds, English cricket will continue to be at a disadvantage against Australia while it adheres to its conservative policy of maintaining an amateur captain and a purely amateur selection committee.

Norman Yardley is a very pleasant individual and cricketer, most popular with Australian players and Pressmen. The fact that he headed the English bowling averages need not be taken too seriously because it is, in itself, an indictment of the general weakness of English bowling, but though Yardley often showed himself possessed of good batting ability, he never made the scores that England was entitled to expect from the batting position he occupied. Nor was there any other amateur in England, I think, who could have batted as well. If Yardley was not good enough for England as a batsman, would English cricket have been disgraced had a professional been chosen as captain? One of the hardest working newspaper executives I met in England was Viscount Kemsley, who certainly carried out the duties of a professional business man, and his innumerable newspaper ships were all the better, I should imagine, for his own personal leadership. And, apart from upsetting a tradition (many of which have been rudely shattered in England in the past decade), would there have been any ignominy in having former professionals with balanced and experienced minds, like Jack Hobbs, Sutcliffe, Duckworth and others, to act as selectors?

But Jack Hobbs, who has been one of England's richest blessings on the cricket field, is not even welcome in the Long Pavilion at Lord's—not because, personally, he would not conduct himself as a fitting member of Lord's, but purely because he happened to be in life a professional cricketer.

It does seem to Australian minds that in the maintaining of age-old traditions, English cricket is losing much that it cannot afford to lose. The cricketing system does not seem to have changed, as most other concerns have, with the times. England has seen vast changes in social provisions for the masses in the past decade, but professional cricketers with whom I have discussed the subject tell me that their calling has not been made more attractive and, with the doubtful future attached to playing cricket, they say it is no wonder that a cricket career is failing to attract young men. So dependent are the counties on older players, that in the season of 1948 there were 27 players over forty actively concerned in county sides.

There is no dearth of cricketers in England. Figures will show that more are playing cricket to-day than ever before. During a Sunday club game at East Moseley, the president of the club told me that there were over one thousand club teams in Surrey alone, but the county draws nothing from this colossal strength because in England to-day there seems to be no half-way mark between professionalism and amateurism—and the man who plays club cricket likes the game as such, not as a means of earning what is a precarious livelihood and a livelihood, moreover, which allows him comparatively little home life.

In an article for the London *Sunday Times*, I suggested that the county officials should make strenuous endeavours to get some of this club strength and club spirit into the decaying county ranks. I further suggested, as a trial, that as few people work nowadays on Saturdays, one whole round of county games, with extended hours, should be played on Saturday, thus giving club players the chance of winning a county cap and bringing a totally different technique into county games. This scheme, or something like it, would also give the professional a few days during the week to do something else besides playing cricket, for I often wondered in England whether cricket officials realised how damaging it is for a married cricketer to have little home life (I thought that many county players, through boredom, "bent the elbow" more on tour than was good for them or the game) and, moreover, how this continuous playing of cricket dulls the intellect and the form of the most gifted player.

The attraction, undoubtedly, in English cricket is the benefit match which the average professional receives. In 1948, Cyril Washbrook, of Lancashire, had the best ever. As we were leaving England it was approaching £13,000 and that sum is tax-free.

Washbrook had the advantages of a season in which interest was unparalleled; he was given the game against the Australians at Old Trafford; he was fortunate in that the Lancastrians regarded the £8,000 record sum achieved by the Yorkshireman, Bill Bowes, the preceding season, as a challenge to their county, and he was fortunate, also, in that two dropped catches at Old Trafford during a Test saw a change in his cricketing luck because such things do count. Apart from these factors, Washbrook was also fortunate in that innumerable games were arranged on his behalf on Sundays and on afternoons of long twilight after the county games had finished for the day.

These additional games fall upon both amateurs and professionals, and as benefit games, for somebody or other, occur frequently, the games-after-play take considerable toll of a player's time and energy. It seemed lacking in taste, too, to have men walking around the playing field with a tarpaulin for coins while the game was in action and to have the recipient leave the ground, the game stopping, while he made a pretty speech of thanks over the amplifier (oh, those amplifiers!), but, in addition to all this, the whole principle of benefit games seems wrong. One day, in London, I was with Larwood, Duckworth and Paynter—three pretty reputable names in English cricket—but the sum totals received by the three out of their benefit games was but a small fraction of that by Washbrook. Washbrook was fortunate in having his in a big season, with everything favourable, but I think the players themselves would welcome a less chancy way of having their years of service recognised.

In my *Sunday Times* article, I compared the cricketing lives of English and Australian players. In Australia, for three of the six months of the season, the leading players are engaged only in Saturday afternoon club games. With Western Australia now admitted to the Sheffield Shield competition, the first-class season is enlarged, but formerly a leading Australian player would be concerned in only six or so first-class games in an average season (there are more with an English tour). When the Australian, therefore, comes to his first-class games he does so with a fresh mind and he is out to enjoy his inter-state tours and the cricket. This is to be noted because the difference in outlook between the Australian and English Test teams of 1948 was most marked. The Australians, as I pointed out in the article, certainly brought more zest and zeal into their play.

The *Sunday Times* received many letters about that article and they printed one, quite a friendly one from a person who said he recognised that I was a good friend of English cricket and cricketers, but he questioned the wisdom of revolutionising English county cricket for the winning of Test matches. Most of the thousands who went to see the Test matches, he contended, knew little about the game and went for the spectacular side of it. The real cricket-lover was to be found in calmer walks of the game, and, as he saw the Australian "zeal and zest" on the field of play, he did not wish to see English teams emulating it.

Now, I can imagine that those ideas are shared by many cricket-lovers in England and one must grant the validity of their reasoning. His distaste of what I called zeal and zest, possibly, was brought about by the many bouncers the Australian fast bowlers delivered, and this brings me to a discussion of the Australian tactics of 1948, whether Test cricket is, so to speak, worth the candle and, also, whether the game of county cricket could continue were it not for Test matches and their revenue-producing gates.

A leading English cricketer at Scarborough succinctly put the issue on bouncers when he said, "You chaps used Bren-guns; we replied with water pistols." That sums up what has happened in post-World War Two cricket. The Australians have given it; the English, so used to taking it during the war years, have continued to take it at cricket.

A retired first-class cricketer, blind in one eye and none too sure in the other, can recognise intimidation immediately when he sees it on the cricket field. There has been almost as much intimidation in Australian cricket in the past two series as there was in the bodyline series; the only difference is that the intent has not been backed by the close leg-side field that Jardine set.

Have the Australians acted unfairly with all these bouncers? If they have sometimes pricked the spirit of the game, they have always been within the laws, because the instructions to umpires since the bodyline days clearly puts responsibility upon the umpires and I have seen no umpire caution Miller or Lindwall for bouncers. But the effect of these bouncers upon English batsmen, Hutton, in particular, has been there for all to see. Miller and Lindwall were the Bren-guns the Englishman spoke of; Edrich and Pollard were the water pistols the English used in reply.

29. *The Australian Press team. Lord Kemsley entertains the visiting writers at Kemsley House*

BOWLER	WKTS	RUNS
RANGNEKAR		
ADHIKARI		
KISHENCHAND		
GUL MAHOMED		
SARWATE		45
NAYUDU		19
HAZARE		
AMARNATH		23
MANKAD		43
SOHONI	1	56

INDIA 1st INNS	326
AUS.1st INGS	

No. OF OVERS	47

BATSMEN	
BRADMAN	99
MILLER	63
2 FOR	187

BATSMEN	OUT	F OF W.
BROWN	8	11
ROGERS	16	31

WANTED AT
MEMB's GATE

SUNDRIES 1

BAR

In the third Test in Melbourne, in the 1946-47 season, Voce deliberately set out to bowl bouncers at Bradman in retaliation for the bouncers the Australians had bowled in the preceding Tests. Voce did bowl several beauties, which caused Bradman noticeable concern, but Voce was fourteen years past the time when he first bowled bouncers in Australia and he retired from the field with an injured groin. He had busted himself in the bouncer process. At odd times Edrich tried to bowl bouncers at Bradman, but Edrich is too short in stature and not fast enough to be a hostile bouncer. Pollard bounced one at Miller in the Manchester Test but Miller is afraid of nothing in this life. Pollard is only medium-fast and so the ball was hooked like fury to the ropes and Pollard tried no more. This, also, was the Test when Edrich bounced the ball at Lindwall and our fast bowler looked none too happy about things.

If one side has not the means of retaliation for all things, then that side is at an extreme disadvantage and, so to speak, the Australians have had the Englishmen at their mercy in post-war cricket because of their fast bowlers. And they have shown little mercy. It must have been obvious to Hammond in Australia in 1946-47 that England would simply have to find a fast bowler to stand a chance in England with the Australians, but the English officials either didn't, or couldn't, find a fast bowler. It seems unbelievable that one did not exist in England in 1948. It was said that many Notts fast bowlers owed their speed to back muscles developed by work in the coal-mines, but the truth is that even if a fast bowler were discovered, the life of a county fast bowler is not an attractive one.

The three Australians, Miller, Lindwall and Johnston, spelled one another during the county games. Over a period of twelve games before the first Test, Lindwall had bowled only 166 overs. Pollard had bowled about three times that number, so that a lone fast bowler in a county side cannot reckon on a long life in the game—as the gifted Larwood can testify. Whereas a class batsman might receive several benefits in his career, a fast bowler does well with one.

Would a fast bowler have made much difference to England's team in 1948? I think that is easily answerable. He would have been invaluable. Keith Miller on England's side would have about balanced the teams. It is well to remember that apart from the few Voce bounced at him in Melbourne, Bradman has been singularly free from bouncers in his post-war cricket. He has

30. *Bradman's 100th run of his 100th century in first-class cricket, made against the Indians at Sydney*

never played against either Miller or Lindwall.[1] He has just not been available for games in which he might have played against these two express men, and I don't think there is the slightest doubt that had Miller played against Bradman he would have plied him with as many bouncers as he gave Hutton. Miller is no respecter of persons or reputations in the cricketing world. Miller was one of whom Bradman said at Manchester: "These chaps get out of control." And a bouncing Miller in opposition would have robbed Bradman of much relish and runs in his post-war career—as he did Hutton.

England simply must produce fast bowlers if she is to stand level with Australia again on Test ground, and Australians can never again complain against bouncers. I don't like the flavour they bring into a game. In his series of articles, Bradman denied that the Australian tactics brought feeling between the teams, but I don't agree with him in this. They inevitably give rise to feeling, but the best means of preventing them or keeping them in check is to possess the means of retaliation. In 1948 Larwood confessed to me that he was scared stiff one day in Sydney when Alexander brought one up under his chin. "That was close, Harold," said Oldfield, as he passed Larwood. "Poof," replied Larwood, "that was nothing." "But," he told me, in 1948, "it certainly gave me a hell of a fright."

I cannot see eye to eye with those English people who believe that Test victories count for nothing. An English victory in 1948 would have been of incalculable value to the country from the morale viewpoint, and those in charge of the game must well ponder whether record crowds will continue to pay huge sums of money to watch a beaten team and, also, whether Australian tours will continue to pay their way if England does not measure up to standard. Then, too, those admirable hundreds of thousands of spectators who flocked along to see the games with great tolerance and suffering amazing inconveniences deserve the best out of cricket and from their representative sides. I never tired of admiring English people in 1948. They were generous in everything—their praise of the Australians and their acceptance of continued defeats. The highest in the land went

[1] This, obviously, was written before the Australian season of 1948-49, in which Bradman played once against Lindwall and Miller. Lindwall bowled only one bumper against the champion in his Testimonial game, but Miller, who took his wicket, bowled three bumpers against Bradman in Sydney, one a particularly nasty one which obviously displeased Bradman. At the end of this game Miller was not chosen for South Africa, to my mind the worst selecting blunder in Australia's cricketing history. Was Miller dropped because of his bowling tactics?

up and down in spirit with the good and the bad days of the English team, and I refuse to believe that several English Test victories would not be for the common good.

It would be wrong for an Australian touring during an English cricket season to consider that he is qualified to express dogmatic opinions on most matters. There is so much background to English cricket that it cannot be quickly assimiliated, but of one thing I am convinced. There must be a pretty sudden revision of ideas and systems because it must be apparent to all that English cricket can do with a good overhaul—and in that opinion I have tried to take into full account the distressing times the Home Country has known in the past decade.

It is against this backdrop of the English standard that one must try and assess the strength of Bradman's twentieth Australian team. In one regard, I think it ranked superior to all other Australian teams, and that was in its capacity to bat, on good pitches, down to number nine. The tricky pitch at Bradford showed some in an indifferent light and that is why I qualify them on a good pitch. In 1905, Syd Gregory was going in to bat at number eight; in 1921, his nephew, Jack Gregory, was number nine, but there are good reasons for believing that this twentieth Australian Eleven had no superiors as a batting team on a good pitch, though here again one does well to remember that some batting reputations stand in the light of a poor period in English bowling.

The openers, Morris and Barnes, were magnificent and would have done well against any bowling. I have a tremendous regard for Morris. He had his taste of hesitancy in England but he overcame the strangeness of the pitches in the manner of a champion, and will be always remembered in England as a batsman of the highest calibre. He has defence; he has all the scoring strokes and he has, also, a most graceful style. His temperament was superb. Barnes is a tenacious fighter who has established himself as one of the greatest batsmen of his age. Had the games been closer, both he and Miller would certainly have made many more runs.

Bradman continued the ideal number one wicket down and Hassett, though mostly a defensive batsman and strangely obsessed with the run-storing complex against weak opposition towards the end of the tour, was a reliable number four, though not comparable, in attacking stroke-play, with some who had occupied that essentially attacking position in Australian teams.

Miller was magnificent. This series, and the preceding one in Australia, did not see him at his best because Miller steadfastly refuses to take a game seriously unless it is a fight, and there were Test innings in which he absolutely refused to concentrate because of the position of the game. But Miller was always on hand when wanted. He was the best-equipped and most spectacular batsman in the side, being dominant on a bad pitch. Barnes, too, possessed bad-pitch ability well above the ordinary.

Harvey was a glorious success, and it was evident early in the tour that he was qualifying to step into Bradman's shoes as a crowd-pleaser. He did not turn twenty until travelling home on the *Orontes*, and it amazed English crowds that one so young and inexperienced should be such an instantaneous success in Test matches. Harvey has the ideal temperament. Nothing worries him and he walked out to bat in that crucial Leeds position as if it were a friendly game back home in the bush with not a single spectator. He is one of those natural champions which come to light every so often in Australian cricket. Bradman was one, Jackson another, McCabe, Clem Hill and Trumper—all flourishing immediately as youths in a Test arena of tried and experienced men. Compton was an English counterpart in 1938, but generally Australia produces its champions at a much younger age than England.

This is not solely due to climate but also to the differing circumstances of the game in both countries. An English champion can blush unseen for many years but the young Australian rubs shoulders with Test heroes in the Saturday afternoon club games and, too, the Sheffield Shield is a more advanced and appropriate step to Test cricket than county games. Thus the young Australian is better fitted for Test cricket. He is more tried and experienced and it is, undoubtedly, because of this that there is a much smaller percentage of Australian Test flops or failures than there are English.

Harvey is a most attractive cricketer. He drives and pulls with tremendous vigour and shares with Bradman the urge to hit fours all the time. Singles and twos come to him more by accident than design. He has a completely different outlook to the game from Bradman. Bradman tossed back his head in dismay on the Leeds balcony the day Harvey played an inglorious cross-bat sweep. Bradman would never have done this. He would have cemented his score and the side's position after making a century, but Harvey was quite content to call it a day after his hundred. His inclusion in the Test team strengthened it considerably, with the bat and in the field, because I really think he is the most spectacular fieldsman I have ever seen. Some might like him to have proved himself against a good slow-spinner,[1] but I think he had the ability to do this because it has to be remembered that he rose superior to the changes in English pitches—and only a naturally great player can do that at nineteen years of age. I feel sure Harvey will shine in the cricket world for years to come, and Australia is indeed fortunate that as Bradman goes out, another star, of tremendous and different attraction, has worked his way to fame.

Loxton was ruggedly honest in his play. His rise to Test circles didn't worry him one little bit and he gave the ball the full swing of his bat and the power of his broad shoulders as soon as he got to the middle. A good spinner, conceivably, might have upset Loxton, but he was a gloriously free and successful player against the medium stuff which England presented. His driving was magnificent and he hit sixes with such regular abandon at Leeds that one wondered whether it was really a Test match going on in the centre. He is the type the crowd loves, and his presence in the side (he was one of the final choices in the original seventeen) gave the Australian team of 1948 much sparkle and dash.

Tallon and Lindwall were not often required as batsmen, so well did their predecessors score, but each, in his sphere, was an outstanding success. I have never seen a stumper to equal Tallon in speed. He missed a number of chances but he suffers from sore hands and I had noticed in Australia that his form deteriorated as the season advanced. Some of his leg-side catches bordered on the miraculous.

Lindwall was the spearhead of the attack and, at the finish, he shared honours with Bill Johnston with a Test tally of 27 wickets each. No Australian speed man has exceeded this. Wisely, the English umpires ignored the hubbub about his dragging over the line, a legacy of the previous Test series in Australia. Lindwall continued to drag in England but the umpires, generally, took the view that they could not watch his hands and feet at the same time and so they were satisfied with him if his back foot came down behind the crease-line. He is the nearest

---

[1] Harvey, and Loxton, also, knew only mediocre seasons on their return to Australia. The spinners *did* worry Harvey—but for all that he is still a grand batsman.

approach I have seen to Larwood, and there were times when I
thought I was looking at a bowler equally as great. Perhaps he
was a little under Larwood's pace but he varied his speed more
and the change was never easy to detect. He found in England
that he could do much more off the pitch than in Australia. He
could cut and seam the ball and so a batsman could never feel at
home with him. He was intensely wise in his approach to the
game and always loosened himself first and then gradually
worked up to top speed. Even then, he only let his fast ball go
every now and then. Lindwall had a slightly round-arm delivery,
and it often interested me that he could get the ball up so high
off a short length.

Lindwall shared much in common with Miller but nothing
more so, strangely, than his dislike of bowling. This is very odd
—that two such gifted fast bowlers should so hate fast bowling.
All his cricketing life, Lindwall preferred batting. As a youngster
in the Sydney third-grade competition he batted and bowled
slows, when wanted, and when he rose a grade it was as a batsman.
He did not bowl at all, and when he came into the first-grade side
(which had O'Reilly as captain and also included Morris) it was
as a last-minute replacement for a bowler and Lindwall bowled
medium-paced against the wind. His love was still batting, but
when he did not receive an innings in three matches (jocularly,
Lindwall says he will never forgive O'Reilly for this!) he thought
he had better think a little more about his bowling if he was to
keep his place in the side. O'Reilly gave him advice on his run-up
to get a smoother action. O'Reilly told him not to worry about
bowling no-balls but to make sure his action was smooth, and
to-day there is no more graceful bowling action in the game.
Lindwall saw McCabe get his immortal 187 not out in the Sydney
Test of 1932; he saw Larwood bowl; he read Bradman's book
on cricket and noted what he had to say about swingers; he
sighed, because there was still no room for him in his club team
as a batsman, and he took up fast bowling in earnest.

But, to-day, Lindwall still prefers to hear the ball crashing
against a picket fence off his bat than to hear the stumps pinging
to his bowling. He'd rather make fifty in a Test than take five
wickets. He practised during the New Guinea campaign on
improvised pitches in the jungle, and he returned from war just
two days before the Australian team was chosen for New Zealand.
He was an immediate choice and, modest, peaceful, smiling young
fellow that he is, has been hurling along his thunderbolts for

Australia ever since. But talk batsmanship to him and he gets a far-away look in his eyes.

Miller absolutely detests bowling and, amazingly, thinks very little of his ability in this direction, but I am certain that the Lindwall-Miller fast-bowling combination is as good as I have seen in Test cricket. Miller delivers from very high and gets the ball up quickly off a good length. He runs it away and he changes his pace cleverly. His bouncers are world-famous but, apart from bowling a string of them every time he gets hit for four, Miller thinks little of them. He showed the Trent Bridge crowd, when they were complaining one day, what he would do with bouncers. As he walked back to bowl, tossing his hair, he went through the motions of a vigorous hook-shot and I do believe that bouncers would not worry Miller in the slightest. If he can deal with them, he sees nothing wrong in bowling them at others, but there are few batsmen in the world as gifted as Miller.

In a B.B.C. broadcast before the first Test, I expressed the opinion that Miller and Lindwall were fit to compare with the greatest fast bowlers of all time. Irate and elderly gentlemen wrote protests, going back practically to Noah in their recapitulation of the names of fast bowlers, but I am quite satisfied that these two modern Australians are really great fast bowlers and that their presence in the Australian team in the 1948 series made success assured. Then, too, Miller was one of the greatest slip-fieldsmen I have seen.

Bradman was most fortunate in that he had smiling Bill Johnston to take over in an emergency or relief. Here, indeed, was another great Australian bowler on English pitches. It might be that Australia has never sent a greater left-hander to England because Johnston was a two-in-one bowler. He bowled fast-medium with great hostility, swinging the new ball both ways, and then, when necessary, he could swing into the groove of a length left-hander with turn from the leg. Johnston's outstanding success with the ball was one of the features of the tour because he was the only one of the bowlers to achieve a hundred wickets and he did this with no favours of cleaning up the tail. He earned every wicket. He was, moreover, as likeable a personality as ever walked on a cricket field. He never stopped smiling the whole tour and never shirked a job, no matter how tiring. He was the perfect tourist.

Toshack joined the three I have mentioned as the fourth member of a well-balanced attack until his knee, which almost stopped him from making the trip, gave out in the Leeds Test. The Englishmen considered him a negative bowler, but I prefer to think of him as a "nagging" type. His attack was at the leg-stump with a leg-side field, but he was so adjacent to the stumps that he could not be ignored. He pegged away, too, with great consistency and kept the runs down, getting a good share of wickets, while the fast men rested. It was Toshack who enabled Bradman to exploit to the full that incongruous rule of the past few years in England of a new ball every 55 overs.

This rule bounced against the English side. It played right into the hands of the Australians because with Lindwall, Miller and Johnston, Bradman could stage sharp periods of attack and then swing Toshack into action to wait until a new ball came along again. This rule is absurd because it whittles down the importance of a leg-break bowler in modern cricket and it results in much negative cricket, the change bowlers simply wasting the ball outside the leg-stump to while away the overs. In the Cambridge-Oxford game only 78 runs had been scored one innings when a new ball became available.

Under the circumstances, a spin-bowler was not a necessity for the Australians, and McCool, who had been the paralysing factor in the early Tests of the 1946-47 series, was completely unwanted. It was an unhappy tour for McCool, who found, also, that he often spent whole county innings in the field without being asked to bowl. He became so much out of favour that Bradman even moved him from his slip position. Though McCool suffered from worn spinning fingers and found the English pitches too slow for him, I would not be inclined to write him down as a tour failure—nor would I Ring. It was, I think, an error of judgment that Bruce Dooland was not chosen in this team. He is a most promising slow-bowler, but he, too, would have shared the fate of McCool and Ring in getting little work to do. Ring did get a game in the final Test and performed with credit, but it was not a tour for slow-bowlers. They were ousted in the first place by the speed men and, secondly, received little encouragement.

A spinning bowler of the calibre of Grimmett or O'Reilly would have pushed himself to the front, even in competition with successful fast bowlers, and one, therefore, must have qualms about giving the highest honours to a side which was deficient in slow spin-bowling. Ian Johnson did the off-spinning in four Tests but was not a success, his seven wickets costing 61 runs apiece, so that for a country which has produced some of the greatest spinners in history, one feels that Bradman's side possessed a marked deficiency in not having a slow-spinner. This lack of balance in attack was twice shown up by what everybody conceded to be a weak English team. Once was at Old Trafford on the Saturday of the Test and the other was at Leeds. On both occasions, the pace attack was collared. Had England been experiencing one of its best seasons, this lack of a class spinner would have run the Australians into much trouble.

On the Manchester and Leeds occasions I have mentioned above, Bradman's team slipped quickly from the heights. It was in a very poor way at Manchester, and only Lindwall's adoption of the role of a stock-bowler at Leeds stopped it from being torn to shreds. Apropos of this innings, it was strange that several English critics should have razed Bill Edrich for his century innings. Edrich often was out through playing across the line of flight of the ball, but he was a supreme fighter and I found this innings full of merit. The same critics, making fast run-getting their excuse and overlooking the fact that Bradman, even on the first day, tried to place negative fields, made nought of the fact that Denis Compton in the second innings was once 25 minutes without scoring.

It was significant that four of the leading batsmen in Bradman's team, Bradman, Hassett, Barnes and Brown (who would have scored as well as any if given a Test opening position) were men who were at their top in pre-war cricket. That, I think, is a guide to the prevailing standard of English cricket and induces us not to rush away with rash ideas of this being the best Australian team ever; but, perhaps, the best test is whether many of Bradman's team would find places in, say, the best Australian Eleven since 1921. I chatted this over one day with a distinguished cricketer of those days, and the team we arrived at was: Ponsford, Morris, Bradman, McCabe, Macartney, Jackson, Miller, Gregory (Jack), Tallon, O'Reilly and Grimmett.

The men we had most pangs in leaving out of this 1948 side were Barnes, who is a most capable cricketer; Lindwall who, though magnificent, could hardly excel Jack Gregory, who was one of the game's most colourful personalities of all time; and finally, Johnston. We found it hardest in omitting Lindwall and Johnston, but, with the former, consoled ourselves with the fact that a pretty good one in Ted McDonald was also omitted. If the side needed only a left-hander, Johnston would be chosen of a certainty, but Macartney was a handsome left-hander, plenty good enough to do the work which Gregory, Miller, O'Reilly and Grimmett would leave to do.

Bradman's opinion that this was the greatest Australian team he had played with must, as I write, be given every respect, but, personally, he was very attached to this 1948 side and, in putting on the coat, one is possibly justified in wondering whether he hasn't strained the seams. On good pitches, it would have been difficult to oust the 1930 batting side which had Bradman himself at his very greatest, and the second most prolific scorer in Ponsford in modern cricket history. It had, too, Woodfull, Jackson, Kippax and McCabe. This 1930 side, of a certainty, would have been far superior to the 1948 one on a wet pitch, for instance.

CHAPTER NINETEEN

RETREAT FROM BOWLING GLORY

IT was in a side street in Blackpool that we found him. George Duckworth, one of his best friends in his playing days, knew the way. "It is a neat little mixed shop," said George, "but you won't find his name on it." And we didn't, which was strange, because in his day his name was possibly even as famous as Bradman's, but he had not only finished with all that. He had not the slightest wish to be reminded of it.

His eldest daughter saw us first. She recognised George and gave him a great welcome, smiling broadly and motioning towards the back of the house. And there in a homely room, its walls festooned with photographs of some of the most stirring times known to the game of cricket, he gave me a quiet but a warm welcome. He recognised me immediately though I was the first Australian cricketer he had met since those stormy days of 1932-33 when his name was sprawled across the columns of newspapers in much the same manner as he sprawled his victims across the cricket field, but in 1948 he was much thinner. Walking behind him, one would never guess that here was the greatest fast bowler of the modern age; the possessor, in his time, of as lovely a bowling action as the game has ever known. But his face, though thinner, had not changed much. He was still the same Harold Larwood.

The conversation, for a time, was circumspect. Not only was I one of the "enemy" of 1932-33 but I was a newspaperman, and Larwood had memories of how he had been publicised over the years by the stunting gentry of my profession. Then, in addition, he wanted to bury the dead. You saw that, clearly, in his refusal to have his name shown in the slightest manner over his shop. Dozens of former cricketers throughout the world, whose claim to fame could not compare with his, have capitalised their glory by having their names over balls or bats, by having it in books, by having it up in big letters outside their places of business, but not in the slightest manner, and certainly not by having his name blazoned to the outside world, did Harold Larwood wish to recapture the past. He wanted only to forget it and so his business, to all appearance, was no different to thousands of similar businesses throughout England that are run by the Joneses, the Browns, Williams and Smiths.

It was a pinch of snuff, so to speak, that broke the ice. He took his box out and offered it to me. I declined. Not so George Duckworth. "Aay, laad," said George, taking a copious pinch. He placed it on the back of his hand, slapped it with the other, sniffed simultaneously and forthwith began to sneeze so vigorously that tears ran from his eyes. Larwood smiled and took his with the air of a man long accustomed to the art.

"You know," he said to me, "I always had snuff in my pocket when I was bowling. I often used to take a pinch of it on the field in Australia. It used to freshen me up. And it's much better for you than cigarettes."

An eminent medical authority in the last century, Dr. Gordon Hake, would have approved of that. "Snuff," wrote Dr. Hake to a critic of his habit, "not only wakes up that torpor so prevalent between the nose and the brain, making the wings of an idea uncurl like those of a new-born butterfly, but while others sneeze and run at the eyes my schneiderian membrane is impervious to the weather or, to be explicit, I never take a cold in the head." Soon after the introduction of snuff into Britain in the eighteenth century, the "Gentlewoman's Companion," noble production, was advising its gentle readers whose sight was failing to use the right sort of Portugal snuff "whereby many eminent people had cured themselves so that they could read without spectacles after having used them for many years."

As Larwood was snuffing, I thought his Australian opponents might have been a little better off in 1932-33 had somebody got his box away from him. He might not have sighted his target or his victim so readily, but here at Blackpool, in 1948, it cleared also the atmosphere and when, at long last, George had got his schneiderian membrane to behave, the three of us fell to discussing the old days in a reminiscent manner. There was no bitterness. I had taken many on the ribs from Larwood and Voce in those bodyline days, but all that was forgotten as we recalled the players of those days and the many incidents —for incidents happened in the bodyline series every other minute.

One has not to talk long with Larwood to realise that he is still embittered over those days. I don't think it is with the

Australians, but rather with those English officials who were glad to have him and use him before bodyline became ostracised, and then, conveniently, put him aside. He finds that impossible to forgive. Like the prodigal son, he would have been welcomed home by the M.C.C. in 1935 and had all forgiven, but Larwood is a man of strong beliefs. To satisfy all and sundry, the M.C.C. wished Larwood to apologise to them. Had he done that, like Voce, he would have been chosen again for the Australian tour of 1936-37, but Larwood could not see that he had anything to apologise over and so he remained adamant and went out of the game under a cloud.

He did not say so, but I gathered that he considered himself badly treated, and many who know the story of those bodyline days will agree with him. With us, he recalled only the happy memories of the most distressing tour in cricket history, though when we talked of Bradman I detected again the same old glint of battle I had seen in his eye when I had faced up to him as a batsman.

"When I bowled against Bradman," he said, "I always thought he was out to show me up as the worst fast bowler in the world. Well, I took the view that I should try and show him up as the worst batsman. But, laad, he was a good 'un."

We fell to looking through his photographic albums and the reminiscences among the three of us came thick and fast. His eldest daughter (and Larwood has five beautiful daughters, the youngest between our legs on the floor) had just begun to take an interest in cricket, and only a few days before Larwood had got out his souvenirs to show her, and they included innumerable balls with silver rings about them describing how in many places he had performed grand bowling feats.

Larwood made some pretty shrewd observations about batsmen. He reeled off the names of famous batsmen who, he considered, couldn't play the hook stroke and were thus at a disadvantage against him. The cricket world would be amazed if I repeated the men he named but, like Keith Miller, the Australian, he considered himself fully entitled to prove their weaknesses with bouncers. But how the wheel has now turned full circle! Here, in 1948, under Bradman, the Australians exploited the bouncers to the full (though without the packed leg-field of Jardine), and members of the Nottingham County Committee, the same committee which was forced to apologise to Woodfull and his team in 1934 because Voce had bowled bumpers, now admonished their own spectators for barracking against Australian bumpers. The cricket world, surely, is as crazy and as inconsistent as the outside one.

It was with difficulty that we induced Larwood to come with us to a cricket game for charity which we were playing on the Blackpool ground. He compromised to the extent of promising to come down after afternoon tea. He had not seen either the 1934 or 1938 Australian teams in action. He had not seen his C.-in-C., Douglas Jardine, since Jardine had played in his benefit game in 1935. He had not seen this present Australian team in action, though he had a hankering to see Lindwall bowl. He could not remember the last time he had seen a game on his old home ground, Trent Bridge. Cricket had lost all its appeal for Larwood.

He came to the charity game, forced into it, we thought, by his family, who liked to see him with old associates. He told me there a story I loved. It was about Sir Pelham Warner and myself and concerned the bodyline tour. It happened during the Adelaide game, where feeling was tremendously high, and where Woodfull used strong words to Warner over the tactics of the M.C.C. team. That story ran quickly to the Press, and Sir Pelham, jumping to conclusions because I was a pressman, wrongly blamed me for the breach of ethics.

"As we were going out to field in your second innings," said Larwood, "Sir Pelham said to me, 'Larwood, I will give you a pound if you bowl Fingleton out quickly.' If you remember, I did, and when I came off the field Sir Pelham was waiting there at the door with a pound note in his hand."

I will never forget that ball. It was the best ever bowled to me in cricket. At Larwood's top speed, it changed course in the air from leg and, continuing on that course, pitched about the leg and middle stump and took the off-bail. It was absolutely unplayable. A batsman never minds being dismissed by a good ball, even for nothing, as I was that day.

"Ah, well," said Larwood, "those days are gone for ever, but here's a pound note. Let's all go and have a drink and we will say it is on Sir Pelham."

There were times, during the Australian tour of bodyline, when Larwood thought the game not worth the candle. He knew abuse. The tumult was overpowering, the work of fast bowling hard. He has a very sensitive side to his nature and often wondered whether it was worth it, but then he allowed his mind to revert to his coal-mining days before he played cricket and that was sufficient.   Strangely, on that tour, his stomach revolted against food.   He found that beer, with his occasional pinch of snuff on the field, gave him all the sting he wanted.   From the Australian viewpoint, it gave him more than enough, but he will always be remembered in Australia, tactics of that M.C.C. side apart, as the Prince of Bowlers.

It was a coincidence that very day that Larwood should have received from Australia a long letter from a youth on the art of bowling.   It was an interesting letter, asking for advice.   It was fitting, even though this lad had never seen Larwood bowl, that he should have written to such a one for advice, though I smiled to myself as I read this delightful piece of youthful folly: "Do you think, Mr. Larwood," wrote this ardent theorist, "that you might have been a better fast bowler if you had begun the swing of your right arm from lower down?"   As if any Australian would have wanted Larwood to be better than he was, but perhaps the oddest thing of all about this letter was that it came from Bowral, home town of Bradman.   How quaint if Bowral, through Bradman's greatest antagonist on the field, should produce another Larwood!

When we parted we had extracted from him almost a half-promise that he would come to Old Trafford and see and meet the Australians.   He wanted to meet O'Reilly;   he wanted to see Lindwall particularly, but Larwood never came.   I think the inside of an English first-class ground contained too many sad memories for him.   He deserved better of the game;   he deserved better, particularly, of English cricket because, in tactics, he was only a cog in the wheel.   He was, for a certainty, the only bowler who quelled Bradman;   the only bowler who made Bradman lose his poise and balance, departing from his set path of easeful centuries into flurried and agitated movements.

I left Blackpool glad that I had seen Larwood, and I think that he, for his part, was pleased again to meet an Australian cricketer, the first since the field of battle in 1932-33.   There is something tragic about his finish in cricket and the fact that he wishes to have no ties with the game now at all.   It is interesting, too, to look back to those days of 1932-33 and reflect what time has done for the central figures, Bradman and Larwood.   The game has been over-kind to one; unkind to the other, but that has ever been the ways of cricket.   It is a game, mostly, for batsmen, and I thought of all this as I left Larwood on the note, of all things, of migration. He thinks hard these days of bringing his lovely family of five daughters to settle in a country which once flamed from end to end over his bowling. That, surely, must be the oddest thought of all—Larwood settled in Australia! But he would be doubly welcome. Australia has never held anything against Larwood.

CHAPTER TWENTY

OLD TRAFFORD, RAIN AND SMOKE

THE name Old Trafford is nothing if not euphonious. It runs trippingly off the tongue and conjures in the minds of those who know their cricket the names of the Tyldesleys (Johnnie, Ernest and Dick), Johnny Briggs, Mold, Parkin, George Duckworth, our own admirable Ted McDonald, whose name and deeds are still fresh in Old Trafford Pavilion talk, Spooner, one of the old school who still watches the young with an unjaundiced eye, Makepeace, Hallows, Iddon, Hornby, MacLaren, Brearley, Pollard, Paynter, Washbrook and the rest. A formidable list of names, indeed, to have associated with a famous ground; few other grounds can boast a better.

My own introduction to Old Trafford was through Neville Cardus, whose name in cricket, I dare say, will remain as long as any of the above. He was as much part and parcel of the ground as any of the others. They showed their artistry and revealed their Lancashire characters on the field; he interpreted it for the masses in the columns of the *Manchester Guardian*, a newspaper as reliable and as entertaining to read in 1948 as it was, undoubtedly, in the early days of the century, and few modern-old newspapers, whose fads and fancies change with the generations, have that reputation.

Cardus was rich in his knowledge and history of the game, but, as his Autobiography reveals, he was particularly rich in his appreciation of the way of life of his fellow-Lancastrians. Using the cricket field as a medium, he gave us in lucid prose the mannerisms and the characters of Lancashire cricketers in much the same way as Dickens did with Mr. Pickwick, Sam Weller and Micawber. Cardus made his types live in print, and all this I devoured avidly as a youth in the Sydney *Guardian* when, as a small cadet reporter, I spent much time in the File room scanning the file of the *Manchester Guardian* and, finding the lure of Cardus's articles too much for me, sometimes taking my newspaper future in my hands with a blade as I ignored stern warnings that "anybody found cutting these files will be instantly dismissed." Outside newspaper files eventually go into scrap. The

Sydney *Guardian* itself went into oblivion, but I still have Cardus's articles of the 1920s preserved in a scrapbook.

One of the most pleasant days in my newspaper life was in 1948 when the Editor of the *Manchester Guardian* asked me to write a double-column article on *the* Leader Page of the *Guardian*. That meant more to me than making a century on Old Trafford which, incidentally, I missed by some three or four runs in 1938.

Who is the typical Lancashire cricketing type? Probably many would name Cecil Parkin, but I knew him only by repute and stories. Makepeace, who stands behind the county nets these days with his "do's" and "don'ts" to the coming generation, is another who looks and acts typically Lancastrian, but, above all others, I would name George Duckworth, who was famous in Australia for his piercing "*OWZAT*," his sense of humour and for putting raw pieces of steak in his wicket-keeping gloves to take the sting out of Larwood's deliveries. The Australian batsmen said George encouraged the flies with his meat, but possibly they had heard of the time when the great Ranji blamed a fly in his eye for his dismissal and it was handy to have such an excuse on hand.

Although it sounds apocryphal, it is true that Duckworth almost missed playing for Lancashire. He was on the ground staff at Edgbaston, Warwickshire, before he linked with the county of his birth, and from 1923 until his end with Lancashire he claimed 852 victims behind the wickets for the Red Rose—268 stumped and 584 caught. Impressive as this total is, goodness only knows what it would have been had all his appeals been answered in the affirmative. Laid head to feet, his victims would surely have extended from Old Trafford to Liverpool, through the Mersey Tunnel and up to Northop in Flintshire, yet that voice was as characteristic of Duckworth as his rotund, squatting figure behind the stumps.

Heredity took Duckworth into the glove and pad business. His father was a stumper. When George went to practise with his school team for the first time his captain asked whether he was the son of the village wicket-keeper. "Yes," replied George. "Well," said the captain, "that settles the stumping position. You are in the first eleven for to-morrow." George had never kept wickets before that but he's never stopped keeping them since, and any charity game within fair distance of Warrington will always find him ready and eager.

Duckworth is intensely proud of his county and his home

town of Warrington. No identity is better known in the county, and often, as O'Reilly and I travelled with him, I would delight in asking George which county he were in. "This is all Lancashire, Jack," he would reply, warmly and with pride in his voice. "Ooh, aye, laad. This be all Lancashire." There is no better Lancashire guide. He knows all the canals, the churches, the old houses (and points out one where Cromwell slept the night before he gave somebody or other some of his own brand of bodyline of that day), and he knows the history of all the towns adjacent to Warrington. He seems to know everybody, and there's no better company in all England than George and his warm-hearted wife, Bessie (who refers to George in an aside as "him"), when they are with their Warrington friends.

The Duckworths had O'Reilly and me to stay with them on their farm during the Lancashire match and fed us like Test cricketers. Bessie always had a "bit o' sup" waiting for us when we returned, and I never tired of watching her make a pot of tea. She would warm the teapot, naturally, but then she would put hot water in the cup to warm it, and then even stand the spoon in the cup to warm it also. The North of England women are proverbially thorough in their household duties, and I was sometimes fearful, as I watched Bessie in her tea-making duties, that she might want to pour some hot water down me to warm me for the tea.

George the Farmer was another study. He was at his richest best when the village children, by their own infallible grapevine system, knew that Uncle George had been to the cricket because he always returned from Old Trafford with a canister of ice-cream, which was liberally ladled out.

"Ooh, aye, Kennie," George would say to the bright little lad from the next farm (who was tragically drowned several weeks later), "thou must sing for sup of ice-cream, laad." And Kennie would soar to shrill and trembling heights, his eyes the while on the ice-cream in George's hands. And diminutive Margaret, quaint three-year-older from across the way, feeling that a little gossip (or chunnering, as they say in Lancashire) should repay the Duckworth largesse, would tell with rolling eyes of how her store-keeping mother would fob off passing strangers who sought the elusive cigarette. "Ooh, t'hyp'crite, Bessie," would say the mite, not understanding that in days of shortages first people come first, "and ye know she has un under counter all t'time." Margaret came across every morning for her gossip with the Australians. The morning we were leaving she said to Mrs. Duckworth, "Aye, Bessie, but doon't tha' 'Stralians toalk foony."

Just up from More, the village, is where Lewis Carroll wrote *Alice in Wonderland*, and out from Warrington towards Cheshire, reputed the greenest county in all England, is some lovely country, the lanes rich with the blooms of rhododendrons. We drove under lowering skies to look at one of George's potato fields. He pointed out ash and oak trees in close proximity. This, he said, was done purposely as the budding of the trees supposedly led one to anticipate the summer.

> *Oak before the ash, in for a splash ;*
> *Ash before the oak, in for a soak.*

Manchester is a depressing city, heavy, like all the industrial towns of the north, with the smoke of industry, but it has character with women of the side streets still dressing in clogs and shawls. The fronts and walls of impressive public buildings are seamy-black from the coal-laden air. So, too, are the innumerable statues, and in the middle of the city is one of Gladstone with finger up and looking for all the world as if he is an umpire, answering one of Duckworth's appeals in the affirmative. Huge gaps have been carved in the city buildings by the war blitz, and Manchester's Piccadilly on a wet day is a dreary, puddly place with all its middle flat to the ground. There is an air of sad resignation about the horses, resigned to their life and the weather, as they clip-clop along the cobbles which Morton once aptly described as so many brown loaves of bread. The horses get a grip with their shoes in the openings between the bricks, thus offsetting the wet and slippery surface.

The bus ride from the heart of the city to Old Trafford is along dingy streets, through the poor quarter of the city, where ragged little urchins eke out their games between passing traffic and bombed buildings. And the bombs, too, played such havoc with Old Trafford itself that in 1948 it looked like a man who had had his head shaved—almost nothing was left on top. Bombs hurled up most of the pavilions and hurled up the pitch too, leaving a crater there that would be rather reminiscent of Dick Pollard's if all his bowling holes at the end of the season were placed pit upon pit. Old Trafford now is very open to the weather, and of all cricketing places in the world that which should be least open to the weather is Old Trafford.

Manchester's bad weather is a cricketing perennial. Cricket writers vied in vituperation when the rain came again and washed out the third Test of this series. They recalled that not a single Manchester Test had been finished since 1905; they recalled that not a single ball had been bowled in the Tests of 1890 and 1938; they noted that insurance companies charge more to insure against rain in Manchester than any other part of the British Isles.

"Not only sunshine figures are hard to obtain about Manchester," wrote John Macadam in the *Daily Express*. "Casualty figures are equally difficult to get. Things like . . . the number of times the Old Trafford lifeboat has put out to mid-wicket; the number of batsmen saved by breeches buoy; the number of umpires marooned and thereafter lost to human ken; the incidence of pneumonia in the weeks following any Test; the compensation paid every fourth year to Manchester parents for the recovery of small boys from the Deansluicegate."

Macadam claims that the oldest horror story in the world is told of George Duckworth, who was seen one fine day standing up to his neck in water over towards the outfield. He was invited to come over and join the gang. "I can't," George is reputed to have said, "I'm on top of a bus."

"But what's the use," Macadam concludes in his lament against Old Trafford weather. "Anything we say will slide off like water from a Manchester man's back."

The Mancunian takes all the criticism of his weather very nobly and refers you to the time of the all-dry Test in 1934, when people fainted in all directions and the players became infected with a dry-weather throat ailment. "Don't take my word for this," he says, knowing that what he speaks is true, "but in the Old Trafford pavilion is a foot-high green jug, specially moulded for the occasion, on which is inscribed full particulars." The commemoration of a fine spell is, surely, a commentary upon all the wet stuff, but the Mancunian will tell you seriously that Bolton has twice as much rain as Manchester, and that sometimes there is play at Old Trafford when there's none elsewhere in England.

And the Mancunian will tell you, just as seriously, that that admirable film, *The Lady Vanishes*, left a bad impression of Manchester weather that has never been effaced. In this film

Naunton Wayne and Basil Radford manage to survive innumerable dangers as they flee through crisis-ridden Europe. Their talk, as they dodge bullets, is of the Manchester Test and what is happening there. They conjecture all manner of cricket happenings and dash for a newspaper as soon as they arrive in England. They open the page only to read "Rain at Manchester. No Play."

Old Trafford was still licking some of its war wounds in 1948, but it improved greatly during the season and, when building becomes easier in England, will soon be back to its former greatness. It is a ground around which revolves many of the best cricketing stories, most of them relating to the Yorkshire-Lancashire Wars of the Roses, which have not yet recaptured their pre-war bitterness and tenacity.

I like, particularly, the story of the Yorkshire defeat at Old Trafford once when Abe Waddington, in a tight finish, was sent in with strict orders not to do anything "foony." The Yorkshire rot had begun when Emmot Robinson had permitted himself a cut—a stroke proverbially ostracised and shunned in such a game —and was caught in the slips by Charlie Hallows. Nothing, then, would go right for Yorkshire and Waddington carried a big responsibility. He played quietly for a time but then pranced up the pitch, made a huge hit, missed, fell flat on his face and was ignominiously stumped by Duckworth. Lancashire had won.

The dressing-rooms told their own post-game stories. From the Lancashire room came sounds of song and the popping of champagne corks. In the Yorkshire room there was glum silence. As Waddington was tying his tie at the mirror, Emmot Robinson said to him, "Laad, they would'st have had to kill me before they got me oot like they got thee." And Wilfred Rhodes chimed in with, "Thou'st fine one to talk, Emmot. Fancy indulgin' in fancy coots at thy time o' life."

There's a looseness about Lancashire cricket at present which is out of type with the county, but the tightening-up will come again. A lady in Grindleford once told me of her first Yorkshire-Lancashire game. "It was all so very clever," she said. "The batsmen were clever, the bowlers were clever, the fieldsmen were clever—everybody was so very clever that nothing happened."

But the War of the Roses still has an appeal all of its own. It is a war, mostly, of attrition. A cricketing enthusiast, who obviously didn't belong to either county, sat and watched slow stuff for a very long time once. Eventually he turned as if in conversation to relieve the boredom and remarked to his becapped neighbour in a friendly manner, "It's a bit dull, isn't it?"

"Is't fra Lancashire?" gruffly asked the other spectator.

"No," replied the stranger.

"Is't fra Yorkshire?"

"No."

"Then what's it to do wi' thee?"

You have to know your Yorkshire and Lancashire types to appreciate them. Better still, you have to play cricket against both counties to appreciate just what a War of the Roses is to them. There was one game at Headingley, I am told, which was just bedlam because the game, for once, departed from type. Hopwood and a young Lancastrian, who obviously had not been educated in such games, hit out furiously and runs came at a terrific rate, a rate which caused the Yorkshire bowlers and fieldsmen to bicker and castigate themselves in no uncertain manner. Of a sudden, umpire Morgan raised his hand and made a general appeal. "Stop, stop," he said, "I can't hear myself count. It's like a bloody parrot-house."

It was the same umpire who had cause once to take Emmot Robinson to task. Robinson, now an umpire, is one of Yorkshire's greatest characters, but at this time he had retired from the game. Verity had just been inoculated to go to Australia and couldn't field. Out came Robinson, from retirement, with his bandy walk, his trousers drooping in characteristic style, to take a place in the gully. To the very first ball bowled while he was on the field he let out an isolated and outrageous appeal. Umpire Morden was grievously offended. "Not out and keep thy bloody mouth shut, Emmot," he called down the field. "Why, thou's not even in the game!"

But back to Old Trafford. On the day of no-play during the Test I walked into the pavilion and, with Thomas E. Henry, Editor of the Manchester *Evening News*, as my quiz-master, joined the hundreds of others down the years who have failed to detect what was wrong with the wicket-keeping picture on the wall (and I'll not give the secret away here). With the rain pouring outside, it was cheering to look at photographs on the wall which showed Test teams taking the field at Old Trafford with not a solitary player in a sweater. As at Lord's, they put up the scores of other games in the pavilion, and I thought I detected a flourish about the office girl as she put up "Rain—No Play" opposite several of the games that day. Manchester, so her gesture seemed to say, was not the only place in which it rained, and there's some Old Trafford self-defence to be seen, also, in the case which houses the Dry-Test jug. Alongside it, nestling close to an incendiary bomb picked up on the ground after a blitz, and a lucky tooth charm that was given to Johnny Briggs by a South African native chief, is a black round ball of soil. This was taken from the wet Brisbane pitch of 1946, as fierce a pitch as one would ever wish to see.

The Wednesday night of November 23, 1904, must have been an unforgettable one in Lancashire history. This was the night when the county and its good friends celebrated Lancashire's unbeaten championship win under MacLaren's captaincy and the presidency of Hornby. This Wednesday night was one to read about on the pavilion wall, and especially in the rationed days of 1948. Nothing was rationed then, not certainly the speeches, because there were six toasts and these were interlarded with musical selections of love, ballads and humour. This was the menu of 1904: Oysters; Clear Soup, Thick Game; Fillets of Sole Dieppoise, Devilled Whitebaits; Capon à la Stanley, Vol au Vent of Sweetbread Toulouse; Roast Saddle of Mutton, Larded Fillet of Beef, Braised Celery, Potatoes; Roast Quails on Toast, Salad; Tutti Frutti Ice, Pastry, Cheese straws; Fruits, Coffee. As I left this and wandered along to the crowded Press pavilion for the meagre lunch of 1948 I thought that, perhaps, it was as well the wine list was turned to the wall. But what a night of jollity, comradeship and speeches that night of '04 must have been!

I have written that most of the Old Trafford roofs went sky-high during the war. On the top of a remaining one is now built a long Press-box, and from it one gets a grand view of this industrial city. On a grassless square outside the ground, bare-legged lads play cricket (as they did all through the momentous Saturday of the Test when England's cricket fortunes turned the corner); a railway line runs adjacent to the ground on the other side and, as at Nottingham, all windows are crammed as the trains go by and slow down for the occasion. I often thought how pleasant it would be for these passengers if something happened as they passed by so that they would be left to ponder the reason for the noise, but nothing ever seemed to happen at train-time.

Over to the right of the ground, from the elevated Press-box, are the Derbyshire hills, a long, low line 16 miles away. A Press friend, Bill Bailey, told me that it's ominous when the hills are seen because clarity comes into the atmosphere just before rain. So that Old Trafford, open as it is now, can keep a weather-eye well cocked, and the crowd, darkly clad and overcoated, generally comes prepared for the worst.

They told me here, too, that from this elevation one can count at least a hundred Mancunian spires on a fine day. Now that could possibly be true. Innumerable ones mingle with the tall chimneys of the industrial north but I don't think the claim can ever be disputed. It is based, you see, on a fine day and—well, don't let's talk about the Manchester weather again!

TEST SCORES AND AVERAGES

First Test

ENGLAND

FIRST INNINGS		SECOND INNINGS	
Hutton, b. Miller	3	b. Miller	74
Washbrook, c. Brown, b. Lindwall	6	c. Tallon, b. Miller	1
W. J. Edrich, b. Johnston	18	c. Tallon, b. Johnson	13
Compton (D.), b. Miller	19	hit wkt., b. Miller	184
Hardstaff, c. Miller, b. Johnston	0	c. Hassett, b. Toshack	43
Barnett, b. Johnston	8	c. Miller, b. Johnston..	6
N. W. D. Yardley, l.b.w., b. Toshack	3	c. and b. Johnston	22
Evans, c. Morris, b. Johnston	12	c. Tallon, b. Johnston	50
Laker, c. Tallon, b. Miller	63	b. Miller	4
Bedser (A. V.), c. Brown, b. Johnston	22	not out	3
Young, not out	1	b. Johnston	9
Extras (b. 5, l.b. 5)	10	Extras (b. 12, l.b. 17, n.b. 3)	32
Total	165	Total	441

BOWLING.—FIRST INNINGS.—Lindwall, 13—5—30—1; Miller, 19—8—38—3; Johnston, 25—11—36—5; Toshack, 14—8—28—1; Johnson, 5—1—19—0; Morris, 3—1—4—0.

SECOND INNINGS.—Miller, 44—10—125—4; Johnston, 59—12—147—4; Johnson, 42—15—66—1; Toshack, 33—14—60—1; Barnes, 5—2—11—0.

FALL OF THE WICKETS.—FIRST INNINGS.—1—9, 2—15, 3—46, 4—46, 5—48, 6—60, 7—74, 8—74, 9—163, 10—165.

SECOND INNINGS.—1—5, 2—39, 3—150, 4—243, 5—264, 6—321, 7—405, 8—413, 9—423, 10—441.

AUSTRALIA

FIRST INNINGS		SECOND INNINGS	
A. R. Morris, b. Laker	31	b. Bedser	9
S. G. Barnes, c. Evans, b. Laker	62	not out	64
D. G. Bradman, c. Hutton, b. Bedser	138	c. Hutton, b. Bedser	0
K. R. Miller, c. Edrich, b. Laker	0		
W. A. Brown, l.b.w., b. Yardley	17		
A. L. Hassett, b. Bedser	137	not out	21
I. W. Johnson, b. Laker	21		
D. Tallon, c. and b. Young	10		
R. R. Lindwall, c. Evans, b. Yardley	42		
W. A. Johnston, not out	17		
E. R. H. Toshack, l.b.w., b. Bedser	19		
Extras (b. 9, l.b. 4, w. 1, n.b. 1)	15	Extras (l.b. 2, w. 1, n.b. 1)	4
Total	509	Total (2 wkts.)	98

BOWLING.—FIRST INNINGS.—Edrich, 18—1—72—0; Bedser, 44.2—12—113—3; Barnett, 17—5—36—0; Young, 60—28—79—1; Laker, 55—14—138—4; Compton, 5—0—24—0; Yardley, 17—6—32—2.

SECOND INNINGS.—Bedser, 14.3—4—46—2; Edrich, 4—0—20—0; Young, 10—3—28—0.

FALL OF THE WICKETS.—FIRST INNINGS.—1—73, 2—121, 3—121, 4—185, 5—305, 6—338, 7—365, 8—472, 9—476, 10—509.

SECOND INNINGS.—1—38, 2—48.

UMPIRES.—F. Chester and E. Cooke.

Second Test

AUSTRALIA

FIRST INNINGS		SECOND INNINGS	
S. G. Barnes, c. Hutton, b. Coxon ..	0	c. Washbrook, b. Yardley	141
A. R. Morris, c. Hutton, b. Coxon ..	105	b. Wright	62
D. G. Bradman, c. Hutton, b. Bedser	38	c. Edrich, b. Bedser	89
A. L. Hassett, b. Yardley	47	b. Yardley	0
K. R. Miller, l.b.w., b. Bedser.. ..	4	c. Bedser, b. Laker	74
W. A. Brown, l.b.w., b. Yardley ..	24	c. Evans, b. Coxon	32
I. W. Johnson, c. Evans, b. Edrich ..	4	not out	9
D. Tallon, c. Yardley, b. Bedser	53		
R. R. Lindwall, b. Bedser	15	st. Evans, b. Laker	25
W. A. Johnston, st. Evans, b. Wright	29		
E. R. H. Toshack, not out	20		
Extras (b. 3, l.b. 7, n.b. 1)	11	Extras (b. 22, l.b. 5, n.b. 1) ..	28
Total	350	Total (7 wkts. dec.)	460

BOWLING.—FIRST INNINGS.—Bedser, 43—14—100—4; Coxon, 35—10—90—2; Edrich, 8—0—43—1; Wright, 21.3—8—54—1; Laker, 7—3—17—0; Yardley, 15—4—35—2.

SECOND INNINGS.—Bedser, 34—6—112—1; Coxon, 28—3—82—1; Yardley, 13—4—36—2; Edrich, 2—0—11—0; Wright, 19—4—69—1; Laker, 31.2—6—111—2; Compton, 3—0—11—0.

FALL OF THE WICKETS.—FIRST INNINGS.—1—3, 2—87, 3—166, 4—173, 5—216, 6—225, 7—246, 8—275, 9—320, 10—350.

SECOND INNINGS.—1—122, 2—296, 3—296, 4—329, 5—416, 6—445, 7—460.

ENGLAND

FIRST INNINGS		SECOND INNINGS	
Hutton, b. Johnson	20	c. Johnson, b. Lindwall	13
Washbrook, c. Tallon, b. Lindwall ..	8	c. Tallon, b. Toshack	37
W. J. Edrich, b. Lindwall	5	c. Johnson, b. Toshack	2
Compton (D.), c. Miller, b. Johnston	53	c. Miller, b. Johnston..	29
Dollery, b. Lindwall	0	b. Lindwall	37
N. W. D. Yardley, b. Lindwall ..	44	b. Toshack	11
Coxon, c. and b. Johnson	19	l.b.w., b. Toshack	0
Evans, c. Miller, b. Johnston	9	not out	24
Laker, c. Tallon, b. Johnson	28	b. Lindwall	0
Bedser (A. V.), b. Lindwall	9	c. Hassett, b. Johnston	9
Wright, not out	13	c. Lindwall, b. Toshack	4
Extras (l.b. 3, n.b. 4)	7	Extras (b. 16, l.b. 4)..	20
Total	215	Total	186

BOWLING.—FIRST INNINGS.—Lindwall, 27.4—7—0—5; Johnston, 22—4—43—2; Johnson, 35—13—72—3; Toshack, 18—11—23—0.

SECOND INNINGS.—Lindwall, 23—9—61—3; Johnston, 33—15—62—2; Toshack, 20.1—6—40—5; Johnson, 2—1—3—0.

FALL OF THE WICKETS.—FIRST INNINGS.—1—17, 2—32, 3—46, 4—46, 5—133, 6—134, 7—145, 8—186, 9—197, 10—215.

SECOND INNINGS.—1—42, 2—52, 3—65, 4—106, 5—133, 6—133, 7—141, 8—141, 9—158, 10—186.

UMPIRES.—C. N. Woolley and D. Davies.

APPENDIX
Third Test

ENGLAND

FIRST INNINGS		SECOND INNINGS	
Washbrook, b. Johnston	11	not out	85
Emmett, c. Barnes, b. Lindwall	10	c. Tallon, b. Lindwall	0
W. J. Edrich, c. Tallon, b. Lindwall	32	run out	53
Compton (D.), not out	145	c. Miller, b. Toshack	0
Crapp, l.b.w., b. Lindwall	37	not out	19
Dollery, b. Johnston	1		
N. W. D. Yardley, c. Johnson, b. Toshack	22		
Evans, c. Johnston, b. Lindwall	34		
Bedser (A. V.), run out	37		
Pollard, b. Toshack	3		
Young, c. Bradman, b. Johnston	4		
Extras (b. 7, l.b. 17, n.b. 3)	27	Extras (b. 9, l.b. 7, w. 1)	17
Total	363	Total (3 wkts. dec.)	174

BOWLING.—FIRST INNINGS.—Lindwall, 40—8—99—4; Johnston, 45.5—13—67—3; Loxton, 7—0—18—0; Toshack, 41—20—75—2; Johnson, 38—16—77—0.
SECOND INNINGS.—Lindwall, 14—4—37—1; Miller, 14—7—15—0; Johnston, 14—3—34—0; Loxton, 8—1—29—0; Toshack, 12—5—26—1; Johnson, 7—3—16—0.
FALL OF THE WICKETS.—FIRST INNINGS.—1—22, 2—28, 3—96, 4—97, 5—119, 6—141, 7—216, 8—337, 9—352, 10—363.
SECOND INNINGS.—1—1, 2—125, 3—129.

AUSTRALIA

FIRST INNINGS		SECOND INNINGS	
A. R. Morris, c. Compton, b. Bedser	51	not out	54
I. W. Johnson, c. Evans, b. Bedser	1	c. Crapp, b. Young	6
D. G. Bradman, l.b.w., b. Pollard	7	not out	30
A. L. Hassett, c. Washbrook, b. Young	38		
K. R. Miller, l.b.w., b. Pollard	31		
S. G. Barnes, retired hurt	1		
S. J. E. Loxton, b. Pollard	36		
D. Tallon, c. Evans, b. Edrich	18		
R. R. Lindwall, c. Washbrook, b. Bedser	23		
W. A. Johnston, c. Crapp, b. Bedser	3		
E. R. H. Toshack, not out	0		
Extras (b. 5, l.b. 4, n.b. 3)	12	Extras (n.b. 2)	2
Total	221	Total (for 1 wkt.)	92

BOWLING.—FIRST INNINGS.—Bedser, 36—12—81—4; Pollard, 32—9—53—3; Edrich, 7—3—27—1; Yardley, 4—0—12—0; Young, 14—5—36—1.
SECOND INNINGS.—Bedser, 19—12—27—0; Pollard, 10—8—6—0; Young, 21—12—31—1; Compton, 9—3—18—0; Edrich, 2—0—8—0.
FALL OF THE WICKETS.—FIRST INNINGS.—1—3, 2—13, 3—82, 4—135, 5—139, 6—172, 7—208, 8—219, 9—221.
SECOND INNINGS.—1—10.
UMPIRES.—F. Chester and D. Davies.

APPENDIX

Fourth Test

ENGLAND

FIRST INNINGS		SECOND INNINGS	
Hutton, b. Lindwall	81	c. Bradman, b. Johnson	57
Washbrook, c. Lindwall, b. Johnston	143	c. Harvey, b. Johnston	65
W. J. Edrich, c. Morris, b. Johnson ..	111	l.b.w., b. Lindwall	54
Bedser (A. V.), c. and b. Johnson ..	79	c. Hassett, b. Miller	17
Compton (D.), c. Saggers, b. Lindwall	23	c. Miller, b. Johnston	66
Crapp, b. Toshack	5	b. Lindwall	18
N. W. D. Yardley, b. Miller	25	c. Harvey, b. Johnston	7
K. Cranston, b. Loxton	10	c. Saggers, b. Johnston	0
Evans, c. Hassett, b. Loxton	3	not out	47
Laker, c. Saggers, b. Loxton	4	not out	15
Pollard, not out	0		
Extras (b. 2, l.b. 8, w. 1, n.b. 1) ..	12	Extras (b. 4, l.b. 12, n.b. 3) ..	19
Total	496	Total (8 wkts. dec.)	365

BOWLING.—FIRST INNINGS.—Lindwall, 38—10—79—2; Miller, 17.1—2—43—1; Johnston, 38—13—86—1; Toshack, 35—6—112—1; Loxton, 26—4—55—3; Johnson, 33—9—89—2; Morris, 5—0—20—0.
SECOND INNINGS.—Lindwall, 26—6—84—2; Miller, 21—5—53—1; Johnston, 29—5—95—4; Loxton, 10—2—29—0; Johnson, 21—2—85—1.
FALL OF WICKETS.—FIRST INNINGS.—1—168, 2—268, 3—423, 4—426, 5—447, 6—473, 7—486, 8—490, 9—496, 10—496.
SECOND INNINGS.—1—129, 2—129, 3—232, 4—260, 5—277, 6—278, 7—293, 8—330.

AUSTRALIA

FIRST INNINGS		SECOND INNINGS	
A. R. Morris, c. Cranston, b. Bedser..	6	c. Pollard, b. Yardley	182
A. L. Hassett, c. Crapp, b. Pollard ..	13	c. and b. Compton	17
D. G. Bradman, b. Pollard	33	not out	173
K. R. Miller, c. Edrich, b. Yardley ..	58	l.b.w., b. Cranston	12
R. N. Harvey, b. Laker..	112	not out	4
S. J. E. Loxton, b. Yardley	93		
I. W. Johnson, c. Cranston, b. Laker..	10		
R. R. Lindwall, c. Crapp, b. Bedser ..	77		
R. A. Saggers, st. Evans, b. Laker ..	5		
W. A. Johnston, c. Edrich, b. Bedser..	13		
E. R. H. Toshack, not out	12		
Extras (b. 9, l.b. 14, n.b. 3)	26	Extras (b. 6, l.b. 9, n.b. 1).. ..	16
Total	458	Total (3 wkts.)	404

BOWLING.—FIRST INNINGS.—Bedser, 31.2—4—92—3; Pollard, 38—6—104—2; Cranston, 14—1—51—0; Edrich, 3—0—19—0; Laker, 30—8—113—3; Yardley, 17—6—38—2; Compton, 3—0—15—0.
SECOND INNINGS.—Bedser, 21—2—56—0; Pollard, 22—6—55—0; Laker, 32—11—93—0; Compton, 15—3—82—1; Hutton, 4—1—30—0; Yardley, 13—1—44—1; Cranston, 7.1—0—28—1.
FALL OF WICKETS.—FIRST INNINGS.—1—13, 2—65, 3—68, 4—189, 5—294, 6—329, 7—344, 8—355, 9—403, 10—458.
SECOND INNINGS.—1—57, 2—358, 3—396.
UMPIRES.—F. Chester and H. G. Baldwin.

APPENDIX
Fifth Test

ENGLAND

FIRST INNINGS		SECOND INNINGS	
Hutton, c. Tallon, b. Lindwall	30	c. Tallon, b. Miller	64
J. G. Dewes, b. Miller	1	b. Lindwall	10
W. J. Edrich, c. Hassett, b. Johnston	3	b. Lindwall	28
Compton (D.), c. Morris, b. Lindwall	4	c. Lindwall, b. Johnston	39
Crapp, c. Tallon, b. Miller	0	b. Miller	9
N. W. D. Yardley, b. Lindwall	7	c. Miller, b. Johnston	9
Watkins, l.b.w., b. Johnston	0	c. Hassett, b. Ring	2
Evans, b. Lindwall	1	b. Lindwall	8
Bedser (A. V.), b. Lindwall	0	b. Johnston	0
Young, b. Lindwall	0	not out	3
Hollies, not out	0	c. Morris, b. Johnston	0
Extras (b. 6)	6	Extras (b. 9, l.b. 4, n.b. 3)	16
Total	52	Total	188

BOWLING,—FIRST INNINGS.—Lindwall, 16.1—5—20—6; Miller, 8—5—5—2; Johnston, 16—4—20—2; Loxton, 2—1—1—0.

SECOND INNINGS.—Lindwall, 25—3—50—3; Miller, 15—6—22—2; Loxton, 10—2—16—0; Johnston, 27.3—12—40—4; Ring, 28—13—44—1.

FALL OF WICKETS.—FIRST INNINGS.—1—2, 2—10, 3—17, 4—23, 5—35, 6—42, 7—45, 8—45, 9—47, 10—52.

SECOND INNINGS.—1—20, 2—64, 3—125, 4—153, 5—164, 6—167, 7—178, 8—181, 9—188, 10—188.

AUSTRALIA
FIRST INNINGS

S. G. Barnes, c. Evans, b. Hollies	61
A. R. Morris, run out	196
D. G. Bradman, b. Hollies	0
A. L. Hassett, l.b.w., b. Young	37
K. R. Miller, st. Evans, b. Hollies	5
R. N. Harvey, c. Young, b. Hollies	17
S. J. E. Loxton, c. Evans, b. Edrich	15
R. R. Lindwall, c. Edrich, b. Young	9
D. Tallon, c. Crapp, b. Hollies	31
D. Ring, c. Crapp, b. Bedser	9
W. A. Johnston, not out	0
Extras (b. 4, l.b. 2, n.b. 3)	9
Total	389

BOWLING.—FIRST INNINGS.—Bedser, 31.2—9—61—1; Watkins, 4—1—19—0; Young, 51—16—118—2; Hollies, 56—14—131—5; Compton, 2—0—6—0; Edrich, 9—1—38—1; Yardley, 5—1—7—0.

FALL OF WICKETS.—FIRST INNINGS.—1—117, 2—117, 3—226, 4—243, 5—265, 6—304, 7—332, 8—359, 9—389, 10—389.

UMPIRES.—D. Davies and H. G. Baldwin.

Test Match Averages

Matches Played 5 : Australia Won 4 Drawn 1.

AUSTRALIA

Batting

	Matches	Innings	Times not out	Runs	Highest score	Average
A. R. Morris	5	9	1	696	196	87.00
S. G. Barnes	4	6	2	329	141	82.25
D. G. Bradman.. ..	5	9	2	500	173*	72.57
R. N. Harvey	2	3	1	133	112	66.50
E. R. H. Toshack ..	4	4	3	51	20*	51.00
S. J. Loxton	3	3	0	144	93	48.00
A. L. Hassett	5	8	1	310	137	44.28
R. R. Lindwall.. ..	5	6	0	191	77	31.83
D. Tallon	4	4	0	112	53	28.00
K. R. Miller	5	7	0	184	74	26.28
W. A. Brown	2	3	0	73	32	24.33
W. A. Johnston ..	5	5	2	62	29	20.66
I. W. Johnson	4	6	1	51	21	10.20

Also batted.—D. Ring 9, R. A. Saggers 5.

Bowling

	Overs	Maidens	Runs	Wickets	Average
R. R. Lindwall..	222.5	57	530	27	19.62
K. R. Miller	138.1	43	301	13	23.15
W. A. Johnston	309.2	92	630	27	23.33
E. R. H. Toshack	173.1	70	364	11	33.09
S. J. Loxton	63	10	148	3	49.33
I. W. Johnson	183	60	427	7	61.00

The following centuries were scored for Australia in Test matches:—
A. R. Morris—196, at the Oval; 105, at Lord's; 182, at Leeds.
D. G. Bradman—173*, at Leeds; 138, at Nottingham.
S. G. Barnes—141, at Lord's.
R. N. Harvey—112, at Leeds.
A. L. Hassett—137, at Nottingham.
    Also bowled.—Barnes (S. G.), 5—2—11—0 ; Morris (A. R.), 8—1—24—0 ; Ring (D.), 28—13—44—1.

* Not out.

ENGLAND

BATTING

	Matches	Innings	Times not out	Runs	Highest score	Average
Compton (D. C.) ..	5	10	1	562	184	62.44
Washbrook (C.) ..	4	8	1	356	143	50.85
Hutton (L.)	4	8	0	342	81	42.75
W. J. Edrich	5	10	0	319	111	31.90
Evans (T. G.)	5	9	2	188	50	26.85
Laker (J. C.)	3	6	1	114	63	22.80
Bedser (A. V.) ..	5	9	1	176	79	22.00
Crapp (J. F.)	3	6	1	88	37	17.60
N. W. D. Yardley ..	5	9	0	150	44	16.66
Dollery (H. E.).. ..	2	3	0	38	37	12.66
Young (J. A.)	3	5	2	17	9	5.66

Also batted.—Barnett (C. J.), 8 and 6; Coxon (A.), 19 and 0; K. Cranston, 10 and 0; J. G. Dewes, 1 and 10; Emmett (G. M.), 10 and 0; Hardstaff (J.), 0 and 43; Hollies (W. E.), 0* and 0; Pollard (R.), 3 and 0*; Watkins (A.), 0 and 2; Wright (D. V. P.), 13* and 4.

BOWLING

	Overs	Maidens	Runs	Wickets	Average
N. W. D. Yardley	84	22	204	9	22.66
Hollies (W. E.)..	56	14	131	5	26.20
Bedser (A. V.)	274.3	75	688	18	38.22
Pollard (R.)	102	29	218	5	43.60
Laker (J. C.)	155.2	42	472	9	52.44
Young (J. A.)	156	64	292	5	58.40
W. J. Edrich	53	4	238	3	79.33
Compton (D. C.)	37	6	156	1	156.00

Also bowled.—Barnett (C. J.), 17—5—36—0; Coxon (A.), 63—13—172—3; K. Cranston, 21.1—1—79—1; Hutton (L.), 4—1—30—0; Watkins (A.), 4—1—9—0; Wright (D. V. P.), 40.3—12—123—2.

The following centuries were scored for England in Test matches:
Compton (D. C.)—184, at Nottingham; 145*, at Manchester.
W. J. Edrich—111, at Leeds.
Washbrook (C.)—143, at Leeds.

* Not out.